The Shadow Negotiation

How Women Can Master the Hidden Agendas That Determine Bargaining Success

Deborah M. Kolb, Ph.D.
and
Judith Williams, Ph.D.

SIMON & SCHUSTER

NEW YORK   LONDON   TORONTO
SYDNEY   SINGAPORE

SIMON & SCHUSTER
Rockefeller Center
1230 Avenue of the Americas
New York, NY 10020

SIMON & SCHUSTER and colophon are registered trademarks
of Simon & Schuster, Inc.

Designed by Kyoko Watanabe

Manufactured in the United States of America

10   9   8   7   6   5   4   3   2   1

Library of Congress Cataloging-in-Publication Data

Kolb, Deborah M.
      The shadow negotiation : how women can master the hidden agendas that
   determine bargaining success / Deborah M. Kolb and Judith Williams.
         p.   cm.
      Includes bibliographical references and index.
      1. Negotiation.   2. Women executives.   I. Williams, Judith.   II. Title.

   BF637.N4 K655 2000
   658.4'052'082—dc21   00-032195

ISBN 0-684-83840-0

Contents

PART ONE

The Power of Advocacy: Promoting Your Interests Effectively

PART TWO

The Promise of Connection: Building a Collaborative Relationship

PART THREE

Putting It All Together:
Balancing Advocacy and Connection

The Shadow
Negotiation

Preface

Negotiation is a hot topic today. "Win-win," in fact, has become a coded buzzword for good results. Scarcely a month goes by without numerous magazines running "features" on negotiation, often complete with quick multiple-choice tests we can use to monitor our proficiency. If we feel the need to hone our skills more sharply, we can go on-line and load up a virtual shopping cart. A click of the mouse produces reams of advice on how to negotiate that next raise on our way to opportunity and leadership. Amid all this redundant wealth, do we really need yet another book on negotiation—and one for women no less? The simple answer is yes, on both counts.

Every year *Working Woman* magazine surveys women's salaries in various industries to keep us up-to-date on the *wage gap*. Currently, women take home seventy-four cents for every dollar that men earn.[1] In the twenty-five years since President Kennedy signed the Equal Pay Act, the disparity has narrowed by only fifteen cents. Progress, clearly, but the rate slowed during the 1990s. Commentators point to various factors to explain the decreasing momentum. They highlight the occupational segregation of the labor force. Women still cluster in low-paying jobs and industries. They account for 90 percent of registered nurses but only 20 percent of physicians. They make up 99 percent of dental hygienists and over 98 percent of secretaries, typists, and kindergarten teachers. They fill three quarters of the clerical positions in U.S. companies but only a little better than 30 percent of the managerial slots.[2]

This occupational clustering, however, explains only part of the wage gap. The experience of one of our colleagues helps tell us why. She was negotiating with a major university for a prized teaching post. Despite her newly minted Ph.D., her initial meetings with the dean left her unsatisfied. Though the salary the dean eventually quoted was a far cry from her graduate student stipends, neither the amount nor the other perks felt right. So she decided to do a little surveying of her own. She asked all the women hired during the past five years about their meetings with the dean and then informally polled a comparable group of men. What she learned surprised her. Each of the women accepted the dean's original offer. Their male colleagues, on the other hand, proceeded to negotiate not only for a higher salary, but also for research support and office space.

This story reflects a pattern familiar to many of us. Grateful for the opportunities we are given, we often just accept the terms that are offered. People expect us to be amenable, and they keep that expectation in mind when they negotiate with us. Furthermore, when a woman negotiates, and not just about salary, she encounters another unspoken assumption: that work is her choice, a luxury rather than something she both needs and wants to do. The person on the other side of the table sometimes takes it for granted that a woman, no matter what her circumstances, will put family and relationships first and not bargain hard. When that happens, she is offered less from the start and generally ends up with less.

These results accumulate over time, widening a gap that is no longer measured in money alone. She might not be considered for an assignment that would stretch her abilities or give her broader visibility. Or she might remain with a department—human resources, accounting, or community relations—where her chances of moving up in the firm are not so promising. For our colleague, initial negotiations that produce limited resources for research and onerous teaching hours make publishing that important professional book or article all the more difficult down the road. Along the way, she might be asked to shoulder extra administrative duties that somehow never figure so much in tenure decisions as publication does. Hard work, professional expertise, and long hours don't count for everything. We should not be surprised that women hold less than 9 percent of the most senior positions in our major institutions today.[3] Women have to negotiate not harder, but smarter.

As we talked to women all over the country about how they experience negotiation, they spoke of specific difficulties and specific situations. But beyond these idiosyncratic circumstances, their collective comments revealed something about the negotiation process itself. And it is this "something" that is missing in the many books on negotiation we can load into our virtual shopping cart. The advice available concentrates on what to do when you are in the throes of bargaining or getting ready. It helps you approach the issues systematically, rationally, and analytically. What you won't find is any guidance on dealing with the kinds of assumptions our colleague faced or those lurking behind the wage and opportunity gap. To do that you must confront what we call the "shadow negotiation."

The shadow negotiation is where hidden agendas and masked assumptions play out. Often it is defined by a whole array of attitudes of which the participants are only dimly aware. These hidden agendas drive the negotiation as much as explicit differences over the issues. Before you can reach a good agreement on the issues, these unvoiced views must be brought to the surface so that misguided impressions and unrealistic expectations—including your own—can be revised.

The Shadow Negotiation emerged from our interviews with women precisely because gender is one of the triggers that set unvoiced expectations in motion in a negotiation.[4] The women we talked to mastered the intricacies of the shadow negotiation often without realizing its existence. They recognized that if they failed to negotiate for the perks and support demanded by a new assignment, they would find themselves working long and unappreciated hours to complete it. They told us of times when they had problems being given credit for what they had done or sparking enthusiasm for their ideas. But they also reported how they changed people's minds and got negotiation on serious issues off the ground. They spoke of times when, put at a disadvantage, they turned the situation around. They negotiated maternity leaves against unfavorable odds and job offers even when their résumés did not exactly fit the positions.

More often than not their negotiations involved change. Creating a flexible work schedule or developing a new project or securing a loan for a new business meant that they had to move the negotiations beyond simple yes-or-no propositions. The issues they faced were often difficult and made uncomfortable demands on the other side. Working collaboratively and constructively even when pushed in the opposite direction, they were able to fashion creative agreements. Their stories show us what win-win looks like when people truly collaborate.

The Shadow Negotiation lays out the lessons we learned from the experiences of women when they negotiate.* But these insights can help all negotiators. People—men and women—rather cavalierly assume that everyone negotiates pretty much the same way and that gestures or signals will be read the way they are intended. This is far from the case. A social worker operates in a different negotiating universe than an investment banker. Whether a doctor is in private practice or affiliated with a university teaching hospital affects how she negotiates. To test how one's situation influences strategic choices and styles, we spoke with women in many fields. We talked to development professionals and management consultants, loan officers and caterers, doctors and writers, engineers and nurses, lawyers and salespeople, real estate agents and child-care workers, physical therapists and secretaries.

The following chapters are not the story of Everywoman. They tell the stories of many women and reflect the diverse choices women make as they negotiate through the myriad issues that come up in today's workplace. To get a sense of how the demands on negotiating skills change over time and how bargaining styles evolve, we interviewed women who were at different points in their careers—just starting out, making mid-career changes, or downshifting, trying to stay afloat in their old companies, or putting together their own firms. We talked with the "stars," but we were as interested in their stumbles as their successes. Despite this range, these women in no way constitute a scientific sample.

Typically, at the beginning of each interview we would ask our contributors to describe what they considered their worst and best experiences at negotiation. They were equally forthcoming with both, although perhaps more generous with their disasters than their successes. Often nothing about the problem itself suggested an inevitably disappointing outcome. Sometimes they were unaware that negotiation was taking place. Only after the exchange, after the meeting was over, did they realize they had been engaged in a negotiation. Other times, the situation snuck up on them, and they could not reclaim the initiative. In certain instances, they felt outgunned and overpowered from the beginning, un-

---

*We have built this book from these "negotiating" stories, but to respect the women's candor and to protect their privacy, we have disguised their identities. We have neither "prettied up" nor sanitized their accounts, but rather have tried to convey them in a way that is both undistorted and unidentifiable. To make our points, we sometimes isolate certain aspects of a woman's story; other times we telescope details from various accounts into one.

able—for psychological and practical reasons—to marshal the resources needed. Success hinged on the extent to which they recognized what was going on in the shadow negotiation and were able to manage their side of the process. We hope you will read our stories from that perspective, constantly asking yourself: Do I do that? Would I do that? What would I have done? Would this approach work for me?

All the change that is taking place around us has upped the ante on negotiating skills. On the domestic front, husbands once brought home the only paychecks and controlled the purse strings. Today nuclear families are fragmented, as likely to be headed by a woman as a man. Not long ago, bosses and their lieutenants decided who would do what work and for what pay. Employees had little room or incentive to negotiate. As organizations have become flatter and leaner, it is up to the employee to negotiate her next job. She cannot count on the one she has today being there tomorrow.

The choices we make (or our colleagues make for us) during negotiations shape our careers and our lives into the future. Isolated negotiations fold into larger and more important ones. A good starting salary secured, a dispute resolved with a colleague, a concession made in pricing our consulting services, working relationships established with other departments—all define the situation in which we find ourselves at a given point in time, but their impact ripples forward. The women in our stories strove to meet the challenges of negotiation in ways that built support for them and their issues, but they also sought an approach that would foster collaboration. Mary Catherine Bateson has made the provocative and convincing suggestion that women compose their lives as works in progress, improvising as they go along. If so, then negotiation is an instrument of that improvisation.[5]

We have accumulated many debts in the course of writing this book. First and foremost we are deeply grateful to the many students, friends and colleagues, casual acquaintances and complete strangers who were willing to share their experiences and perspectives with us. This book would not have been possible without their generosity. Several people were especially important in influencing our ideas. Lotte Bailyn, Sara Cobb, Joyce Fletcher, Debra Meyerson, Linda Putnam, the late Jeffrey Z. Rubin, and our other colleagues at the Program on Negotiation at Harvard Law

School and the Center for Gender in Organizations at the Simmons Graduate School of Management provided continuous support. Kitty Pell and Christine Power helped us with their early enthusiasm and willingness to conduct initial interviews. Without the patience of our agent Loretta Barrett or the deft eye and gentle guidance of Fred Hills, our editor at Simon & Schuster, *The Shadow Negotiation* would never have seen the light of day. Jonathan Kolb pored over the many drafts with good humor, sharpening our ideas and our prose as he went along. But it is from our children—Samuel, Elizabeth, Megan, and Tamsen—that we probably learned most about how to thread our ways through the multiple shadow negotiations in our lives.

RECOGNIZING THE SHADOW NEGOTIATION

The alarm goes off at six. By six-thirty coffee is brewing along with an argument. The contractor has finally agreed to look at the storm damage. You cannot get away this afternoon. Besides, it's your husband's turn. You covered the last crisis. Do you risk delay and reschedule, come up with a workable alternative, or hold firm?

First on the agenda at the office is a meeting with your boss. As you suspected, she rejects the team's proposed media campaign. You think she's wrong. How can you convince her? Should you try? What happens to the team's morale if you don't?

Office space is being reorganized. Last time around you compromised. Everyone expects you to be equally amenable this year, but they're in for a surprise. Your department has run out of room for new hires.

At lunch you go over a new contract. Your client keeps making sly innuendoes while his lawyer ignores your suggestions on revisions that protect your firm's rights. What do you say? How do you get them to focus on the business issues? To take you and your demands seriously?

You get a late telephone call from your most important supplier. He's having second thoughts about those price revisions that the two of you talked about. Can you find a solution—perhaps a slower schedule for the increases—so that he's comfortable and you don't blow your budget projections?

You finally head home. You will tackle that one tomorrow.

Sound familiar? A day on the job seldom goes by without the need to negotiate cropping up. We routinely deal with conflicting priorities and conflicting demands on our energies. Our responsibilities often exceed the "official" authority we have to get things moving. We cannot tell people what to do. They are usually under no obligation to listen, let alone follow orders. In fact, whenever we need something from someone else—a job, more cooperation, more time, or more money—we negotiate.

Conflicts of any consequence between people must be worked out *with* people. Most of this bargaining plays out in the informal exchanges that are part of the warp and woof of daily life. We drop by a colleague's office for a chat or enlist a mentor's help over coffee. Circumstances are more likely to find us vying for a raise or trying to restore a fractious team to equilibrium than taking part in the public drama of a mega-merger or a UN peacekeeping effort. Yet we often let these visible high-stakes negotiations shape our notions about negotiation and, in turn, the abilities and skills needed for success.

Nightly, larger-than-life figures parade across our television screens, the charismatic leaders and brilliant tacticians who have just pulled off some negotiating wizardry. The news summary zeroes in on the unexpected coup or the adroit posturing. It is not surprising that along the way we elevate negotiation to an "art form" practiced by the innately talented. A real estate developer with the instincts of a street fighter attaches the article *the* to his first name and labels what he does *The Art of the Deal.*[1] We watch Secretary of State Madeleine Albright shuttle between capital cities or trade representative Charlene Barshefsky hammer out a tough agreement with the Chinese government and can be silently pleased at her success. But conscious of the distance between this rarefied world and our own more mundane concerns and less stellar achievements, we mythologize the negotiation process and the people who negotiate.

The myths that have grown up around skillful negotiators need to be taken with a large grain of salt. Exceptional bargainers seem to have the magic touch, but that touch comes from a lot of practice. By training and from taking some not-so-public knocks, they have become adept at figuring out how to navigate the thorny situations that demanding circumstances or taxing people can create.

There is nothing magical or mystical about negotiation. People get better at it with practice. Ordinary people. Yet the mythologized negotiator makes us doubt what we can accomplish. Suspecting that we are neither sufficiently artful nor naturally persuasive, we let opportunities to negotiate slip by us unclaimed or unnoticed. Cramped by circumstance, with no magic up our sleeve, we don't consider negotiation a possibility. We just make do and move on, not realizing that we might have bargained. Often, from lack of training or experience, we fail to recognize that we are in the midst of a negotiation until it is too late to change the outcome. Even when we are well aware that we are negotiating and we know the stakes involved, we might have trouble getting the person we're negotiating with to listen, much less cooperate with us.

For the last several years we have been talking to women about what happens when they negotiate. Some of them buy into the mythology of the great negotiator and naturally assume their innate abilities come up short. Others have taken some hard knocks at the negotiating table and have become discouraged or disillusioned. Remembering what occurred the last time they asked for a raise or their running battles with another department for staff support, they find negotiation an unpleasant experience. They much prefer to avoid difficult situations altogether than get into heated disputes. If they cannot figure a way to sidestep the problem, they approach negotiation with sweaty palms and a high level of anxiety.

This wariness is not groundless. Despite the tremendous successes individual women have achieved, as a group we have not fared well when we must bargain hard. We pay more for our cars, new and used, and come out of salary talks with less in our pockets than men do. Although the vast majority of households depend on two paychecks, men make more of the money and women do more of the chores. With the odds stacked against us, it is only human to avoid negotiation on occasion. When you calculate the chances for success and find them slim, you settle for what is offered rather than negotiate for what you can legitimately demand.

Avoidance or acquiescence only *seems* to be an easy way out. In the

long run, bit by bit, it silences you. The happy fact is that effective negotiators are made, not born. Even professional negotiators learn their trade.
And success feeds success.

The Problem Is Only Part of the Story

Most popular advice on negotiation recommends that you focus on
solving the problem and provides a blueprint for attacking it. Rather than
wage a battle over a single issue, the advice suggests, think of the problem
as a series of trade-offs among many issues. With a single issue at stake,
any negotiation lurches toward a win-lose proposition. Someone is going
to come out on top. If, however, you can break down a monolithic problem, discover it is actually made up of many different issues, those differences give you room to find a compromise. No one wins everything, but
no one loses everything either.[2]

This advice is useful. A realistic assessment of the problem always
helps you formulate your strategic options. An emphasis on problem solving often leads to an agreement that produces some benefit for everyone.
The fable of the two oranges bears out what these mutual gain or win-win
solutions can offer. At the same time, it brings into sharp focus what the
problem-solving orientation leaves out.

The fable takes place at Christmastime and involves two sisters. One
plans to bake a chiffon cake for the festivities; the other, a fruitcake. Both
recipes call for two oranges. But when the sisters check the larder, they
find only two, not the four they need. An argument immediately erupts
over who gets the oranges. One sister complains that chiffon cake is wrong
for the season. The other retorts that fruitcake may be traditional, but nobody likes it. Obvious solutions are out of the question. It being a holiday,
they cannot borrow from the very neighbors who will later be their guests,
and the stores are closed. The sisters, unwilling to compromise and bake
only half a recipe, become more and more entrenched in defending their
rights. It is an all-or-nothing contest. They cannot both get what they
want. Or can they?

Preoccupied with winning, each overlooks the actual ingredients
specified in the recipes. Amid the heat in the kitchen some pertinent facts
emerge. The traditional fruitcake requires only the rind, while the deli-
cate chiffon cake uses just the juice. If one or the other sister was to pre-

vail, either the rind or the juice would go to waste. By focusing not on who wins but on the problem itself, both sisters can get what they want. One sister carefully grates the rind off the two oranges, then hands them over to her sibling for squeezing.

What a great solution, you think. If you just adopt this problem-solving approach, you can instantly become an effective negotiator. You have only to look at the problem—for differences in needs and interests—and propose solutions that play on those differences. The techniques are seductive in their promise of success. But consider what is slighted or missing in the orange story. The dispute might mask resentments that have nothing to do with oranges. Our sisters might have other issues on their agendas. The older sister might be fed up with always having to accommodate a younger sibling. She might not want to make *any* deal that works for her sister. The younger sister, on the other hand, might not be willing to give an inch just because she really hates fruitcake. Then, too, the solution is almost mythic in its symmetry. There is no overlap in the sisters' needs. Neither one's interest in the oranges impinges on the other's. What happens if the problem is not quite so tidy? The easy win-win solution vanishes if one recipe calls for both rind *and* juice. One of the sisters would be forced to give up something she wants. The negotiation suddenly begins to look a lot more complicated, and agreement requires another level of communication.

Make no mistake. Focusing on the problem can take you further than adversarial win-lose confrontation. The people involved in any negotiation *do* have different interests. By capitalizing on those differences, you *can* come up with trade-offs, rind for juice. You can swap something you don't care about for something that does matter to you. You might have a different appetite for risk or be operating under different time constraints, and you can take advantage of these disparities. You can pay or be paid in different currencies, exchanging part of the raise you want for an extra week's vacation. But no matter how creative you are in searching out mutual benefits, you cannot take the people out of the problem. Sometimes the people *are* the problem.

The problem-solving orientation skews the negotiation process toward rational analysis. It assumes you can pretty much figure out what motivates the other party and trade on that. It's great if you can gain her trust, but you don't really need to work at getting her cooperation. She'll jump at a creative idea that meets her needs. As a rational decision maker, you assume, she is bound to make the right choice.

But negotiators are not always rational. When people bargain, they bring their idiosyncrasies to the table—their disposition toward conflict, their biases, remembered slights or successes, and their feelings about each other. Dirty dishes in the sink and an overflowing laundry basket can have more impact on where a family decides to spend its vacation than its frequent flyer miles. Bargainers can have concerns that have nothing to do with the problem but affect its resolution. They might be worried about a sick child or the extra time they have to spend with a frail parent. They might think they are losing their edge at the office and feel obliged to take a strong stand.

Negotiation *is* a vehicle for problem solving. But any negotiation is also a form of social interaction; it involves a *you* and a *them.* Unspoken wants and expectations come into play that interfere with "getting to yes." In order to solve the orange problem in the real world, each sister would have to work to bring the other to the point where she saw the value of compromise. Good ideas, good trades, are not enough. You might have more creative solutions to your own particular orange problem than you know what to do with. Your real challenge might be getting the other party to give your proposals a hearing, particularly if he or she is perfectly content with things as they are.

The Shadow Negotiation

As we talked to women about what happens when they negotiate, we learned that a good idea alone rarely carries the day. Negotiations are not purely rational exercises in problem solving. They are more akin to conversations that are carried out simultaneously on two levels. First there is the discussion of substance—what the bargainers have to say about the problem itself. But then there is the interpersonal communication that takes place—what the talk encodes about their relationship.[3] Yes, people bargain over issues, but they also negotiate how they are going to negotiate. All the time they are bargaining over issues, they are conducting a parallel negotiation in which they work out the terms of their relationship and their expectations. Even though they seldom address the subject directly, they decide between them whose interests and needs command attention, whose opinions matter, and how cooperative they are going to be in reaching an agreement. This interchange, often nonverbal and masked in the positions taken on issues, has a momentum all its own, quite apart from the substance of what is being discussed.

We call this parallel negotiation the *shadow negotiation*. This shadow negotiation takes place below the surface of any debate over problems. As bargainers try to turn the discussion of the problem to their advantage or persuade the other side to cooperate in resolving it, they make assumptions about each other, what the other person wants, his or her weaknesses, how he or she is likely to behave. They size each other up, poking here and there to find out where the give is. They test for flexibility, trying to gauge how strongly an individual feels about a certain point.

How you resolve the issues hinges on the actions you take in the shadow negotiation. If you don't move to direct the shadow negotiation, you can find the agreement tipping against you. The shadow negotiation is no place to be a passive observer. You can maneuver to put yourself in a good position or let others create a position for you.[4] Your action—or inaction—here determines what takes place in the negotiation over problems.

Impressions count. Slight changes in positioning can cause a major shift in the dynamics within the shadow negotiation. You want to move into a position from which you can claim your place at the table. At the same time, you need to encourage your counterpart to collaborate with you in fashioning an agreement that works for both of you.

The Twin Demands of the Shadow Negotiation: Advocacy and Connection

To hold your own in the shadow negotiation, you don't have to be brash or aggressive. You do need to be an advocate for your interests. Through strategic moves you position yourself in the shadow negotiation so that the other party takes your demands seriously. You also turn any attempts to put you on the defensive. In effect, your advocacy defines your claim to a place at the table. It tells the other side not only that you are going to be an active player, but that you will not and do not need to settle for less than you deserve.

Active positioning is critical to how you negotiate the issues. The impressions you create in the shadow negotiation determine how much give and take there will be over the issues and influence any agreement you make. If you are unsure of yourself or doubt whether your demands are justified or legitimate, you will have a tough time convincing others to give them much weight. Bargainers are quick to ferret out points of weakness, where you are tentative or vulnerable. You must be ready to move in the shadow negotiation not just to promote your interests but to block any attempt to undermine your credibility.

The messages you send in the shadow negotiation establish your advocacy. But you cannot pay attention only to gaining an advantage for your demands and to how you are positioned in the negotiation conversation. Any good solution requires compromise, concessions, and creativity on both sides. Concentrate only on your agenda, promote it at the other party's expense, and she has little incentive to cooperate. Regard her as an enemy and pretty soon she starts acting like one—blind to the interests you share.

To find common ground, you have to work together, not against each other. This is where the *skills of connection* come into play. It takes sensitivity and responsive action to draw out what other people have on their minds in a negotiation. Often these hidden agendas are their real agendas. Unless bargainers are explicitly encouraged to talk about them, they will hesitate, fearing that any candor will be used against them. They don't want to tip their hand.

There is a pragmatic reason behind this attentiveness to relationship building in the shadow negotiation. Show the others involved that you value them and their ideas, and there is a good chance they will reciprocate. You'd be surprised how quickly they become more open in voicing the reasons for their demands *and* more receptive to listening to yours. But establishing a connection with the other party does a good deal more than facilitate equal airtime. When you each feel free to engage in an open exchange that flows both ways, you can confront the real issues rather than their proxies. Different perspectives surface and point to other, more creative ways of resolving the issues than either of you can contemplate on your own.

Advocacy and connection go hand in hand in successful negotiation, and you establish the terms of both in the shadow negotiation. Using strategic moves and turns, you create your own space in the conversation. You cannot let a need for responsive and open exchange hold your own interests hostage. You must lay the groundwork for dialogue with a forceful advocacy. The other person has to have something and someone to connect with for the skills of connection to work. But those skills hold a larger promise. They enable you to build a relationship across differences so that you are both committed to working collaboratively on a mutual solution.

What Does Gender Have to Do with Negotiation?

Almost without exception, the women we interviewed could analyze a problem or a situation with great skill. Yet they stumbled in the shadow negotiation. The reason became clear the more we talked with them. Problems can be and often are gender neutral. But surprising things happen in negotiations. Unrecognized expectations and unwarranted assumptions come into play. And gender often sets them off.

Because we experience negotiation in such a personal way, we look for personal reasons why being a woman matters more at some times than at others. Something in the chemistry of this particular negotiation, we figure, makes gender an issue. But even when we don't have a strong visceral reaction, gender colors our experience.[5] Any negotiation is caught in a web of influence, social values, and informal codes of conduct. Social norms or standards that seem at first blush to have nothing to do with gender might generate troubling expectations about what we should and can do as women. Resources are often unevenly divided along gender lines. As a result, what appears to be a benign or even playing field might, in fact, slope against us.

Gender Frameworks

To a great extent, how we see gender determines how we deal with its effects in the shadow negotiation. We can consider being a woman a hindrance in negotiation and take seriously Professor Higgins's exhortation in *My Fair Lady:* "Why can't a woman be more like a man?" Alternatively, we can celebrate our differences and adopt the approach of Sally Field and Dolly Parton in the movie *Steel Magnolias.* When Steel Magnolias negotiate, they tap feminine strengths to temper confrontational impulses and encourage collaborative exchange. Or we can focus on the social dynamic set in motion when common yardsticks used to measure performance don't fit a woman's experience.

Professor Higgins's advice. For the Professor Higginses of this world, the gender glass is half empty for women. They are not, by nature, bad negotiators. Socialized to be mothers and caretakers, they have never been schooled in the art of hard-nosed bargaining. They can, however, learn the "rules of the game."[6] A woman need not fare badly in a salary negotiation or put in a double shift at home and at work. If she has not been able to argue her case for equal pay for equal work or prevent her colleagues from talking over her, she can study how to be more assertive, more strategic in her thinking, and less emotional.

The Professor Higgins approach is a remedial one. It assumes that individual deficiencies can be patched up with sufficient study and rigorous discipline. Passivity, for example, is a personal liability that can be corrected by training. The fault rests squarely on the particular woman's shoulders. She needs a "cure." Conveniently overlooked is the extent to which that cure will always be incomplete. No matter how hard a woman tries to learn the rules of the game, she will always play the game *as* a woman. Adopting aggressive behavior or a more "masculine" way of speaking in a negotiation can backfire. Instead of gaining her a voice and acceptance, it can provoke censure or backlash.[7]

Remedial programs like these hold out a dubious promise: If you patch yourself up—fill in your obvious deficiencies and acquire the necessary skills—you can play the game as well as, or better than, many men. By recommending the wholesale assimilation of "good" masculine qualities, however foreign, advice like this encourages a woman to blame only herself when she is underpaid, overworked, or simply overlooked, invisible. The fault lies with her—in some inadequacy, in something she did or failed to do—not in the imbalances in the system itself.

The Steel Magnolias' answer. Wait a minute, some critics say. Femininity is *not* an encumbrance. It gives a woman an edge, assets she can use to her advantage. Rather than lament the lack of assertive independence or competitive drive in women, why not celebrate an expressive, emotional, caring femininity? Women, through their capacity to mother and from their subordinate status at work, have developed not just coping mechanisms but real strengths. Empathy, an intuitive aptitude for collaboration, the ability to connect with others rather than to remain distanced as an independent actor, an instinctive feeling for "relationship"—these skills and inclinations carry an unrealized advantage in the new interconnected world of business. Women, it is suggested, build rapport and reach joint solutions more easily than men do precisely because they cooperate and empathize more naturally.[8]

This thinking successfully challenges the notion that women are in some way deficient or inadequate. It runs into difficulty, however, when it assumes that a constellation of certain traits and qualities makes up the "female essence." This premise washes out differences among women. The problem is not that women do not have these special qualities. Many do. But others enjoy the challenge of competition; they are not by nature *only* concerned with others.

There is also some wishful thinking involved in declaring feminine attributes unqualified assets uniformly useful in negotiation. These "feminine" skills, far from being an advantage, can undermine a woman when she negotiates. If she is not careful, her attachment to relationship can be exploited and used against her. Of course, the helpful female colleague does not mind shouldering the lion's share of the work and ending up with none of the credit. Of course, a woman negotiating a severance package will sacrifice her financial interests to maintain cordial relations with her former employers. Taken to extremes, the feminine advantage does not gain a woman much credit when she negotiates. While her empathetic male counterpart earns praise for his "people" skills, she is just acting like a woman. And if she is *really* successful, she is accused of being manipulative, of using feminine wiles to get her way. That is the flint behind the honey in a Steel Magnolia's voice, the reason for the hint of the pejorative in the term's common usage.

There is a more damaging objection. Praise of the "feminine," when unqualified, makes it easy to discount or ignore the extent to which influence follows gender lines. As one commentator put it, an emphasis on women's special qualities of caring and nurturing amounts to a "setup to be shafted."[9] In an unequal world, such critics argue, difference will always mean less and women will generally get less when they negotiate. In other words, the doubts women experience about their ability to do well often tell more about status, about bumping up against seemingly immovable walls and ceilings, about having less clout, than they reveal about underappreciated skills and abilities.[10]

We are using the exaggerations of Professor Higgins and the Steel Magnolia for effect. They point to the extremes in the advice directed at women, but they also illustrate the extent to which we personalize the challenges gender creates in negotiation. On the one hand, it is *our* weakness and so we need to remedy it. On the other, it is *our* strength, but we must be wary in how we use it. But not all the challenges gender poses in negotiation are rooted in personal causes. However inclined we as individuals might be to view supposed differences as a handicap or a strength, a woman quite simply has to work harder than a man to get what she wants in a negotiation. When others automatically assume she will not push her own interests, they offer less, are more difficult to bring to the table, make unreasonable demands, and say no more freely. They might doubt her competence, her ability to be forceful and stand her ground under pressure. The power dynamics in the relationship or the organization might work against her. To counter this momentum, she might repudiate those qualities that have traditionally been associated with women—an ability to connect with other people, the capacity to listen. Empathy, she reasons, is not going to get her very far when she faces a hard bargaining situation—particularly when the other person interprets her concern as a sign that she will not put up much resistance. But being tough or hard-nosed does not seem to solve the dilemma either.

The yardstick explanation. Gender is not a "woman's" problem—a question of whether women have deficiencies or special qualities. Although gender figures in most human relations, we deny its pervasiveness, preferring instead to see egalitarian gender neutrality in our relationships and in our organizations. Yet to a large extent, we still maintain implicit standards for behavior that can have a different impact on women than men. Standards generally reflect the experience of the people setting them. And, by and large, men do the setting in our society. As a result, their experience becomes the yardstick for measuring what is normal. And, in a masked exercise of power, that standard is then rather cavalierly assumed to be gender neutral.[11]

Think, for a minute, about the criteria most often used to decide whether an employee is on a fast track and ripe for promotion. He or she puts work first. Loyalty and ambition are gauged by the time committed to the job. A woman who has primary responsibility at home, which is often the case, inevitably faces distinct disadvantages when measured by this yardstick. She might be a valuable employee precisely because of her ability to juggle conflicting demands on her time and to set priorities, but these abilities have not been factored into the definition of the "ideal employee."[12] When she goes to negotiate a promotion or a salary increase, that unspoken standard follows her into the room. It does not matter that the yardstick narrows the talent pool and might actually encourage bad work practices, a self-perpetuating crisis mode where pulling an all-nighter or emergency after-hours meetings becomes the norm rather than the exception. Late at night nobody stops to question the norm or how it gives an advantage to anyone who measures up but penalizes those who don't.

Yardsticks like these can be demoralizing for a woman negotiator if their gender bias is not recognized. When the standard provides no room for what a woman brings to the table, she often stops seeing what she does right. In the middle of a seminar, Liz, a consultant in a national firm, confessed that she was a terrible negotiator. Always, she said, she failed in her efforts at self-promotion. After a sales call on a prospective client, for example, Liz's boss used the cab ride back to the office for an impromptu lecture on her "passive" approach. To attract clients, he stressed, Liz had to emphasize the "value-added" she contributed. Liz had always felt uncomfortable concentrating on *her* role. As a rule, she preferred to find out what the client needed and only then to talk about the ways in which the firm could help. Because Liz's practice of negotiation went so against the grain at the firm, she considered herself out-of-step and inept. Even by her own tally, her quite considerable skills had little value. That she met with such success she attributed not to her deft handling of clients but to the luck of the draw in ending up with a disproportionate share of congenial ones. Liz was actually a terrific negotiator. More often than not, a sales call would be followed by a request from a client that she handle the account. Her boss passed along these messages, but his manner encouraged her to discount them and she did.[13]

Yardsticks like these make us question our notions of what it takes to be an effective negotiator. Like the proverbial fish unaware its environment is wet, we often swim in gendered waters in negotiation without realizing it.[14] The more aware we are of just how wet the water can be, the better able we will be to handle the gendered backwash. Should we be so quick to assume, as Liz did, that the conventional wisdom about the effective negotiator is gender neutral?

The "Model" Negotiator

A good deal of ink has been spilled about the personal characteristics that make for success in negotiation. Most of it starts with the premise that the effective negotiator is a results-oriented problem solver. Here, too, the emphasis on problem solving causes trouble. Let's look at the person who emerges once we make that assumption.

- Effective negotiators are tough, tireless, and determined. They promote their interests aggressively and need persuasive reasons to temper their demands.

- Effective negotiators are prepared. They know going into a negotiation what they want and identify any roadblocks ahead of time.

- Effective negotiators are decisive and clear.

- Effective negotiators are versatile in their tactics. They don't hesitate to bluff or stonewall if it gets them a better deal. But they can be concerned and caring if that works to their advantage.

- Effective negotiators are objective and unemotional. They employ emotions, such as anger or disappointment, tactically.

- Effective negotiators are focused. They keep their eyes on the goal.

The image of the effective negotiator as a problem solver succeeds on one front: It quite nicely debunks the mythology that skillful bargainers are the result of a felicitous genetic combination. The model negotiator sketched above does not rely on God-given talents. Successful results come from hard work—analyzing the situation, planning a strategy, thinking through options, and making constant adjustments. But what about the person actually doing all this work?

Problems and their analysis may be gender neutral, but the conventional wisdom about the model negotiator as problem solver is decidedly not. The effective negotiator turns out to look remarkably like a man. He has all the positive qualities we associate with masculinity: competitiveness, independence, objectivity, self-confidence, and coolness under pressure. Of course, the model doesn't fit every man. There are the bullies who dominate by force rather than the forcefulness of their arguments. Then there are the avoiders who run for cover at the first sign of conflict. But, by and large, the effective negotiator is measured by a masculine yardstick. That standard shadows the male negotiator whenever he bargains, whatever his negotiating style. He can afford to be conciliatory because it is assumed that when the going gets rough, he'll get tough.

But what about a woman? Some of us have no difficulty seeing ourselves in the description of the model negotiator. Still, the model poses problems—for men and women alike. A *Barron's* cartoon encapsulates the dilemma. Two businesspeople, a man and a woman, are standing, briefcases in hand, outside an ominously closed conference room door. The woman has a word of caution for her male colleague: "Just don't let them see your feminine side." Clearly the cartoon woman subscribes to the conventional wisdom about the model negotiator. A man and a woman can only gain from an ability to stand up under pressure and let their competitive juices flow, while expressing concern for others is apt to undermine their efforts.[15]

But the model negotiator can have more significant consequences when the person showing that feminine side is a woman. Consider the following items taken from the Extended Personal Attributes Questionnaire, a test to measure an individual's femininity or masculinity.[16]

MASCULINE	FEMININE
independent	helpful
self-confident	aware of others' feelings
competitive	warm to others
stands up under pressure	gentle
active	emotional
makes decisions easily	devoted to others
never gives up easily	kind
feels superior	understanding

Questions in tests like these are posed as forced choices. They look for differences and not surprisingly they find them. In real life, people are more complicated than simple either/or categories. We are all an idiosyncratic mix of personal traits and characteristics, and none of us fits uniformly into one column or the other. Despite the exaggeration the tests produce, however, they do catch something of our beliefs about men and women.[17] Women are expected to fall more often in the right column and men in the left. And the traits on the left have a different orientation than those on the right. They support individual autonomy.

Although negotiation takes place between and among people, requiring some degree of cooperation, the model negotiator is essentially an independent actor calculating how to achieve his ends. The stress falls squarely on talents that contribute to individual success and excludes others that are needed to make interactions work. When we pay attention only to the analytic or independent components of a negotiation, the shadow negotiation disappears—and with it, to a large extent, the call for relational skills. The effective negotiator drawn to these specifications deploys only certain qualities and abilities. Other—equally important—skills get erased. And the skills that disappear are those traditionally associated with women.

Something else falls out from comparisons like these. No woman, however competent, can pull off what is essentially a male performance. She will always be considered somewhat deficient, lacking the objectivity and competitiveness necessary to stay in the negotiation. This sleight of hand presents a real quandary for a woman when she negotiates. She cannot, by definition, fit the model. However she chooses to do her bargaining, she is caught in a Catch-22. Her behavior will be deviant when she tries to adopt the standard *and* when she doesn't. If she acts like a woman, her skills are devalued. Her intuition, concern for others, and emotionality interfere with any logical discussion. If she patterns her behavior on the model, she pays attention only to the rational or autonomous side of the negotiation and fails to bring into play her relational skills. At the same time, she might be judged harshly for being unfeminine, pushy, and unsympathetic. We are by no means implying that she should refrain from forcefully pursuing her interests—only that a negative reaction can be anticipated and has to be managed in the shadow negotiation.[18]

As women, we take our differences *and* our competence into every negotiation. These can be turned to our advantage, but they have to be recognized as valuable, not erased—by us or by our counterparts. We need, in effect, to revise the standard.[19] Even the terminology that we use to describe negotiation betrays the need for revision. Participants in a negotiation are characterized as "adversaries" or the more distanced but chilly "other party." The words themselves evoke either a competitive contest or a faceless battle of wits. Some negotiations are contests, but not all, and some that are do not need to be. In fact, so long as negotiators operate with this mental metaphor in mind, the rapport necessary to settle disputes collaboratively remains elusive. Without a genuine responsiveness to the other person, we cannot draw out his or her perspectives. As a consequence, we deprive ourselves (and the other person) of any chance to explore ideas that just might lead us to a creative solution.

The issues gender raises in negotiation are not about either/or choices—between adopting a "masculine" or a "feminine" style. We need not so much a gender-neutral understanding of effectiveness but one that allows us to use all our skills and intelligences. Certainly we must cultivate an aptitude for analysis and self-promotion. But it is equally clear we need to hone our relational skills.

The influence gender exerts on the negotiation process varies greatly. It can be a nonissue, or its effects can be exacerbated, particularly if imbalances in power exist. But whenever gender insinuates itself into the shadow negotiation, we can take steps to lessen the impact. As empowered advocates *and* connected negotiators, we can move to bring other people's perceptions into alignment with our sense of who we are and what we want to accomplish. The job at hand for any woman negotiating is to be aware of these perceptions and to manage them actively.[20]

Inside a Shadow Negotiation

Let's take a look inside a shadow negotiation and chart how it affects the way in which the issues are framed and resolved. Elizabeth and Will are physicians in a small HMO located in a suburb outside Atlanta. The two, both in their early thirties, get along well. One or the other must be on duty when the center is open, and they routinely split weekend and evening shifts. But friction erupts over the summer vacation schedules.

Will: I'm going on a fishing trip with three other guys the last week in June. Pencil me in for that time slot.

Elizabeth: Well, um, actually, that's not okay. That week is a problem for me. My mother's moving into a new apartment. Remember? She has to be out of our old house by the end of the month, and I've promised to help pack up and get her settled in her new place.

Will: I can't change my plans. If I don't go, the trip gets canceled and our deposit's down the drain. Shift your mother's move back a week.

Elizabeth: I feel terrible about this, but that would really frazzle my mother. We'd have to put everything in storage. She can't move into the new place until the first.

Will: So? She's going to have to put some stuff in storage anyway, and she could stay with you for the week.

Elizabeth: Now, *that* I really don't want to do. How about splitting the week? I could move her in over the weekend. . . . It would be a hassle, but then you could leave on Monday.

Will: You gotta be kidding.

Will slips his claim into a casual conversation with no warning, catching Elizabeth off-guard. He also introduces the issue not as a request to be negotiated but as a statement of fact. By suggesting a compromise, Elizabeth makes it clear she has not been fooled. They are going to negotiate their way to a solution.

The two go around and around, Will holding out for the week and Elizabeth putting out suggestions for compromise. Will gets increasingly angry and loses his temper. Upset, Elizabeth starts to waver. She hates it when anyone yells at her. To buy some peace, she says she'll put on her thinking cap.

She not only thinks about what they should do, she spends a sleepless night worrying. Her mother, although difficult, can stay for a week. The experience just won't be pleasant for either of them. If Elizabeth is going to shuffle things around, suffer the inconvenience, she wants something in return. Summer is coming. She'll trade first choice on the duty roster for July and August. That seems fair to her.

Elizabeth: You can have the vacation week. (Will smiles.) But I want first dibs on the summer schedule. (Will stops smiling.)

Will: No way. What does the call schedule have to do with
                vacation? You don't really need that week. You just said so.
                Done. Finished. Thanks.

Elizabeth: Not hardly. You get the week. I get first choice this summer.
                That's a fair trade. If you don't give me the summer, you can't
                have the week.

Will: This is going nowhere. I'm not going to tie up my summer.

Will and Elizabeth have reached a pivotal moment—that point when a negotiation can move forward along various paths or become deadlocked. How did they get there? The situation has all the ingredients needed for some horse-trading. Surely they can work out a deal.

Both Elizabeth and Will have been remiss, making plans without clearing the vacation schedule first. So they have a mutual problem. Neither can solve it independently, although Will makes a valiant attempt. He raises the issue as a nonproblem— "Pencil me in." He might have been trying to slip one by Elizabeth, getting her consent before she even realized what was happening. That's a common ploy in the shadow negotiation. We've all emerged from casual encounters like these wondering how we agreed to something or even if we had agreed.

Even though Will's maneuver does not hoodwink Elizabeth, it does gain him a tactical advantage. He frames the negotiation, staking out a definite position. The week should be his. His subsequent comments put the onus of making that happen on Elizabeth: "*You* could shift. . . . She could stay with *you*."

Elizabeth and Will talk about their problem, but what they say and how they say it betray a lot about their interpersonal relationship. When Will says "You could *shift your plans*," he is sending a message about how they can resolve the argument. But he is also sending another message that communicates quite specific things about the relationship he thinks exists between the two of them. This message says "*You* could shift your plans." Will assumes Elizabeth will be the one to do the adjusting, the one to come up with a solution. And she reinforces his impression when she agrees to put on her thinking cap. All he has to do is wait.

Will fits the image of the model negotiator. He conducts himself as an independent actor and concentrates on furthering his own interests. Sensing no compelling reason to compromise, he doesn't deviate from his plan. He also uses emotion strategically, knowing his shouting will throw Elizabeth off-stride and put her on the defensive. His angry rejection of Elizabeth's trade is calculated, rather than real. He aims to get her to accommodate him.

Elizabeth, by contrast, pushes for a solution that is acceptable to her, but she also wants Will to feel good about it. It is Elizabeth who worries when they cannot agree. It is Elizabeth who takes on the burden of producing the solutions. Rather than insist that she get her way, 100 percent, she proposes a compromise—splitting the week—and then comes up with a creative trade—priority on the summer schedule for the week.

Both Elizabeth and Will get tangled up in gendered expectations—the independent male and the caring female. If Will assumes Elizabeth will be the concerned one, Elizabeth just as readily concludes that Will will not. Not only does Elizabeth take on the more caring role, Will expects her to do so. Ironically, Elizabeth's efforts to accommodate Will's needs signal to him that she probably won't put up more than a token fight for the week. In a way, her flexibility feeds his intransigence.[21] He waits for Elizabeth to flinch, then summarily dismisses her first compromise. When she does not relent and puts conditions on her subsequent proposal, he gets angry. She, meanwhile, silently disparages his inflexibility and the greater importance he attaches to going fishing with his buddies than he accords her family responsibilities.

Will and Elizabeth have come to an impasse. Impatient with going around in circles, Will decides to bluff. "We'll flip a coin," he says. "Heads and the week's mine." His stratagem trips him up. Elizabeth, rather than giving in as he expects, goes along. The toss turns up tails, but Elizabeth frets over the outcome.

> *Elizabeth:* I'm sorry. I feel terrible. You have to cancel your plans. Tell
> me you're not mad. Friends?

A few days later, a business conference comes up for one of Will's friends, and the fishing trip gets rescheduled anyway. But Will never tells Elizabeth.

Advocacy, Connection, and the Shadow Negotiation

Even though the toss goes Elizabeth's way, she remains dissatisfied. They didn't do such a good job of negotiating, she thinks, if the two of them were forced to let chance resolve their dispute. As many of us do, Elizabeth replays the negotiation in her mind, looking for where she went wrong, wondering whether she could have discovered the right solution if she just kept at the problem.

Elizabeth does not go astray in how she approaches the problem of the vacation schedule. That is pretty simple. She stumbles in the shadow negotiation. While she concentrates on the problem, searching for a workable compromise, Will puts all his efforts into getting his way. By taking sole responsibility for the problem, she leads Will to believe that she will be the one making all the concessions. Once Will solidifies this position in the shadow negotiation, no amount of creative problem solving on Elizabeth's part can change the perceptions at work. Will simply interprets those efforts as signals that she will give him what he wants.

In the following chapters we lay out a different path to becoming an effective negotiator than the problem-driven one Elizabeth chooses—one that equips you to position yourself in the shadow negotiation through empowering moves and connecting overtures. Our blueprint for success draws equally on advocacy and connection. A thoughtful advocacy gets you into a position where you can be comfortable and effective in pressing your demands. An equally important part of this advocacy comes in convincing your counterpart that it is perfectly natural for you to promote your interests.

In the best negotiations, strong advocates connect with each other. The person with whom you are negotiating must be able to see your efforts to get connected as something more than a prelude to concession. Collaborative dialogue requires some reciprocity, some give-and-take, and openness to other perspectives. As a forceful advocate you establish your voice in that dialogue. As a connected negotiator you engage the other side in a conversation in which differences can surface without personal discord. The relationship-building implicit in connection should not, however, be confused with creating a superficial harmony. It does not demand that you satisfy the interests of others at the cost of your own. You do not foster a climate in which innovative proposals can be generated by making concessions unilaterally nor by being the only one cooperating. Both advocacy and connection require disciplined and deliberate efforts. They build on each other.

To give you a preview of how advocacy and connection support each other, let's rewind Elizabeth and Will's negotiation back to where Elizabeth proposes to trade the vacation week for first choice on the summer call schedule. In this replay, Elizabeth moves to check Will's efforts to cast her in the role of accommodating female.

> *Will:* You gotta be kidding. *(angry exchange)* This is going nowhere. I'm not going to tie up my summer.
>
> *Elizabeth:* Okay. Time out. *We* have a problem. I'm fresh out of ideas. And you don't have any. Maybe we should just let Joe [the medical director] decide.

Elizabeth figures Will won't under any circumstances want to appear to his boss as someone who cannot work out a simple conflict in vacation schedules. Of course, Elizabeth doesn't either, but she uses the implicit threat to put Will on notice. She is not going to do all the compromising and produce all the ideas. Will has to pull his weight and be more flexible if he doesn't want to involve the medical director. Simultaneously, she takes away Will's veto power and restores balance to the shadow negotiation.

Having a repertory of strategic moves is essential when you are negotiating, particularly with someone like Will whose natural inclination is to play the strong male against what he assumes to be your accommodating female. The people you negotiate with need to know that they cannot push you around before you can convince them to take you and your interests seriously. Elizabeth achieves this objective. Will immediately begins to backpedal.

> *Will:* Let's not be so hasty. We don't need to drag Joe in.

Elizabeth can take her victory and run. But Elizabeth's charge in the shadow negotiation is to do more than get the upper hand. She needs Will's cooperation to reach a decision that they both can accept. After all, they are still going to be working together long after Elizabeth's mother is settled into her new apartment and summer is over. Elizabeth cannot rest with issuing a threat. An outcome forced by her is just as unproductive as one imposed by Will. Under either scenario, resentments would fester. She is after Will's participation, not his capitulation. She couples the strong strategic move with a connected overture to draw Will back into the discussion.

> *Elizabeth:* If we don't ask Joe to intervene, I'm not sure what we can do. We're both in a tight spot. I know I wouldn't want to disappoint my friends. But I wasn't kidding when I said I was tapped out in the idea department. What do you think we should do?
>
> *Will:* I guess I didn't expect this to be such a big deal. It's gotten all out of proportion. Why don't we just . . .

Elizabeth comes right out and asks for Will's cooperation. She is careful to express her concern for his predicament. She never tries to apportion the blame for letting the situation deteriorate. Rather, by acknowledging Will's concerns, she creates an opening for him to respond in a more constructive, participatory way. He might not. But she has given him the chance, and she still reserves the option of forcing the issue.

Negotiating skills are critical for us as women. We depend on them in specific situations—to get a raise or a good price on a car, say. But we also call on them more generally just to get done what needs doing at work and at home. Negotiating skills are not a magic wand, however. No matter how adept we become, we will continue to juggle time and conflicting responsibilities. When all is said and done, there will still be only twenty-four hours in a day. Skillful negotiation cannot change this simple fact of life. But it does allow us to exert greater control over what happens during those twenty-four hours.

The more skillful we become as advocates in a collaborative process, the more we can expand our opportunities. When we use advocacy purposefully, not to overpower the opposition but to establish credibility, we lay the groundwork for building mutual respect. Negotiators who trust each other can probe more deeply and more candidly, and the prospects for innovative solutions increase geometrically. In a complex and rapidly changing world, no one can have all the answers. The opportunity to create dialogue, to benefit from other viewpoints and other people's skills—this is part of the promise of negotiation. It is one that women are well poised to realize.

PART I

The Power of Advocacy: Promoting Your Interests Effectively

1

STAYING OUT OF YOUR OWN WAY

A reporter once asked Yogi Berra what advice he would give aspiring ballplayers. After puzzling for a minute, the veteran catcher produced one of his signature comebacks: "Ya gotta dress for every game." Berra, seldom out of the Yankee lineup, was talking about more than just putting on his pads and mask. To play well, you had to be ready, pumped up, and prepared to face what was thrown your way. That's what the tools of effective advocacy do for you in a negotiation. They don't just put you in the game. They help insure that you will be ready to hit whatever is tossed your way, be it a sneaky curve or an unexpected fastball.

Part of that readiness is confidence in yourself and your ability to hold your own. Before you can convince the other person of anything, you first have to believe that you are in a good position to push for your demands. It's tough to get up for a negotiation when you look at your chances of success with a jaundiced eye. Why bother to negotiate at all? Who wants to get into a struggle she is just going to lose? Pushed by a colleague, pressured by a boss, or just limited by circumstances, it often seems easiest to acquiesce quietly or keep quiet altogether. Why risk the unpleasantness? It's tough to be persuasive when you think your case is shaky. Unconvinced of its merits, you are bound to have a hard time convincing anyone else. Better, you think, to cave before the other side pokes holes in your argument or laughs. Then again, maybe if you come on strong, assume an assurance you don't really feel, they won't notice the holes in your case.[1] It's toughest of all to force yourself to negotiate when you have been burned in the past or feel uncomfortable pressing for something you want.

Before you can negotiate effectively with others, you might have some negotiating to do with yourself. Successful advocacy begins with preparation—both psychological and factual. You must convince yourself that your demands are legitimate and believe that you have both the right and the ability to push for them. You need to see a negotiation as an opportunity that opens up choices, not as an occasion that forces you to take what is offered. Many successful negotiations begin with a resounding "No." But to get past that no, you must first see the possibility of a yes. Once you step back and take a realistic look at what is possible, you would be surprised how often you can turn around even a seemingly no-win situation.

Sometimes the enemy is us. As women, we often don't take the simple steps needed to empower ourselves in a negotiation. At times, we get in our own way even before the actual bargaining starts. Underestimating our strengths is as deadly as overestimating those of our bargaining counterpart, but we do it all the time. When we think we are on tenuous ground, we pull back on our demands and narrow our options from the beginning. When outflanked or outgunned, we silence ourselves because we don't see much point in speaking up anymore. At the other extreme, our dander up, we dig in our heels, substituting rigidity for persuasiveness. And now and then we just walk away. We don't attempt to even the odds.

The negotiation process is difficult enough without carrying a self-imposed handicap. Others try to gain the upper hand at our expense. They prod here and poke there in the shadow negotiation, looking for an advantage or searching for a vulnerability to exploit. We don't have to volunteer either or unwittingly hamper our chances for success. Men are as liable to commit acts of self-sabotage in negotiation as women. Women just tend to trip themselves up in different ways. Let's look at a sampling of common pitfalls we have winnowed from our interviews. The first step on the way to becoming an effective negotiator is to recognize how you get in your own way.

Opportunities for negotiation go unrecognized. To negotiate, you have to realize that it is possible. Otherwise the moment slips by. Opportunities are missed for lots of reasons. Sometimes, confronted with what seems to be a final decision, it's easy to forget that no decision is final until it is accepted. Faced with what seems to be an immovable barrier or just plain stubbornness, we are quick to hear that no as the last word. The office manager flatly refuses to discuss health-care benefits. Part-time workers are never included on the company policy. Your new co-worker has an annoying habit of vocally second-guessing your decisions on major accounts. You mention the need for some ground rules, but she cuts you off. When you accept that no as the end of the conversation, you foreclose on the possibility of negotiating through the problem.

Other times, the situation does not seem to lend itself to negotiation. Both these reasons converged for Karen when she was given a new and exciting account at her advertising agency. Karen saw the assignment as a vote of confidence and hesitated to mention the heavy load she was already carrying. She put in longer and longer hours. Challenged by the new account and aware of its visibility in the agency, she kept on top of it, but gradually her other accounts began to slip. Copy was late getting to the designers. She had to reschedule several important meetings with other clients. Over the course of several months, the slippage raised eyebrows. No one in the agency contested her performance on the new account, but it was not the unalloyed success she expected.

Karen missed a negotiating moment. She considered the new assignment a flattering fait accompli. Presented with a terrific opportunity (and one she considered an order from the top), she did not see the possibility of negotiation—let alone its necessity for her overall success. She could have bargained to lighten her current responsibilities or to take an oversight role on certain accounts. She could have requested an assistant and actively sought the managing partner's guidance on the account. Having secured none of these preconditions, she could not shine on all fronts and her great assignment produced mixed results.

Even within peremptory decisions there is generally room for some give-and-take, but you have to be aware of the possibility and act on it. Before going along with imposed solutions and shutting down your options, try to get behind the rationale. Less onerous answers may be available, but to uncover them you have to get the discussion going. Negotiation is always, or almost always, a possibility.

Being pushy is not my style. Some opportunities to negotiate are not so much missed as dismissed. The practice of negotiation does not square with the sort of person we want to be. It is not so hard to go after support for a project or to defend a team member or a child. But when it comes to asking for something for ourselves, that's a differrent matter. We might want a raise or a high starting salary or more time to work up a proposal, but it just doesn't feel right to push too hard. The self-promotion involved, we think, borders on selfishness. Besides, it is a waste of time. We find it more pleasant and efficient to spend that hour getting our jobs done or being with our families and friends than jockeying for an edge. The gamesmanship is off-putting. If what it takes to be an effective negotiator is self-absorption and fluency in boasting, the price is too high.

Distaste leads to avoidance. Better not to play the game, we think, than feel like a fraud. A museum curator in her mid-twenties, for example, carries around an image of herself that makes negotiation painful. "All my life," she says, "I have been taught to put others ahead of myself. I still have trouble seeing myself as a negotiator. It feels very foreign and uncomfortable to sit down and decide what I want and how to get it. Whenever I do this, I feel as though I am being selfish."

Naomi Wolf labels the pressures women feel to accommodate others the "Dragons of Niceness."[2] These invisible monsters, to her mind, constantly urge women to put the pleasure of others ahead of their own and to take their reality from that pleasure. Negotiation will always feel unnatural so long as being sensitive to others is confused with giving in to their demands. It will always be distasteful when defined as a selfish activity in which people beat each other up for a bigger slice of the pie.

People do make demands in negotiation. That is why we negotiate in the first place. But we have a choice in how we put those demands. When we avoid negotiation because we see it only as an exercise in aggressive self-aggrandizement, we not only prevent ourselves from finding our own voice, we deprive others of the opportunity to hear what we really think. The issue is not whether to negotiate but how to negotiate in a way that feels authentic and still gets us what we want.

Seeing only our weakness. Many women go into negotiations suspecting they will lose. This expectation then drives their thinking. Why should my customer meet my terms, they reason, when so many other vendors are waiting in line? I have spent too many years in a low-paying job in a nonprofit agency. I will never get the salary I want in the private sector. My boss is going to do what he wants anyway. Why should I raise a cautionary voice? He will just accuse me of not being willing to take a risk, even a calculated one. Negativity like this is an almost surefire guarantee that we will start a negotiation psychologically one-down. Even more troubling, it discourages us from negotiating in the first place.

Once we rivet our attention on weakness, we exaggerate everything that works against us. We blind ourselves to real strengths and cannot recognize, much less use, what we actually have going for us. Barbara's re-entry into the job market is a good example of the damage negative thinking can do.

After taking a decade off to be at home, Barbara was grateful for the job interview. It was just luck that she heard about the opening from a friend. Obviously any one of the other candidates would jump at an offer. Barbara obsessed over the gaping holes in her résumé until they were all she could see. When the offer came, disappointing as it was, she grabbed it. Barbara would have been surprised to learn just how pleased the principals in the firm felt when she accepted. They wanted an older person and put a premium on the connections she had made in her volunteer work. But Barbara's negative focus prevented her from parlaying those advantages into a higher salary.

With our weaknesses looming so large, we may not draw on strengths that we actually have and that supply the resilience necessary to stay in the negotiation. When intimidated or challenged, we might rigidly defend our claims or take the path of least resistance and retreat. Women are not alone here. Most people harbor doubts about being able to reach their goals. What makes the difference is whether we allow these natural doubts to control our actions. We shortchange ourselves when we focus only on weakness and don't use the assets we do have.

Bargaining ourselves down. Self-doubt creates another problem. We don't wait for the other side to whittle us down. We do it ourselves. Before we even start to negotiate—for a new job, a shift in career path, or more open communication with a client or a co-worker—chances are good that we carry on a private debate with ourselves. What do I want? What are my chances of getting it? Am I up to fighting that battle once again? Do I have a choice?

All too often we do more than set goals in these internal dialogues. They are where we make the first concession of the negotiation. Before we open the "official" discussions, we start bargaining ourselves down. We know what we have contributed to the group's effectiveness and to bottom-line profits. A 10 percent raise seems justified and realistic. But then the second-guessing starts. "My boss will never agree to that," we argue mentally. "I'm good, but maybe not that good. I'd probably be making more than the rest of the group. I'll start a bit lower—8 percent sounds more like it."

This private rationalizing might be faultless. The boss might consider a 10 percent raise totally out of line. But the point is that we don't even give her a chance to react to our request. Once we make that first concession in our heads, we limit our choices. We decide ahead of time what response we will provoke. We never test whether our anticipated scenario is, in fact, what will happen.

By making that first concession in our heads, we lower our aspirations and lose ground before the negotiation even opens. We ask for less than we want in the hope that we'll get something and avoid a messy confrontation. These diminished goals become self-fulfilling prophecies as the shadow negotiation plays out.[3] Once we settle for an 8 percent raise in our head, that figure usually turns out to be the most we can get, regardless of what we might deserve. When we worry about whether our demands will be hard to swallow, rather than trying to make them more palatable, we handicap ourselves from the start in the shadow negotiation. Self-doubt dominates our thinking. The central issue is not whether you can get something, but how to get what you want.

Making sure everyone is happy. Even when we stand up to that devil whispering in our ear to lower our goals, we can fall prey to another equally insidious voice that gets in our way—the one that insists that we smooth things over. To make everyone happy (or happier), we try to be "nice." Maybe we don't want to appear overly aggressive or unsympathetic. Maybe we have trouble with "winning" when victory comes at someone else's expense or is not masked by a team effort. Whatever the reason, we stumble at the end and give our gains back. That's what Beth did in a negotiation with another editor.

We were fighting over a new title. The book fit nicely on my list and I argued my case pretty strenuously. The other editor finally threw up his hands and said, "Okay, Beth. It's yours." Did I accept that? Oh, no. I tossed the ball back at him. I told him he could keep the book. I could tell just from the look on his face how much the decision meant to him. He'd had a rough couple of months. But I warned him that we needed to set up some guidelines. Otherwise, next time around, I wouldn't give an inch.

Did they ever set up any guidelines? No. Beth smoothed things over with her fellow editor, but at a cost only to her.

Women, often great readers of nonverbal cues, can retreat at the first sign of displeasure instead of using these messages as a wedge to open a dialogue. Looking to be fair to everyone, we sometimes forget about being fair to ourselves. We also up the ante on what it takes for us to say enough is enough and walk away.

Wanting everyone to be happy, our personal stake in a negotiation can become a moving target. We constantly adjust what we want in response to what the other person wants. At the same time, we fail to reckon the end cost of these concessions. Intent on peacemaking, we don't think about the price of that peace until it is too late. If others take advantage of us in the shadow negotiation, it is often because we let them. Caring about the other person in a negotiation is good, but not when it is totally one-sided.

These acts of self-sabotage happen most often in the shadow negotiation when you are uncertain about the situation and doubt your abilities. While a lack of information or understanding prompts some people to overplay their hands, it usually provokes the opposite reaction in women. Uncertainty about the situation feeds our self-doubts and we pull back, re-treating into old and sometimes destructive habits. Before we can put the qualities and skills we as women bring to any negotiation, we must take steps to reduce that uncertainty and doubt.

Confidence in a negotiation comes not so much from knowing you are in complete control but from recognizing what control you do have. The more realistic you can be in assessing the situation, the more effective you will be as a negotiator. A superficial pep talk is not adequate preparation. Successful advocacy depends on a hard-edged appraisal of where you stand and what you can do to improve your situation. There are four steps you can take to prepare yourself. Each step is simple, yet together they provide you with the self-awareness and situational insights you need to negotiate effectively. As your understanding expands, so does your confidence in your ability to deal with the situation.

- **TAKE STOCK**

   Deliberately inventory the skills and experience you bring to the table. Often you will find hidden resources you are not using. Look at what makes you feel vulnerable. Then you can plan ahead to compensate.

- **LEARN AS MUCH AS YOU CAN**

   An informational vacuum creates anxiety. Gather the facts that support your case, but also find out as much as you can about the other person and his or her situation. Pertinent information helps you set your agenda and stick to it.

- **DEVELOP ALTERNATIVES**

   When you have all your negotiating eggs in one basket, you feel (and are) pretty dependent on how the negotiation turns out. Having other options available increases your flexibility. You can objectively decide whether it is better for you to make a deal or walk away. You are not captive to any particular solution.

- **GET FRESH PERSPECTIVES**

   We get trapped in our own thinking. Talking to others whose judgment you trust generally helps you see the situation in a new light. Often you come away with suggestions that orient you more positively or more realistically.

As women, we need to prepare ourselves not only for what we expect others to dish out but also against the self-inflicted strikes we unwittingly launch against ourselves. These acts of self-sabotage frequently do more to harm our position than the other side's tactics even contemplate. Concentrate on you. Take stock of where you are and where you want to go. Probing like this tells you what information you need and where your resources could use a little shoring up. In a nutshell, think long and hard—not just about what works to the other party's advantage but what works to yours. This process not only helps you stay out of your own way, it strengthens your hand.

A Case of Self-Sabotage

Historian Thelma Aronberg faced a situation that made her ripe for self-sabotage. Thelma, at thirty-six, was a tenured professor in the American studies program at a liberal arts college in Ohio. An outspoken perfectionist, she pushed herself on all fronts. Students flocked to her lively and somewhat eccentric classes in pop culture and film. Colleagues had come to expect an original and iconoclastic approach in her publications, but could not quibble with her meticulous research. All in all, Thelma was not a woman you would expect to sabotage herself. But that's what happened when her department head dropped by for what she thought was a friendly chat.

Thelma, away the previous week giving a long-scheduled seminar, had missed the monthly department meeting and was anxious to catch up.

Brad:　　How did your seminar go?

Thelma:　Fine. Great group, lots of interchange, lively discussion.

Brad:　　Well, you missed an interesting faculty meeting. Congratulations are in order. We selected you department chair.

Brad's announcement sent Thelma reeling. After waiting three years to adopt a baby, her new daughter was about to arrive at the same time that her first book was due at the publisher. She could not imagine how she could manage the extra load.

Thelma:　This is a joke, right?

Brad:　　Uh-uh. The vote was unanimous.

Thelma:　That's crazy, insane. I couldn't possibly take on the chairmanship now.

Brad:　　Look, it's your turn. The chair is supposed to rotate every two years. That's department policy. But this is my second stint. I'm not putting in a third.

Thelma:　Can't you get somebody else?

Brad: You're the only one who isn't pulling her weight. Everybody's
                 got their own work to get out. Everybody's stretched. And
                 everybody else has done a stint.

The insinuation that she was not a team player cut. Thelma was not a
freeloader who let others carry the departmental burdens. She did more
than her share of committee work and student advising. Apparently those
efforts did not count. If the department did not consider her a team player,
and her colleagues were prepared to force the issue when she was so in-
undated, Thelma thought, maybe it was time to look for an appointment
somewhere else.

Feeling beleaguered, undervalued, and overburdened, Thelma saw no
way out of the predicament other than to resign. The timing was impossible. She couldn't just go along. The consequences would be disastrous.
From where she was sitting, Brad's request sounded like an order, not the
opening of a discussion. But was it? Had Thelma felt more in control, she
could have turned her negative perspective around. Her position was
stronger than she realized. We will return to Thelma and how she resolved her quandary after we explore the resources she eventually tapped.

Take Stock

Once self-doubt takes over or the choices you have seem equally unat-
tractive, as they did for Thelma, you risk distorting the situation beyond
recognition. Preoccupied with your vulnerability, you might read only
weakness in the picture you see. When you find yourself in a situation
where you see no way out, step back and take stock. What personal resources are you forgetting? What assets do you have at hand that you are
not using? You want this inventory to be as complete and precise as possible. There are four questions you can ask yourself to firm up this self-
evaluation.

QUESTION #1: *Ask yourself why the other person is
negotiating with you at all. What do you have that she or he
wants or needs?*

People don't negotiate without reasons. Negotiation happens because
each of us wants something and stands to benefit from the negotiation.

The other party sees immediate advantages or potential gains in the future. What are those? What do you offer? This line of questioning shifts your focus from why you need them to why they need you. That change in emphasis, by forcing you to look at your strengths, prevents you from getting bogged down in the weaknesses of your position. It gave Pat, a twenty-seven-year-old reporter, a needed edge in a difficult negotiation. Pat was angling to be appointed press agent for a political campaign and had a lot working against her.

> I wanted to break away from pure news reporting. This job opening
> was my first real shot at doing that. But I had no name recognition
> in political circles. I wasn't just green. I was young. Except for the
> volunteers, everyone on the campaign was at least fifteen years my
> senior and seasoned.

Right off, the candidate started testing Pat in the shadow negotiation. He stressed her inexperience. Hiring her, he said, posed some real risks. The press agent in any campaign was highly visible. If she came on board, she would be learning the tricks of the trade at his expense. In exchange, she should be willing to be paid at a bargain-basement hourly rate. Pat wanted the job at any price. The figure he quoted was not much different from what she was earning as a reporter. But few reporters pull down big salaries. In a political campaign low pay meant your opinions did not carry much weight. If Pat accepted the candidate's offer, she risked being silenced before she even started.

But Pat, having taken stock, had a good handle on what she brought to the campaign. Every time the candidate pointed to a weakness, Pat countered. Yes, she was green, but none of the seasoned professionals on the campaign had her journalism skills. No, she was not paid much as a reporter, but she had earned another currency he badly needed: wide contacts among the press.[4] By keeping the candidate focused on her talents and how they met his needs, she was able to negotiate a salary more in keeping with the demands of the job and one in line with the pay scale prevailing among political consultants. She not only got the paycheck she wanted; she earned the respect of the insiders on the campaign.

Knowing your own value, what you bring to the table, gives you a psychological edge. You have the means at hand to divert attention away from areas where you might be a little wobbly. But don't do your inventory in the abstract. Make a list of five good reasons why the other party needs you. This exercise will help you reframe the situation. The realization that the needs don't run in just one direction puts you on a more even footing. You might want something from the other party, but you also have something he or she wants from you.

QUESTION #2: *Ask yourself what happens when you have been successful in a negotiation.*

Experience can be a great teacher in negotiations. The more you negotiate, the more adept you can become. But that only happens if you learn to bank your experiences. You have to see how success in one situation can carry over and fortify you in another. Most of us are better at negotiation than we realize. Look at situations that have gone well and ask yourself why. By exploring the reasons behind your successes, you often gain insights that point to possible ways of getting unsatisfactory encounters back on track.

Emily used this technique to save her business. Emily started her own public relations firm after apprenticing at a large agency in Atlanta. Despite a growing client list, she was barely keeping afloat financially. The mounting pressure on her bottom line forced her to confront why. She did fine negotiating the initial contracts. The problem came later. She did too much unpaid work for her clients. Every time her clients asked for additional services, she undercut her profits. It was a vicious cycle. She couldn't bring herself to say no, and because she couldn't, her clients kept making more and more requests. "In a way, I renege on my own contracts. I cannot say no to clients. I know it and they know it."

Emily was no novice at negotiation. Besides starting her own company, she spearheaded a successful anti-smoking campaign in her community. "I cared about clean air. But the campaign was not personal. It was a cause." Emily felt sure of her ground when she stood up to angry restaurant owners. "When tempers got hot, I could always deflect the personal attacks and my personal stake in the outcome by going to the facts."

Emily realized she needed a comparable fail-safe mechanism when she negotiated with her clients on reimbursement for additional work. She found it by revising her basic contract so that it included an itemization of services that were not covered. Whenever a client suggested expanding the original scope of work, she had everything in black and white. The issue became not whether they would pay for these extra services but how much.

Everyone has a success story she can tell. Such experiences do not have to be drawn from your work environment to be translated to it. Perhaps you convinced the condo association to put in some flowering shrubs or managed to get a great deal on an old brass bed or persuaded the powers that be on the program committee at your synagogue to take up your suggestion for a lecture series. Analyzing those successes gives you insights into what makes a negotiation work for you. Do you prefer to take your risks in small doses rather than all at once? Do you prevail by persistence? Are you so organized that when you begin bargaining your argument contains no loose ends? Or do you rely on your reading of people to come up with a creative solution? Times when you are successful are moments for learning. As your understanding of why they happen becomes clear, you can try to create those same conditions in other situations where you might not feel so confident.

QUESTION #3: *Ask yourself what you know about the other party and the situation.*

Past negotiations can teach you a lot, but so can your wider experience. A curious thing often happens to women when they negotiate. They forget what they know once an encounter gets tagged as a "negotiation." They don't carry over to a negotiation the cues and observations that get them through the give-and-take of their daily routines. They might have been soaking up information about people or group dynamics, but they don't use it during a negotiation. Over time, you gain insights into what motivates people and how they are likely to behave. Tap into those observations. They are incredible resources to bring into play. They helped Amy not just hold her own in a difficult negotiation but to prevail.

After thirty years of marriage, Amy was embroiled in a bitter divorce. The slight, shy librarian worried about how she would fare against her successful and combative husband. Living with such a dominant personality had systematically chipped away at her self-confidence. Over the years, she had gotten out of the habit of making decisions or taking the initiative. Convinced she could not stand up to her husband, she was about to let her lawyer handle the settlement negotiations. Then she hit upon an unexpected asset. She knew her husband inside and out.

I have studied him for thirty-one years. None of his partners knows him
the way I do. He always portrays himself as a good guy, but he's not.
He's tenacious and persistent. He is also a master manipulator. He
uses charm and seduction to get his way. By knowing these things
about him, I could preempt him.

Well aware of how her husband reacted when provoked, Amy consciously created opportunities in the courtroom for him to reveal the man
she knew—someone who never gave up anything unless he got something
in return, who defined *fair* in terms of what he could extract. The judge,
even her husband's lawyers, began to see *him* as a bully rather than *her* as
an ineffectual mouse. Taking charge, capitalizing on a hidden strength,
Amy also came to view herself differently. She was not the pushover her
husband expected to encounter. "At one point a light came on," she recalls.
"I had become a formidable adversary." And the settlement she negotiated
proved it.

Realizing how much you do know about the other party empowers you
in a negotiation. It can be key when dealing with someone difficult, as
Amy discovered. Cues you absorb about negotiating styles contain valuable hints on how to deal with the other person. Understanding the tack
he or she is likely to take helps you plan your own strategy—whether you
are negotiating a difficult divorce or a severance package.

QUESTION #4: *Ask yourself what about certain situations makes you feel vulnerable. Where are you vulnerable?*

Assets and resources have a flip side. You have to pay attention to your
weaknesses too. Knowing you have a gap in your skills or background, you
can figure out ways to bridge it. Look back over your past experiences.
What situations give you trouble? What makes you feel vulnerable? How
do you test yourself? Do you always get what you want? Does that success
mean you are an effective advocate or that you are asking for too little? In
certain circumstances do you tend to avoid conflict, blame yourself, or
take on the burden of making everyone feel good?

Just thinking about troublesome experiences alerts you to occasions
when you slip into self-sabotaging patterns or when you find your confidence threatened. Once you understand what trips you up, you can figure
out what you need to do to compensate. Gina, an entrepreneur, considers

her lack of academic credentials a potential liability when she bargains. A retailing whiz with an uncanny ability to coax money out of investors, she never got past high school. That her backers, her customers, and her staff have long since ceased to care about her educational background is not the issue. Because Gina thinks they do, because she believes it, that perception is a liability. It undermines her confidence in the shadow negotiation.

Recognizing this, Gina masters the ins and outs of any proposal and learns as much as she can about the people she will face. "Most people aren't so thorough," she admits. "But I never got an education. I don't have a college diploma, much less an M.B.A. Preparation helps me fight my lack of confidence. I know I know my stuff, degrees or not."

Being alert to what triggers your vulnerabilities allows you to plan ahead. When warning alarms trip, you can fall back on rehearsed responses. If you discover you have a tendency to bargain away your advantage at the last minute, a mantra—"Keep it, stupid"—comes in handy. It is not an ironclad insurance policy, but it might keep you on your toes. Judy, a former teacher turned investment banker, negotiates large municipal bond deals. Aware that she gets caught up in the pressure to close, she always gives herself a night to go over the fine print once more. Knowing that she has this time in reserve prevents her from making hasty commitments.

Rather than leave to chance whether your vulnerabilities will be exploited in the shadow negotiation, anticipate occasions when that is likely to happen. Forewarned, you can control them, not vice versa. Armed against the worst, you can avoid falling into bad habits and approach any negotiation with confidence.

Learn as Much as You Can

Information is a valuable commodity in negotiations. We've seen what knowing about yourself and tapping into what you know about the other party can accomplish. But imagine what would happen if you had perfect information. You would understand exactly how to present your case and the responses you needed to have ready. You would have a clear idea of where the other person would compromise and where no concessions would be made. Perfect information, in effect, would take away all the guesswork and eliminate the anxiety. Unfortunately, as bargainers, we rarely enjoy this luxury. But the more we can discover, the more realistic our assessment of the situation becomes.

Two distinct kinds of information come into play in negotiations. *Factual information* provides the hard data—the pertinent facts and the intelligence about policies, practices, and precedents—that you use to back up your arguments. *Scouting information* helps you predict the hearing those arguments will get so you can fine-tune your approach.

Factual information. To negotiate effectively, you must believe your argument is defensible. A solid informational foundation helps support that conviction. With the pertinent facts on hand you won't get flustered when pointed questions come your way. You can supply concrete reasons why your proposal makes sense—why, for example, gradual price increases in a contract are more likely to be accepted by a client than a smaller but immediate hike. Factual information also provides a focus for the discussion that prevents it from deteriorating into a debate over personal preferences and beliefs. Facts extend well beyond quantitative data. They cover a whole host of organizational policies and precedents as well as comparisons that can be drawn from other sources. If, for example, you want to propose a flexible work schedule, you can make your argument more effectively if you can point to other examples in your organization or to arrangements at other companies that have worked well.

Facts in this broader sense help you counter challenges. Alison, a banker in her late twenties, had a degree in international finance. Fluent in Arabic and Hebrew, she applied for a posting to the Middle East. Her boss turned her down. Given the status of women in that area of the world, he said, she could not be effective. Alison knew, from a friend's experience in Cairo, that even in conservative countries Western women moved easily within the international business community. Instead of pushing against her boss's mind-set, she pulled together information from government and nongovernmental sources. She was able to show, by industry, just how many American women worked in the Middle East. She also documented the difference in the way "foreign" women were treated in these countries. Her boss, who had been operating on a gut reaction and no concrete information, finally realized that he was on shaky (perhaps actionable) ground.

No place is the need for substantiating factual information clearer than in salary negotiations. A salary request cannot be plucked out of thin air. It has to fall within industry standards. Those standards, in turn, allow you to defend your demands. But a host of personal and organizational factors coalesce when money is the issue and make salary negotiations challenging. Women often compare themselves to other women and do not consider a range of possibilities outside this small sample. There is also an almost universal expectation that women will not push hard on dollars. As a result, offering them less seems a safe bet.[5] Then there is that inevitable question: "What are you making now?" Prospective employers often use an applicant's current salary as a benchmark in deciding what to offer. This practice presents a problem for women when their current salaries reflect neither their abilities nor their actual levels of responsibility. They may, for example, be switching from part-time to full-time work, moving from the public to the private sector, or returning to the workforce.

Whatever your circumstances, the more you know about a job and the salary it should command, the more comfortable you will feel. First off, the information takes away some of the uncertainty. You can distinguish a fair offer from an insult. With a firm salary range in mind, you can focus the discussion on the qualifications for the job and what it should pay, and avoid getting into a more subjective argument over what you are worth.

Concrete information affords solid protection—against both overselling and undervaluing. With a thorough survey of current salary ranges in hand, you can calibrate your options and check the temptation to bargain yourself down in that private debate that takes place in your head. Connie, a talented engineer in her late twenties, had spent six years at a start-up dot.com. Frustrated at a salary that did not begin to compensate for her long hours and doubtful that the firm was ever going to take off, Connie decided to start job hunting. But before she could go out on any interviews, she knew she had to be prepared to justify the big jump in salary she wanted.

> Of course I did my homework, but the right information was not easy to find. I was comparing salaries at a small start-up with those at a big engineering firm. Instead of raises, we got stock options. These were worthless now, but maybe not if the company went public. Still, I needed a logic for the number I put on the table.

To build her case, Connie concentrated on what first-year engineers made at large firms when she graduated. She called the placement office at her university and discovered that salaries clustered in three groupings.

STARTING SALARIES[*]
$37,500–$35,000
$33,000–$30,000
$22,500–$19,000

*These figures are hypothetical.

Given her educational record and experience, she felt secure putting herself just under the top tier. She then projected what that number would be with annual raises—one at the inflation rate and another assuming a higher merit increase. She fixed on an appropriate merit raise, which she was convinced she would have earned, by talking to friends who graduated with her and worked at large firms.

TARGET SALARY RANGE	INCREASE AT INFLATION (3%)		MERIT INCREASE (6%)	
	STARTING LEVEL	CURRENT DOLLARS	STARTING LEVEL	CURRENT DOLLARS
$33,000–$30,000	$33,000	**$38,500**	$33,000	**$44,500**

The higher figure, $44,500, turned into Connie's opening demand. The lower one, $38,500, became her walk-away price. If an offer fell below that figure, she would turn it down. Unless you define this walk-away figure yourself, any prospective boss will mentally fix it at your current salary level. Connie's research not only gave her the ammunition she needed to deflect discussion away from her weakness—her current salary—to what the prospective job should command. It also insured that she could back up the demands she did make with supporting data for engineers with comparable training and experience.

Due to their circumstances, women can enter salary negotiations at a disadvantage. Any equivocation tempts a prospective employer to push an offer lower and lower. To resist, you need a logic for the number you put on the table. That logic translates facts and figures into a cohesive argument. When a demand seems legitimate given what you have discovered, it is much easier to defend to others.

Scouting information. Not all crucial information comes in the form of facts and figures or clear-cut policies. You retrieve an altogether different kind of information by sounding others out for their take on particular personalities or for their reading of an organization's politics and its culture. The more you know about the person you are going to be negotiating with, the more confidence you will have in your approach.

Often the outcome of a negotiation turns on the political environment in which it takes place. Decision-making routines, norms, the informal power structure—all these condition the response you are likely to get. Do your demands fall within normal practices or do you have to take special care? Are there precedents for what you are proposing? Who else will be affected? Are their reactions liable to be negative? If so, what can you do about turning those initial responses around?

This kind of knowledge is generally not public. Nor is it uniform. Different people will have had different experiences with the same person, and these experiences color their opinions. No two people will have the same reading on office politics or the organization's culture. As a result, it is important to let your scouting range widely.

These scouting reports guide you as you figure out how best to approach the other party. Erika used them to get off on the right foot when she argued her case for a specific first assignment after completing the training program at a New York investment bank. Erika wanted to be an options trader, but the decision was taken out of her hands. Instead, she was slated for the research department, a plum assignment. "I'd been a star in the training program, and in some ways the assignment was a reward. But not for me. I had my sights fixed on the trading floor."

Most of the trainees considered these assignment decisions final. Erika wanted to negotiate hers. At the same time, she had little interest in being branded a troublemaker. Before Erika started her scouting, she had no idea how receptive the management committee would be to an alternative suggestion from her. Having spent only a short rotation on the trading floor, she was even less certain how to approach the head trader. She also worried about the head of research. The woman had been something of a mentor, and Erika did not want a change in assignment to alienate her.

Erika, gregarious and not the least bit timid about approaching relative strangers, gathered information informally. To test the feasibility of even proposing a change in assignment, she talked to men and women in various departments who had completed the training program three or four years earlier. To get a better handle on the head trader's likely reaction, she went out for coffee with any options trader under thirty she could corral. Within a relatively short period of time, a clear picture began to emerge: The first assignment was critical to her career path. Requests for reassignment, while not common, had been successful in the past. With this feedback in hand, Erika shared her career plans with her mentor, being careful to make her appreciation of the woman's support explicit.

Scouting information did more than lessen Erika's fears about the risks of putting in for the options desk. It also pointed out how she should couch her proposal so that it would stir the least resistance. By a fortuitous accident, Erika's mentor had just listened to the head trader complain that his department was not attracting its full quota of talented women despite concerted efforts on his part.

Scouting information allows you to anticipate problems. If it looks as if your demands will bump up against entrenched attitudes or established ways of doing things, you know where to fine-tune your request. If current practices come up short as far as you are concerned, you know any proposal must supply an acceptable alternative to those precedents. Bettina, pregnant with her first child, used this kind of information to develop a proposal for a flexible schedule.

Bettina, an operations manager in an automotive assembly plant in Detroit, realized any change in her schedule would automatically affect others. In the past, these arrangements had created problems in her company—both for management and for the women. To get management's side of the story, she quizzed her boss and other department heads about the headaches flexible schedules caused them. At the same time, she drew out women on the challenges they faced when they reduced their hours.

"Face time," it turned out, was a big element in how employees were perceived. The increased emphasis on teams meant that if you weren't around, you gradually became invisible. "I talked to women on flexible schedules," Bettina recalls. "And I watched them. They missed important meetings and gradually got left out of the decision making. Then, feeling guilty about disappointing their bosses and not wanting to be excluded for career reasons, bit by bit they started putting in longer hours. Eventually they were working a full schedule for part-time pay."

With this scouting information in hand, Bettina could address many of management's concerns in her proposal. Her scouting reports also underscored the need to build in safeguards for herself and pointed to where she would be most vulnerable. Any proposal she made had to maintain her level of responsibility *and* prevent erosion of her time at home. To protect against slippage on either count, she incorporated a three-month review so that she and her boss could evaluate how the arrangement was working for both of them.[6]

Information increases your control over a negotiation. The more you know ahead of time, the more realistic you can be in setting your goals and the easier it is to figure out what steps you need to take to get what you want. With the right information at your fingertips—both factual and scouting—you gain confidence in what you are doing. As a result, you are unlikely to sabotage yourself by caving in too soon or settling for less than you should.

Develop Alternatives

Information, in and of itself, bolsters confidence. Going into a negotiation prepared lessens the chances of being caught unawares. It becomes easier to be firm. It is also harder for others to brush off well-documented arguments. But information does more than bolster your case. It forces you to clarify your options. Earlier we suggested you begin to prepare for a negotiation by taking stock and considering why the other party needs you. That is an important step, but you can take it further. You can analyze what will happen to each of you if you cannot come to terms. What are your alternatives? What are the other person's? The answers to these questions reveal just how much flexibility you have in a negotiation. The better your alternatives are, the less your fate hangs on the negotiation's outcome and, paradoxically, the more influence you are likely to have over the terms of any agreement. In parallel, as your counterpart's alternatives worsen, yours improve.

Find other ways to satisfy your needs. When the other party senses that you have no alternative but to take what is offered, he or she will be tempted to give as little as possible. With another job offer or another contract in your back pocket, you don't have to depend on the other party's generosity or go along with any ultimatums. You can decide what is best for you rather than have the other side do the defining. Alternatives, in effect, expand your bargaining power.

The notion of alternatives is captured in the acronym BATNA, which stands for Best Alternative To a Negotiated Agreement.[7] Your BATNA answers the question "What will I do if we can't come to an agreement that meets my needs?" Alice and Meg broadened their alternatives midstream in a negotiation when their firm's contract with its only client came up for renewal. The company the two women ran provided part-time clerical services to a nearby university on a contractual basis. In turn, they filled their roster of workers with lower-income women from a job-training program initiated by the city.

As soon as the talks started, the university's vice president for financial affairs began pressing them on price. "He thought we were ripe for plucking," Meg commented. "Two naïve, overeducated, twenty-something women with lots of heart and no street smarts." Right off the bat, he cited the university-wide cost-cutting program and slashed Alice and Meg's fee until there was barely room in the numbers to cover their overhead. Panicked, they were on the verge of giving in just to secure the contract's renewal.

"Then we called a time-out," Alice said. "We told him we needed a week to think over our decision." The two spent that time not in squeezing the last nickel out of their budget but in lining up other work. By the end of the week, they had secured verbal commitments that, altogether, represented more work than they could handle without staffing up.

The vice president attempted to start the next round of talks where the previous one had left off. "Sorry," Meg interjected. "If that is your budget allowance, we will have to scale back our services." No longer dependent on the university contract for survival, Alice and Meg could hold out for a fair price. Without these other commitments, the temptation to go along with the vice president's ultimatum would have been much stronger. Having viable alternatives strengthened their resolve.

The vice president was surprised. He thought, given their situation, he would be able to dictate terms. Once Alice and Meg disabused him of that notion, they were able to work out a deal each side could live with. The vice president actually became quite conciliatory. An efficient bottom line was only part of his mandate. The university had no interest in jeopardizing a contract that eased its tense relations with the city. He needed an agreement more than Alice or Meg guessed.

Alternatives strengthen your position, but they also serve another important function. They keep you focused on your goals. The discipline of working through what actually is a better alternative forces you to identify why it is better. With other opportunities available, you don't run the risk of getting so caught up in the negotiation itself that reaching agreement—any agreement—becomes the goal. No deal is better than a bad deal—if you have an escape hatch. But don't make the mistake of overestimating the alternatives at your disposal. They must be real. Otherwise, they are just wishful thinking and can tempt you to overplay your hand.

What is the worst that can happen? It pays to think about worst-case scenarios. At times, your fallback position is to leave things the way they are. If you cannot strike a deal, you won't be any better off, but you also won't lose anything. At other times, you have no viable alternative. All your other choices would leave you worse off. When you find yourself in this situation, you don't have much room to bargain. You might have to resign yourself to taking less or paying more than you had hoped—and not just in terms of money. That's okay. There is no point in blaming yourself or faulting your negotiating skills. No one can negotiate effectively without some viable choices.

Jill took charge of her company's travel arrangements and soon discovered she had no flexibility in picking the agent. It was an unwritten rule that the company would use the agency owned by an influential board member. The agency's quoted prices were high enough to border on a conflict of interest. But Jill was stuck. The woman would not reduce her rates and Jill had no other options to explore. Despite her reluctance, Jill had no choice but to continue the well-established precedent.

Don't forget to assess the other person's alternatives. Having a good grasp on your alternatives gives you a realistic picture of your situation. But if you can learn more about the choices at the other party's disposal, the picture becomes even sharper. The reason for this is simple. What we think of our alternatives directly affects our assessment of the other side's position. Once we decide our alternatives don't look good, we almost automatically assume the other person has the upper hand. Marge, a freelance designer in her early forties, almost got caught in this trap. Until she actually investigated the other side's choices, she exaggerated the flexibility it enjoyed.

Marge had done some top-notch design work for ODI, one of the largest furniture dealers in North Carolina. Not long afterward, ODI's owners approached her with a proposal. Instead of continuing to do contract work, why didn't she become a partner? They would supply office space and needed capital. In exchange, she would provide in-house design expertise. On the plus side, the partnership would end her persistent cash-flow problems. On the down side, it might compromise her independence and her ability to work for other clients. The issues between them soon boiled down to one—office layout. The owners wanted Marge's space configured so that it appeared to be an extension of their design department. Marge insisted that her space be clearly defined so that her other clients would feel comfortable coming to the office.

This was a tough negotiation for Marge. ODI dwarfed her shoestring operation. What's more, the owners' enthusiasm for her work masked a veiled threat. Accept or they would find someone else. This hardball tactic made Marge suspicious. She knew there were only two other designers of her caliber in the Greenville area. She called both and discovered that neither would consider the kind of arrangement ODI had in mind. ODI would have to raid a competitor or persuade a designer to relocate— not exactly great alternatives for them. Marge's awareness of the owners' limited choices enabled her to push hard on her space demands. Had she taken the owners' reading of their options at face value, she would have found it much more difficult to resist their attempts to dominate her in the shadow negotiation.

Alternatives—yours and the other party's—go a long way toward answering the question of who needs whom more in a negotiation. They provide a litmus test for the ability of either to walk away. When you have other options, you cannot be held captive to an imposed solution. When you know the constraints under which the other person is operating, you are much less inclined to grab any offer he or she puts on the table. And if your alternatives turn out to be poor, you don't waste time blaming yourself. You try for the best you can hope to realize. Knowing the alternatives on both sides of the table adds to your effectiveness as a negotiator precisely because it gives you a realistic picture of the cards you have to play.

Get Fresh Perspectives

So you have inventoried your assets, come to grips with your weaknesses, learned more about the situation and the players, and still things look pretty bleak. The more you mull over your problem, the worse it looks. Sometimes, caught in our own myopia, we see no way out of a bad situation. But difficult negotiations need not be toughed out alone, nor should they be. Talking through a problem with family members, friends, and colleagues often gives you the support you need to face what you expect to be a troubling experience.

Seek out objective advice. Informal consultants can do more than provide moral support and a safety valve. Removed from the immediate situation, they invariably have a different take on it. Nor are they subject to the same doubts you might have. Their outlook can help you filter out your biases and view your choices objectively.

Meredith, an attorney specializing in trust and financial planning, had built a committed practice among the new breed of entrepreneurs in Silicon Valley's technology start-ups and the Bay Area's biotechnology firms. One of her first clients had recently died of AIDS. He left a large estate, a distraught and loving partner, and an appalled family. A week after his will was filed at probate, the family brought an injunction to remove Meredith as trustee. The grounds were incompetence.

Meredith panicked. Even her wicked sense of humor disappeared.

> I didn't know what to do. If I stepped down as trustee, it was an admission of incompetence and the worst kind of betrayal of James. His family is a powerhouse in this state. If I fought them, I was going to be slaughtered. Either way I would be ruined.

Part of Meredith's strain was financial. She was spending all her time preparing her defense. Her billable hours shrank at the same time that her expenses escalated. She also worried about the quality of the work she had done for James. His condition had deteriorated rapidly, and they had competed against the clock to finish the documents. Had she done a sloppy job in the rush?

Meredith knew she could not allow this state of paralysis to continue. She turned to colleagues at the Women's Bar Association for a detached look at the lawsuit. Not hampered by the emotions and strains she was under, they walked her through the case. She was not in such bad shape legally. The work for her client was solid, defensible on its merits. She was, however, letting the opposing counsel's status overwhelm her. Her fears were understandable, they all agreed, but it was an emotional reaction, one that the lawyers on the other side were all too willing to exploit in the shadow negotiation.

Gradually, Meredith's friends brought her to a new understanding. She was not so vulnerable as she assumed, but she was getting in her own way. Given her involvement and her emotional state, she could not mount a defense by herself. Rather than increasing Meredith's gloom, this objective assessment sharpened her focus. She hired a lawyer to represent her and turned her attention back to her other clients, which relieved her financial stress. Several months later the suit was dismissed.

Tap the experiences of others. It is not unusual when we get into a bind in a negotiation to think "Why me?" Preoccupied with our own difficulties, we assume no one else has ever had the same experience. By talking to colleagues you often discover you are in good company. Katherine looked forward to her performance review. She expected praise for her work and a big raise. Instead she got a reprimand. She needed to cultivate a softer manner. She was too aggressive in her dealings with other members of the firm. Katherine, taken aback, had no idea how to respond. It was not exactly the moment to suggest a raise.

In a smart move, Katherine temporized and told her boss she needed to think about his feedback. And think she did. But she also mentioned the incident at the breakfast women in the firm held each month. Karen was halfway through her description when smiles started to crack around the table. It turned out that most of the senior women had been treated to the same lecture at one point or another. They also thought they had been singled out for negative feedback. As the conversation progressed, it became apparent that what had seemed to be an individual problem was actually a firm problem. That consensus eased Katherine's doubts. She wasn't too aggressive, merely held to a different standard. When she picked up the negotiation with her boss, she focused the discussion not on her behavior but on objective criteria: what she had accomplished for the firm.

Widen your focus. There is one last way fresh perspectives are helpful. Uncertainty about what to do can tempt you to narrow your choices. A troublesome decision seems more manageable when you only have to consider a yes or no answer. At the same time, simplification like this prevents you from considering other options. A wise counselor can often come up with an array of additional ideas. Suddenly you don't see yourself trapped in an either/or decision, whether to accept or to refuse. Esther, a junior partner in a consulting firm, reaped the benefits of an expanded perspective.

Esther's potential caught the eye of the managing partner, and he offered her a special assignment heading up a task force on diversity. This offer was a mixed blessing. Esther cared about diversity, but she also cared about keeping her career on track, and promotions at the firm went to the rainmakers who brought in new business. The task force would eat into hours she could spend on work that would be rewarded. To make matters worse, virtually no one turned down a special assignment from the managing partner.

Esther faced a dilemma. If she said yes, it would take her away from her primary work and hurt her career, but the managing partner would consider her a team player. If she said no, she could get on with her "real" work, but the partner would be offended. Because the assignment appealed to her, she was tempted to agree and deal with the difficulties later. Before she made a final decision, she decided to run the pros and cons by her old business school professor. He quickly passed over the consequences of saying yes or no. Instead, he focused on Esther's real problem. She wanted to take on the assignment but worried about the impact on her career. The dilemma came not from the assignment itself but from the importance the firm attached to it. Esther needed to convince the managing partner that no one would accept this assignment or place much credence on its findings unless the work carried as much value for the firm as rainmaking.

The managing partner had long been an advocate of increased diversity within the firm, and he immediately grasped the core issue when Esther laid out her reservations. As long as the diversity effort bore no relation to the firm's reward systems, no one would pay its results much attention. Together, Esther and the managing partner came up with an estimate of how much time the assignment would take to insure first-rate results, and reduced her other obligations by a corresponding amount. They then began to analyze how those efforts translated to the firm's bottom line. They were after concrete ways of measurement so that organization building as well as rainmaking counted in decisions on who got promoted and who didn't.

It is not always easy to ask for help, and not all advice is equal. Even close friends or colleagues can be tempted to tell you what they think you want to hear. Bent on making you feel better or avoiding an emotional discussion, they mask their real opinions. You might have to contract explicitly for candid advice, and you must choose your consultants carefully. You don't want an overly rosy picture painted, but an unnecessarily bleak view is just as little help. To understand where you stand, you need to corroborate both the good and the bad.

Objective feedback, whether positive *or* negative, invariably gives you a more realistic take on your situation. No matter how scrupulous your self-assessment or meticulous your information gathering, at times a correcting lens is needed. Informal consultants can confirm your suspicion that you are not in a particularly strong bargaining position. They can also encourage you to view the negotiation more positively by pointing out where you have become too narrowly focused or drawn questionable conclusions.

Thelma's Dilemma

We have laid out a series of steps that can prevent you from getting in your own way and help start your advocacy off on the right foot. These steps have a cumulative effect, reinforcing each other. To show how they can work together, we want to return to Thelma's story at the point where she is being pressured to take over as department head. Defensive and stretched to the limit, Thelma at first saw only an insoluble dilemma. She could not manage an infant, her teaching load, and the chair's additional duties. If she accepted, she saw two miserable years ahead. Angry with her colleagues and resentful of the time the chair's job would take away from her new baby, she decided the only way out was to resign.

Thelma called a friend at another school and poured out her tale of woe. Brad had accused her of being a freeloader when the department needed a team player. No one was sympathetic to her situation. She had pretty much made up her mind to resign. Thelma's friend surprised her. Instead of commiseration, she got a mini-lecture. Thelma did not realize she was engaged in a negotiation. And in a negotiation you have to think about what you want. Her friend then posed a question that puzzled Thelma at first. At what price, she asked, would Thelma take the chair's job? What sort of support would the department have to give her? Mulling over that question Thelma took the initial step in preparing an effective advocacy. Maybe, she started thinking, she could bargain after all.

Thelma first looked at where she stood. Her position was actually pretty strong, when she considered it objectively. Without doubt, she was the best person for the chair's job at that moment in time. She had been a moving force on the college's curriculum committee. With her as chair, the department would gain a vocal spokesperson who could push the administration for reform. But, most important, the department needed her—whether or not she accepted the chair's job. One of the college's most popular teachers, she wielded considerable influence with the administration—a big advantage in a budget-cutting atmosphere.

Thelma also realized she had some hidden assets she could bring into play. She was pretty good at reading people and situations—the kind of information all of us pick up but so often discount. She knew the department, and she knew Brad. She had watched him in action for almost a decade. He disliked complaints and looked for solutions, not more problems. He wanted to get rid of the chair's responsibilities and would probably try to find the resources to make the job easier for her.

What's more, she had a lot of scouting information at her fingertips. As soon as the adoption agency notified her about the baby, she had sought out members of other departments to discover how they handled the dual burdens of work and family. But she still needed information on the arrangements other departments made to lessen the extra load any chair took on. Did they supply additional staff support? Were teaching commitments reduced to free up time? A few quick telephone calls yielded the answers. Support staff was invariably provided and teaching commitments reduced by at least one course.

With these arrangements in mind, Thelma began to craft a solution that met her needs and Brad's—his for somebody to take over as chair and hers to have the time and energy to enjoy her daughter. To give herself a fallback position, Thelma approached a colleague she had helped out in the past. Would she be willing to serve as co-chair the first year of Thelma's commitment if Thelma did all the organizational work from home? Yes, the woman agreed, if Thelma returned the favor when her turn as chair came up.

Thelma was left with one thorny question. What demands could she make that were realistic and filled her needs? Just to be on the safe side, she decided to ask for an assistant and for her teaching load to be lightened by one course.

The next morning Thelma put her conditions on the table. Brad did not even blink. He was perfectly willing to bargain.

As Thelma discovered, biased and distorted pictures of where you stand can wreak havoc with your capacity to negotiate. To argue your case effectively, you need to believe that you have something to bargain with and over. Otherwise opportunities slip by. Before you can engage the other party in a negotiation, you have to make sure you are ready—psychologically and practically. A realistic fix on your bargaining position not only enables you to stay out of your own way, it focuses you on the positive steps you can take to support your demands. It's the bargainer's equivalent of being dressed for the game.

2

MAKING STRATEGIC MOVES

Effective advocacy hinges on getting into a good position in the shadow negotiation and staying there. That takes some deliberate maneuvering. You want the other person to be receptive to your demands—or at least grant them a hearing. But just because you are primed to negotiate is no guarantee that your counterpart is anxious to meet you halfway.

More often than not, you have a reluctant bargainer on your hands. She might see no advantage in dealing with you. She stalls or ignores you. Phone calls go unanswered. That important talk keeps being postponed. Even when you wear him down with your persistence, he pays lip service to your ideas and immediately skips to his own agenda or changes the subject. Somehow you never manage to get a two-way conversation going. He has made up his mind before you open your mouth. She thinks that if she holds out long enough you might relax your demands or stop bothering her.

It's perfectly normal to encounter resistance in negotiation. A good part of every negotiator's job is to convince others to take his or her proposals seriously and go along with them. But the process requires some give-and-take. Not all the giving or the taking can come from one side. Strategic moves are the means you use to influence the balance in any negotiation and insure that the give-and-take goes both ways.

A willingness to negotiate is at some basic level a confession of mutual need. People negotiate with us when we have something they want and they cannot count on our falling in with their plans without our getting something in return. These perceptions of mutual need play out in the shadow negotiation, and here is where the rub comes for women. We frequently negotiate in situations where on the face of it we need the other party more than he or she needs us. As a result, our demands can be easy to dismiss, and it takes more effort to persuade the other person that we have something credible to offer.

So long as a loan officer at the bank senses that you don't fit her profile of a good customer (and few entrepreneurial women in service industries do), she is going to think twice about setting up a credit line for your new business. Before she gives your application more than a perfunctory review, she must see you as someone capable of running a company and shepherding the transition from idea to reality. Once you set her thinking in that direction, the needs at the table begin to balance out. She might control the money you want, but she is still in the business of lending it out. She wants new customers just as you want a credit line. Rather than rely on her hunger for new accounts, you must move strategically to convince her that you are worth the risk.

Even when we as women are in a position to press our demands, we can find them being discounted. This happens for lots of reasons. We might have acquired a reputation for going along. Having learned to negotiate in situations where we have less say than other people, we might have hesitated to speak up in the past. Most bosses will keep piling on the work so long as we silently go about completing our assignments on time. Colleagues and clients might simply expect us to be amenable, knowing that we are reluctant to challenge the system. If a co-worker can count on us to pick up the slack, she won't feel inclined to discuss doing her fair share.

The failure of women to make themselves heard in a negotiation is often chalked up to a feminine style of communicating.[1] Women, so the argument goes, cloak their comments in diffidence or hesitate to put themselves forward. But communications skills are seldom the root of the problem. Nor is timidity the only culprit when women are talked over or find their demands and suggestions ignored. Often they have been left out of the earlier informal discussions where the issues are really decided. By the time they offer their opinions, what they have to say is irrelevant. It's not just that they are not heard. Their ideas no longer count.

More than persuasive coaxing is needed when you bump up against attitudes like these in the shadow negotiation.[2] You must bring the people you negotiate with to the point where they realize that they have to deal with you seriously and fairly. Just as there are steps you can take so that you come to the table with confidence, there are strategic moves you can make to convince another party to heed your demands. These moves convey to her just exactly why she at least needs to meet you halfway. Any reluctance she might have to negotiate with you fades once she is forced to admit that she will be better off if she deals with you *and* worse off if she doesn't.

Strategic moves employ both the carrot and the stick. Using incentives, the carrots, you make the other party aware of the *benefits* of dealing with you. You point out the value she gets in return, how negotiating with you works to her advantage. It is always safer for that loan officer to say no. The loans she doesn't write don't appear on the bank's monthly watch list of troubled accounts. She must be convinced that there are clear advantages (and precious little risk) for her if she approves your loan application.

Sticks operate in reverse. By exerting pressure on the other party, you underscore the *costs* to her if she continues to ignore you or persists in giving you a hard time. If she sees few reasons to meet your needs, you supply them by raising the stakes. Increased pressure might be in order when the prospect of negotiation holds some real disadvantages for the other party. He or she might be quite content to let things drift along as they are. A boss accountable to management for the department's cost cutting might be reluctant to give you a raise until you tell him you have another job offer. Business as usual is more comfortable than introducing an alien voice—yours—into the decision-making apparatus already in place—until, that is, the others realize you have a much-needed piece of information. A co-worker who has been successful in persuading you to produce those late-night projections has a vested interest in not negotiating with you until you leave early several nights in a row.

Establishing your voice *as a negotiator* in the shadow negotiation is no small task. You can pretty much take it for granted that your credibility will be questioned and your resolve tested. In situations where you are not the only one involved in making the decision, the other party must understand that you have the authority to commit your organization. A supplier will always defer to the person in the firm he thinks has the final say and controls the checkbook. It doesn't matter that the account is your responsibility and you are the one making the sales calls. Your opinions won't carry any weight so long as he doubts your authority to make decisions or put his requisition through. To be heard—in a meeting with your colleagues at work or by that supplier, anyone—you must marshal some authority for your voice.

At times an overtly self-promoting move would be awkward or your own efforts are not enough to compel someone to negotiate with you. Strategic allies can pave your way by putting their credibility behind you. It also pays to plan ahead when you know an important negotiation is coming up. You can then move to influence its outcome by shaping the process. By anticipating resistance and lobbying behind the scenes, you can position your ideas and issues so that they are heard positively once the negotiation actually gets under way.

- **HOLD OUT INCENTIVES**

  In any negotiation, the other party controls something you need—more money, more time, more cooperation, better communication, an opportunity. That's why you want to negotiate in the first place. But your needs alone won't get anyone to the table. The other party must recognize that you have something of value to him or her. Incentives make that value visible.

- **STEP UP THE PRESSURE**

  The incentives you hold out might not convince someone to negotiate with you. He or she might be perfectly content to let things continue the way they are. In which case you have to raise the costs of *not* dealing with you. You can increase the stakes by letting him know you have other alternatives and don't have to go along with his plans. You can force a decision in your favor by convincing her that taking no action on your demands is not an option. Things are going to change even if she continues to stall.

- **ESTABLISH YOUR AUTHORITY**

  Unless the other party recognizes your authority, she will resist dealing with you. To have any control over the negotiating process, you must establish your credibility and, when others are involved in the decision-making process, your right to speak for them.

• ENLIST SUPPORT

In many circumstances, what you can accomplish on your own is limited. You can reinforce your efforts to influence the other party by enlisting allies. Strategically placed allies can insure you a favorable hearing. They can also bring pressure to bear on your behalf.

• EXERT CONTROL OVER THE PROCESS

You can move to structure the negotiation process by planting seeds for your ideas or gathering support for your agenda. Besides increasing your chances of encountering a positively disposed bargainer, behind-the-scenes efforts can prevent opposition from gaining momentum and make it less likely that your proposals will be rejected prematurely.

Laid down in black and white, these strategic moves seem very "official" and premeditated, manipulative even. It is easy to slip into the mistake of thinking you can hold them in reserve, just for those "big" negotiations. You are not, after all, planning a major peace initiative in the Middle East. You merely want to lower the decibel level at the weekly staff meeting. Just once it would be nice if you could make arrangements with your client without discovering later that he had double-checked them with your boss. With all the cutbacks at work, you don't mind picking up some of the overload, but you would like to participate in the discussions over who is going to do what. None of these situations seems to call out for a strategic campaign. But unless you change how the other party looks at them and you, nothing about the situation will change for you in the shadow negotiation.

Strategic moves are not stiff-arm tactics. They provide the means to increase your influence over a negotiation's course. They help you bring the other party to the table and even the odds once the real bargaining starts. Fiona Sweeney faced a negotiation that turned out to be a pivotal point in her career. She had joined an international computer company when she graduated from college. Over the next eleven years, she steadily moved up the ranks. Calm, pragmatic, and thoughtful, she attributed her success to diligence. Her co-workers singled out her intuitive feel for organizations. Her businessman father thought it was his doing.

Suddenly, Fiona was promoted to controller of operations and transferred from upstate New York to Palo Alto. Never "one of the boys" in a predominantly male environment, Fiona found California a jolting experience. Accustomed to thrashing out ideas with longtime colleagues, she felt isolated. And then her new boss gave her what seemed to be an impossible task. He charged her with negotiating a change in the company's decision-making processes. Despite its professed goal of customer satisfaction, the company was a series of fiefdoms, with little coordination even on major accounts. The system almost guaranteed customer dissatisfaction, but the sales managers had no inclination to change. Instead, to protect commissions and their valued customers, they exerted pressure on production and quality control.

Fiona, new on the scene and ripe for testing, needed all the strategic moves at her disposal to carry out her assignment. First and foremost, she had to convince the various departments to take her seriously. Only then could she begin to negotiate the significant changes demanded by any real shift in the organization's decision making. Once we explore the individual moves that contribute to an effective advocacy, we will return to Fiona's story to show how she integrated those moves into a strategic campaign.

Hold Out Incentives

Incentives entice people to deal with you. These carrots can take many forms, but they have one purpose. They convince other parties that negotiating with you is in their best interests. You cannot just *tell* them that you have something valuable to offer; you have to *show* them. This demonstration requires coming up with the right incentives, and those, in turn, depend on the specific circumstances.

You can have the best product or service in the world, a long list of talents you have scrupulously inventoried, but you won't get far in a negotiation if the other person is not in the market for what you are selling. Value must be perceived to be valuable before you can turn it into an advantage. Your customer says she can get comparable services from other vendors, and she won't pay a premium for yours. If you want that premium, you have to make clear what you provide that other suppliers don't. The product launch comes off ahead of schedule. If no one knows that you made that happen, your contribution goes unnoticed. To be rewarded for it, you have to make it visible in the shadow negotiation. Even when your value is apparent to the other person, he or she might be tempted to discount it simply to maintain the upper hand in your relationship. When you let that happen, you shortchange your contribution and severely penalize yourself.

Make sure you have something the other person needs. Just because you are motivated and see clear benefits in what you offer, you cannot be sure that the other party will jump to the same conclusion. No matter how versatile the talents or services you bring, if the other party doesn't need them, then she won't have an incentive to deal with you. Your incentives must have some resonance with her needs. If you want her attention, you have to create that need.

At forty, Molly was a month away from finishing her M.B.A. Although she had begun her job search early, her prospects were not bright. Her age worked against her, but so did her résumé. Her entire work experience consisted of teaching English as a foreign language when her husband was stationed in Germany. "I was a blank page," she comments, "with a young daughter."

Molly did, however, have considerable motivation: a need for financial security.

I never expected to work full-time. But then my husband died suddenly. I went to business school to make sure that I could afford to send my daughter to college.

Molly also had a game plan. She wanted to carve out a niche for herself in mergers and acquisitions. But after several chilly interviews it was apparent that no one was going to sign her up on a promise to work hard.

Molly decided she needed something concrete to bring to the negotiations. She went back to the drawing board and developed a matrix of Internet software firms. She analyzed what niche each company filled in the emerging e-commerce space. She then looked for synergies with established companies. With this work in hand, she wangled her way into interviews with three investment banking firms. None was interested in hiring her, but one found her project promising enough to give her a trial as a researcher—without pay or any staff support.

After getting her foot in the door, Molly faced the daunting task of creating a perception of value for what she was giving away and translating her trial period into a job. Only when her research began to yield real results did she approach the managing partner.

> Joel didn't even realize how tentative our arrangement was. I told him I could not continue to work for free and had begun a job search. He had no idea they weren't paying me.

Her focus on a hot new market gave Molly leverage, an incentive for the managing partner to deal with her. Her research was just starting to produce results and he couldn't afford an interruption. Keeping her on was easier than training someone new. Once he came to this conclusion, Molly could negotiate terms. She had established her value.

Creating value is a key move in the shadow negotiation. Once you figure out what the other party actually needs, you can tailor your incentives so that they respond to those needs. You suddenly appear more useful than he or she realized. You don't always have to create this value out of whole cloth the way Molly did. But you do have to demonstrate it. You cannot leave it up to the other party to puzzle through how and where your talents or product might be useful. You have to make that connection yourself. The trick comes, as Molly discovered, in knowing what the organization values (or will value in the future) and then making it easy for the other person to see that you can do that valued work or provide the needed service. He or she then has a reason to negotiate with you.

Make your value visible. After assessing your situation, you might conclude, quite rightly, that you have a lot of value to offer. But somehow that value does not seem to be gaining you much ground in the shadow negotiation. Generally it is not working to your advantage because it is invisible. Value can be discounted on both sides of the table. Not only do you have to be aware of your value, you must make sure that it is firmly implanted in the other person's mind.

The value of the work you do disappears unless you claim it. The conference goes off without a hitch. If no one knows about the long hours you put in to make that happen, your contribution goes unnoticed. Unnoticed, it goes unrewarded. If you want to change that situation, you need to make your value visible.

Frequently the people we negotiate with must be reminded of our contributions. Rather than continue to be taken for granted, you can deliberately jostle their awareness. It does not take much; sometimes a delicately administered reality check is enough. You can, for example, interrupt your services for a bit. Toni was a partner in a growing architectural practice. Gradually, she had taken over the responsibility for insuring that the office ran smoothly, that clients paid promptly, and that bills went out on time. She had assumed these duties largely by default. Her partner had no interest in anything other than design. Before long he gave no credit to the effort and time Toni spent keeping the office on an even keel. Then Toni was invited by an old friend to give a talk in London.

About to prepare "instruction" sheets on office procedures for her partner, Toni held off. She thought he might at least be curious about the mechanisms she had put in place. He wasn't. At the last minute, she asked if he wanted to go over them, but he just smiled. "No problem," he assured her. "I'll take care of everything." After a few days, in the course of which he had to make an emergency run to the bank to transfer funds, he had a good picture of what went on behind the scenes in his own office. The work Toni had been doing was no longer invisible. The experience left him with a new appreciation of the burden Toni had been carrying. He was now prepared to talk about sharing the responsibilities so that they were both freer to get on with what they really enjoyed—designing.

For your value to influence a negotiation, you must take steps, however subtle, to insure that it is right there on the table for both of you to see. We cannot stress this point enough. When women's work disappears, so do their influence and their bargaining power.

Make certain the other party pays fair freight for your value. The person you are negotiating with might, in fact, have a good idea of your value. He or she might even appreciate the work you do. The sticky problem here comes not in making your value visible but in convincing him or her to give you credit for it. The shadow negotiation turns into a tug-of-war in which you are pushed to retreat on your demands. You want a promotion; your counterpart pushes you to settle for praise and a pat on the back. Because women are often expected to do more for less, you need incentives at hand to convince the other person that being valued means having your value rewarded.

Chris, a television executive, knew exactly what she contributed at the station. But she still faced two major obstacles when she decided to ask for a raise. She worked in an industry notorious for underpaying and over-working women, and she reported to a boss, a lawyer by training, who prided himself on his reputation as an aggressive negotiator: "Al likes everyone to think he eats nails for breakfast. He would not hesitate to cram a take-it-or-leave-it proposition down my throat."

"Women at the station are the glue that holds things together," Chris says. "But we fade into the woodwork when it comes to making demands." To get the raise she wanted (and deserved), Chris had to force Al to admit that she played a critical part in the station's operations and that she should be paid accordingly.

Chris drew on her flair for the dramatic and a rather puckish sense of humor to orchestrate the interview. She thought out each detail with a feeling for the dynamics in the shadow negotiation.

> Al loved the exercise of power. He always conducted salary negotiations from behind a huge desk. The supplicants sat opposite him on a couch that sank to the ground, making them feel inconsequential. I brought one of the high stools we use in the studio with me to the meeting. From that perch, I wasn't swallowed up in a bottomless couch. I looked down on Al.

The negotiation began amicably. Al agreed to all but one of her re-quests—saying yes to another week of vacation, a company car, and a first-class seat when she had to fly to the network's West Coast offices. He would not budge on her demand for more money.

As they went back and forth, Chris's value to the station became abun-dantly clear.

> I timed the meeting to occur during the busiest part of the day in the newsroom—at deadline, when my presence was crucial. I purposely let producers interrupt us. They broke into the meeting several times to tell me about stories, tape editing, and satellite shots.

Despite these timely interruptions, Al remained adamant: no raise. Chris got off her stool and looked at Al.

After a long silence, I said I hoped there would be no hard feelings. I thought he valued my work. Then I told him I had to get the newscast on the air and walked out of the office.

When Chris left Al's office, she was not bluffing. She knew her value; Al knew her value. If he wanted to keep her, he was going to have to pay her a fair wage. Al sent his secretary after Chris. When she walked back into his office, he was sitting on the couch. "Let's talk money," he said.

Each of us brings different skills and expertise to bear in a negotiation. But, like Al, other people might discount what we offer in a negotiation, generally for a simple reason. They are going to have to pay for it—by giving us more money, or time, or cooperation. You can help them over this hurdle, but you have to do it in a way they understand and appreciate. Chris's high stool and the interruptions she prompted were symbolic actions that Al immediately read. Toni's trip to London jolted her partner, and they were able to come up with more equitable ways to share the office burdens. And Molly's project provided the managing partner with tangible evidence of the future contributions she could make to a firm engaged in mergers and acquisitions. To be effective and to increase your influence in a negotiation, the incentives you hold out must be recognizable and worth something to the other person.

Step Up the Pressure

Negotiation inevitably involves change. You open talks because you want something to be different—a higher salary, a new job, or increased communication. The advantages of the change may be so apparent to the other side that he or she is amenable to negotiating it with you. But holding out a carrot is not always enough. Caught in inertia and a dislike of change in any form, your counterpart may not mind passing up some possible advantage. Things are just fine the way they are. Why risk unsettling them? Abba Eban, Israel's former foreign minister, once observed that diplomats have "a passionate love affair with the status quo" that stills any forward movement.[3] That love affair carries over into ordinary negotiations. To get them off the ground, you often have to unfreeze the situation by making the status quo less attractive.[4] The pressures you exert raise the cost of business as usual. As the other party weighs her choices, she begins to see that things cannot remain the same. She will be worse off if she doesn't deal with you.

These pressure levers run the gamut from outright threats to gentle prods, and must be used carefully. Blurting out a threat to go over your boss's head is likely to escalate the tensions and might get you fired. Sometimes you can make your point simply by letting the other person know that you *can* increase the costs to her. You don't necessarily have to act on that warning. Once she suspects that the current arrangements are going to change whatever she does, she is likely to be more willing to negotiate. That way she insures that she has a voice in any decision. Alternatives can also be used as a pressure lever. If the other party seems reluctant to meet your demands, you should make sure he or she knows you have other options that do.

Issue a credible threat. Threats are the most obvious means of forcing the other person to admit that maintaining the status quo is not an option. A threat commits you to a course of action if your counterpart does not respond in a particular way. A threat can be a powerful tool, but to put real pressure on the other party, the threat has to be real. You must be prepared to follow through on it. If your bluff is called and you don't, you are the one who will be worse off, not the other party. The negotiation tips in her favor if you issue an ultimatum on the minimum salary you will accept and then quickly revise that figure downward at the first sign of resistance.

Abby was more than ready to act on a threat. She and her reporter fiancé had planned an idyllic getaway in the Bahamas before he left on assignment for the Mideast. Abby wanted the long weekend to be perfect and did not even shop around for a bargain. The couple paid top dollar for a suite steps away from the ocean. Both had pulled long hours in exchange for the time away, and they arrived exhausted at the resort. Instead of being shown to their room, they were told the hotel was overbooked. They soon found themselves shuttled off to a dismal lodging house miles from the ocean. They stayed the night and flew back home the next morning.

An irate Abby promptly called her travel agent to complain. She wanted a full refund for the hotel and airfare. The travel agent just as promptly denied any responsibility, commenting that he had no control over the resort's booking policies. Nonsense, Abby responded. There was no way he could compensate her for the lost weekend, but he could make her whole financially. If he didn't, she was going to make sure other clients were spared a similar experience. Either she heard from him by five o'clock or she would file a complaint with the local consumer protection agency and post a reprise of her weekend on the Internet. For good measure she also mentioned that her fiancé was a reporter and friendly with the newspaper's travel editor.

The travel agent could not have cared less about a complaint to the consumer protection agency. It would take years for the agency to get to it. Bad press, on the other hand, would be a disaster. Much of his business came from referrals. He didn't wait until five o'clock to settle with Abby. He agreed right then to credit her MasterCard account in full. Had Abby's travel agent suspected she was bluffing, he might have tried to stonewall her, but he could not take the risk. His bookings might suffer.

Abby had nothing to lose by threatening the travel agent. That is not always the case. In most business situations you need to give yourself and the other person room to maneuver. You might couple a threat with a conciliatory move that lets her know that you would prefer not to go down that path. Rather than issue an ultimatum, from which you cannot back off, you can talk about what you will be forced to do if she does not move on your demands. Say, for example, a co-worker resents being assigned to your team and is being less than cooperative. You can threaten to go to the vice president but cushion the warning with an assurance that you would prefer for the two of you to settle the problem.

Force a choice on the other party. Threats can be masked and issued subtly, but the risk of retaliation remains. Letting the other person know you have other alternatives carries less risk and can be just as effective in persuading her to negotiate with you. Once she realizes you are not captive to her plans or her schedule, she is forced to move on your demands. Karen leveraged her alternatives in order to push a boss who was stalling on her raise.

Karen had been promoted from administrative assistant to department manager, but without an increase in pay. Her old position was never filled, so she wound up doing two jobs. Karen didn't mind the long hours, but she resented the flat salary. Her boss, a nice guy, procrastinated on any decisions that might cause dissension. "He never makes waves. He's not a coward," she says, "but he avoids conflict." When she complained about her salary, he was sympathetic and agreed she deserved a raise. "I'll see what I can do." Every few weeks, he would reassure Karen, "Don't worry. I'm working on it." But nothing changed. Patience was not one of Karen's virtues. Already in a slow burn over the delays, she heard about a similar job in another agency.

After several interviews, she decided the other agency was not a place she wanted to work. Its job offer did, however, provide her with the leverage to unfreeze the talks with her boss. She told him an opportunity had come up that paid 30 percent more than her current salary. She preferred to stay, but only if he could match that figure. Given her boss's obvious tendency to procrastinate, she set a deadline. He had to let her know by the end of the week so she could give the other agency an answer.

Karen used her alternative to raise the cost to her boss of doing nothing. He could no longer delay in order to maintain the status quo. It was the prod (and the justification) he needed to argue forcefully on her behalf with his boss and with the company's human resources department.

Often the people you are negotiating with do not have the authority to make the decision. They must squeeze the resources needed out of a superior. Rather than become embroiled in a contest with a higher-up, they take the path of least resistance. It is easier to stall and see how things play out. To speed the process along, you have to provide them with the ammunition they require to get what you want from their boss.

Make the consequences tangible to the other person. Big sticks like the one Karen wielded are often not at hand and might not work if they were. An indirect approach can exert subtle, less-overt pressure and can be as effective in the long run. Caroline had always been willing to pick up the extra work that needed doing around the office. Resources were tight, and everyone was stretched. Usually, Caroline accepted the extra assignments gracefully, but she had reached her limit. She couldn't take on any more work without producing a shoddy product. When her boss approached her with yet another project, she was ready. She was not going to let herself be positioned as a slacker in the shadow negotiation. On her white board she had listed all her projects and their due dates. She was happy to take on this new work, but she wondered which projects he wanted her to drop or delay. The move immediately shifted the focus in the shadow negotiation from her dedication to an unreasonable schedule. She forced her boss to make a decision. Rather than give the assignment to someone else or delay Caroline's other work, he hired an assistant for her.

When incentives do not get the other party's attention, you need to make these kinds of strategic moves to increase the pressure. Otherwise he or she will predictably remain satisfied with things as they are. By making the current situation less comfortable, you shake up the other person's complacency. When she realizes the costs attached to doing nothing, she will be far more receptive to negotiating with you.

Establish Your Authority When You Are Negotiating for Others

When you are negotiating for yourself with another person, you can direct your strategic moves to him or her. Once you establish your credibility, you are all set. But if you are speaking for others and they are involved in the decision-making process, there is another level of complexity to consider. Not only do you have to be credible in your own right; you must also convince the other side that you have the backing of the group you represent. Whatever incentives you hold out or pressures you bring to bear, it is impossible to get a negotiation off the ground if the other side questions that support. Generally, they consider negotiating with you a waste of time and prefer to deal with the real decision makers.

Whenever you speak for a larger group or represent your organization in a negotiation, the other side needs to understand just how much latitude you have to make a decision or commit your organization. No lawyer in her right mind will allow you to make changes to a joint-venture agreement unless she is convinced you can act for your partners. She wants some proof. Your customer must know whether your boss fully approves of the precedent-breaking agreement you have offered. Unless she has that assurance, she won't care about the terms you offer, however attractive. She is going to entertain quite reasonable fears that the final agreement will be far less favorable once those with real authority get involved.

Secure explicit authorization. Certain elements almost guarantee that your authority will be questioned. If the other people across the table have never negotiated with you before, they naturally want reassurance about your ability to commit. Big differences in status, age, or background can generate unease and sometimes outright suspicion. Dora, treasurer of a utility in Pennsylvania, looked at an upcoming negotiation and knew she would have to establish her authority before any meeting took place. Dora's assignment was difficult enough. She was to extricate the utility from a partnership with a Kentucky coal company that had not worked out.

> I was going to be negotiating our withdrawal with a bank chairman and the president of the coal company. They were angry about how the partnership turned out to begin with. When my CEO told them I was going to handle the negotiations, they took it as an insult, another example of their shabby treatment. They felt quite justified in being offended. I was young enough to be their daughter. They were from the South; I was a northerner. They were heads of their organizations; I was a couple of reports short of being boss.

To establish her authority to negotiate the financial disentanglement, Dora drafted a letter for her CEO's signature. The letter was conciliatory but succinct. Dora had been chosen to conduct the negotiations because she was the person in the organization who knew the most about the partnership. She enjoyed the full confidence of the board and had complete authority to act on its behalf. As Dora suspected, the president of the coal-mining operation attempted to bypass her and called her boss directly. The CEO simply referred back to "his" letter.

By establishing her authority ahead of time, Dora got the negotiations off on the right foot. The others involved in the negotiation recognized that they had no choice but to deal with her. At times you will not have the clear and complete backing that Dora enjoyed. In that case you need to establish the authority you do have. Clarity here serves two purposes: You won't be tempted to overstep your bounds and promise more than you can deliver; and the other party has a better sense of what she can legitimately expect to negotiate with you.

Maintain the backing of your "side." The ability to negotiate effectively often depends on perceptions, and when you are negotiating on behalf of others, the impressions that influence the shadow negotiation multiply. You must address your "opponent" across the table *and* maintain the continued confidence of your own constituency.[5] Real authority is not necessarily conferred by a title or a corner office. It comes from the continued support given your efforts and your approach. Without express backing from your side, the other parties involved invariably doubt your control and your ability to commit. Are you really leading the negotiation? Can they trust what you say?

Debra and her boss decided they could no longer postpone office renovations. They badly needed their space rewired in order to upgrade their systems. Since Debra had just finished a major project, the timing was perfect. She had the time to supervise the changeover. But the engineering contractor was uncomfortable taking orders from a woman when the decisions involved high-tech systems. He kept calling Debra's boss on the pretext of sounding out his ideas. What he really wanted was authorization. Debra's boss thought nothing of taking the contractor's calls. He enjoyed talking about the new fiber technologies. It never occurred to him that he might be undermining Debra. Until she protested. So long as her boss made himself available to the contractor, the contractor would cut her out of the loop and refuse to deal directly with her. Once Debra worked this dynamic through with her boss, he routed all queries from the contractor to Debra.

Consider authorization an ongoing activity. Even when you can count on your side's full support, your authority will be tested in the shadow negotiation. If those involved in the direct negotiations sense that you enjoy less than enthusiastic backing from the people who count in your organization, they will pick up on these doubts and use them. The testing intensifies, and your own constituents, watching this performance play out, become uneasy. They begin to wonder whether you are the right person to manage the negotiation for them. Soon you are in danger of losing credibility on all sides. To break this cycle, you have to confront challenges to your authority as they happen.

Fran, director of human resources in a research center, moved to stop the erosion of her authority on both fronts in the aftermath of a merger. Soft-spoken, with a phobic aversion to severe business suits, Fran radiated approachability. Her self-deprecating humor and attentive listening invited confidences—one of the reasons she was so good at her job. Fran, a great believer in consensus building, went into the talks determined that they not be adversarial. She saw them as an opportunity to build strong working relations.

Confrontation goes against my grain. With goodwill on both sides, I thought we could find a way to work together on the challenges we faced in meshing two very different cultures.

Across the board, existing benefits at Fran's center outstripped those offered by the new partner. As head of human resources, Fran was charged with working out the discrepancies. At the start, she had to set at rest suspicions within the center that she was not "tough enough" to stand up to the other side's team of negotiators. "Some of our people were openly nervous," she says. "Envisioning Bambi coming up against Rambo, they were afraid I would cave when the stakes got high or the pressure mounted and give away their benefits."

These doubts spread through the center's grapevine. Inevitably, they reached the other company's negotiators. Sensing little widespread support for Fran's collaborative approach, they began to distrust anything she said as nothing more than lip service, lacking any real force. Their lead negotiator was already gleeful about facing a woman. Now he became openly scornful, writing off Fran's collaborative overtures as so much "Zen mumbo jumbo."

Fran's ability to negotiate—collaboratively or otherwise—depended on her colleagues' confidence in her and her strategy. To gain their active support, she set up an advisory group with representatives from all departments, including human resources. The meetings of this group furnished Fran with ample opportunity to calm worries. When talks stalled, she explained why she refused to make a concession or what steps she was taking to restart discussions.

Fran next consolidated her authority to speak for the center. "I was getting challenges from the legal counsel and from my own boss," she says. "I couldn't work that way, constantly guarding my back." She went to the center's managing director and asked him point-blank: "Who has the last word?" He said she did. This request for explicit authorization became key. The director was on record as supporting Fran, and she was beholden to him to deliver.

As Fran discovered, an "official" assignment does not automatically convey the backing necessary to carry it out. Without obvious support from her side, Fran would have lacked the legitimacy needed to negotiate the benefits schedule for the merged companies. To get that authorization, she moved to dispel worries within her company that she might be too soft for the job. At the same time, she put in place monitoring mechanisms that prevented doubts from resurfacing later during the negotiations.

Like Fran, most of us have to assume that our credibility will be challenged when we negotiate. Because this questioning is seldom set permanently to rest, it is essential to think about your authority in terms of the strategic moves that you can make—not just to establish credibility but to keep it. Explicit and ongoing authorization from someone with real power gives you visible support that means something to your own team. It also drives home a necessary point to the other party. Attempts to circumvent you and go over your head will achieve nothing. He or she must deal with you. You are in charge of the negotiations.

Enlist Support

At times, the strategic moves you make on your own don't do the job. The other side does not see sufficient benefits in what you offer, and the costs you have raised are not high enough to force a change of mind. No matter what you do you cannot seem to attract his attention or get him to take your demands seriously. If you don't think you have the resources to move the negotiation forward on your own, you can call up reinforcements and enlist the support of others. Just by sheer numbers, strategic allies can add credibility to your cause. Their confidence in you is what convinces the other party to negotiate with you. When an ally's opinion counts with that person, the extra influence often tips the shadow negotiation in your favor.

The roles strategic allies play range from modest to critical. Their interventions can simply open doors for you. A timely phone call from a mentor adds a personal note to a letter of recommendation and can shift your résumé to the top of the pile. An opportune word from a well-placed friend can coax a larger check from a contributor hesitant to support your agency. As allies become more actively engaged, they alter the dynamics in the shadow negotiation even more profoundly. They become, in effect, strategic partners and broaden your impact, particularly if they complement your strengths with other skills or give you access to different spheres of influence.

Allies can also wield sticks you might not want to use yourself and apply overt pressure on the other party. He or she might think twice about incurring a boss's displeasure, alienating a prominent figure, or disappointing a valued colleague or an important client. Resistance tends to evaporate when it carries a penalty.

When enlisting strategic allies, you have to consider two points. The most obvious is whether the potential ally actually supports you and how firmly. The second is the relationship she enjoys with the person with whom you are negotiating. Does she have the clout to make a difference? Does the other party value her opinions?

Use allies as intermediaries. Acting as intermediaries, allies can intervene in a negotiation. They can troubleshoot a proposal ahead of time and insure that its hearing is biased in your favor. When you involve them in the early drafting stages, they have a chance to contribute to the proposal's final shape. Once their suggestions are incorporated, the proposal carries their stamp of approval. In effect, they become its sponsors. Liv's boss, June, served as a critic and buffer during Liv's work/family negotiations.

Liv started from scratch when she carved out a niche for public-interest counseling at a major East Coast law school. With the birth of her first child, Liv had shifted to a 70 percent schedule, trading flexibility to work at home for actual hours. Pregnant with her second child, Liv wanted to bring in a co-director to job-share with her.

Liv was not breaking new ground when she requested a part-time schedule. A job-share, on the other hand, would be a first. For Liv and for the dean, the stakes were higher. A job-share could jeopardize the counseling office, which was universally regarded as Liv's creation. At the same time, it could establish a potentially troublesome precedent in a milieu that was not particularly hospitable to creative work arrangements.

Liv's boss, June, an associate dean, would have loved to work half-time. Identifying as she did with Liv's situation, she acted as a sponsor for Liv. She reviewed Liv's proposal, identifying points where it might provoke the dean's resistance. Just as important, June raised the issue with the dean. That broad-brush and informal discussion colored the dean's first impressions. He respected June and valued her judgment. Not only was he persuaded to consider the proposal, he took seriously June's warning that Liv would resign if something could not be worked out.

"It was very important," Liv stresses, "to have a buffer between me and the dean."

Eventually I had to argue my own case, but June prepared the way. I did not have to go in to the dean cold. And I did not have to threaten him with leaving.

Intermediaries like June position you favorably before talks even begin. At a minimum, their confidence primes the other party to listen to what you have to say.

Use allies as strategic partners. Certain allies are positioned—through personal relationships or status alone—to influence a negotiation. Others bring specific skills that complement yours and increase your value in the eyes of the other party. Anna, the executive director of a social service agency in a depressed New England mill town, drew on allies for both influence and skills. Increasingly troubled by her agency's dependence on state allocations and the United Way, Anna was determined to broaden its financial base. She was especially concerned that the agency secure sufficient funding for its expanding community health programs. Private foundations seemed the logical place to go.

> I became a cheerleader for what my agency could do for the community. I had a specific agenda. I wanted to be known and respected in the private foundation world. That was where the new money was coming from in health care, and I wanted to establish my agency as a "credible vendor."

Anna soon encountered a major stumbling block in this plan. The foundations were not interested. The agency's rapid growth made foundation officials wonder whether she and her staff could handle the larger budgets involved. She also suspected they weren't overly impressed with her. "I just don't come over as a player," she says.

Anna decided she needed to shore up her agency's image. A disconnect existed between what the agency could accomplish and what outsiders thought it could do. At first Anna was baffled. Then she realized her board could provide a bridge to the wider community and to greater legitimacy. To access professional strategic advice on health initiatives, Anna invited the head of the local school of public health and a respected surgeon to join the board. To give depth to the agency's financial planning, she sought out two prominent members of the business community and put them in charge of overseeing the finance and budget committees.

Anna's new board members became strategic partners in the agency's expansion. Anna never went alone to critical foundation presentations. She always arranged to have the appropriate board member accompany her. These moves increased foundation confidence in her programs, and the foundations began to work with her on grants.

Allies are important resources in the shadow negotiation. They can be critical when you encounter difficulties in establishing your credibility. Their support makes your incentives more tangible precisely because they can trumpet your value in a way that you cannot.

Use allies as sources of pressure. Allies are not restricted to working on the bright side, extolling your virtues and the benefits of negotiating with you. They can also bring pressure to bear. Their influence on the other party raises the costs of not dealing with you forthrightly. Not incidentally, it is often easier for them to be the bearer of bad news. June, as an associate dean, could let the dean know that Liv might resign unless a job-share could be worked out. Had the comment come from Liv, the dean would have given it far less credence. He might even have dismissed it altogether as a hollow threat.

During an intense negotiation, it is easy to forget that other people besides you and the person you are negotiating with have a stake in the outcome. These stakeholders represent a potential source of influence. When your interests coincide with theirs, it is not difficult to persuade them to become vocal or exert pressure behind the scenes. Roni deliberately sought out such a stakeholder when she negotiated a part-time schedule.

Roni, director of development for the symphony of a large city in the Midwest, was getting her master's in public policy at night. She found the pace toward her degree frustratingly slow. When her contract with the symphony came up for renewal, she proposed cutting back on her hours in order to finish her degree earlier. The symphony's general manager responded with two options. One: Roni would be allowed to work on a part-time schedule until she completed her degree requirements. The general manager made this option contingent on her commitment to remain with the symphony, full-time and in the same position (that is, for the same salary), for two years after graduation. Two: Roni could leave the symphony when her contract expired.

Neither option was acceptable to Roni. She suggested other possibilities, but the general manager refused to discuss them. Not wanting to leave, but unwilling to commit to two years at a flat salary, Roni tendered her resignation. She then turned to the conductor. His plans for a series of celebrity concerts and a European tour hinged on securing corporate support, an effort Roni was spearheading. When Roni told him of her resignation, his concern was obvious. "My alliance with the conductor was a natural," she says. "I knew what a high priority he placed on fund-raising at that moment."

Although Roni never requested the conductor's intervention, she was not surprised when he asked the general manager to extend her contract and allow her to work part-time until the corporate fund-raising was safely launched. After talking with the conductor, Roni did not press her boss. Instead, she proceeded as if she were departing when her contract expired. She was actually waiting for the general manager to come to her. And he did.

Roni capitalized on her good relationship with the conductor. The mutual interest they shared in the uncompleted fund-raising effort raised the costs to the general manager of her leaving. By accepting her resignation, he would jeopardize the conductor's goodwill. It is important to note how carefully Roni employed this strategy. She avoided the appearance and the fact of exploiting the conductor. At the same time, she protected the general manager from any loss of face. Neither he nor the rest of the organization was ever aware that she had gone "over his head." Rather than bring public pressure to bear, she gave him room to change his mind.

Certain stakeholders are natural allies. But enlisting their aid implies a quid pro quo. Your strategy must take into account their interests as well as your own. These do not always dovetail so perfectly as Roni's and the conductor's. Moreover, the issue of enlisting outside support can be a particularly sensitive one for women. There is often a hidden Catch-22. Calling on allies, instead of being interpreted as a sign of strength—that you have powerful people behind you—is often read as weakness. You obviously need someone to bail you out or fight your battles. The danger can be real, but the benefits of such help so frequently outweigh the costs that it pays to consider ways of offsetting any negative impressions. By enlisting the conductor's support indirectly and informally, for example, Roni maintained the public impression that she was negotiating on her own.

Allies even the odds at the table. Strategically chosen, they set the stage for a favorable hearing. They also alter the consequences for the other party. It is not so easy for her to ignore you or to treat your demands casually when that behavior carries the added risk of offending people whose goodwill and favorable opinions she values.

Exert Control over the Process

Incentives and pressures increase your influence over a negotiation. Incentives pull other parties into the negotiation. You demonstrate just what you can do and are doing for them. Pressure levers push them into dealing with you. They come to see that their situation will only deteriorate if they don't. You—what you offer or can cost them—are the focus. In this sense, incentives and pressures are highly personal and can generate highly personal reactions. The advantages you are demonstrating are your advantages; the threats, however subtle, are threats you are making. The allies defending or supporting you are your allies.

Women sometimes run into trouble using these direct methods. The moves, even when they can be deftly employed, don't fit their negotiating style. Touting their value seems too blatantly self-serving and exerting pressure too heavy-handed. Or, worse, they suspect the remedy will do more harm than good and provoke resistance or retaliation. These circumstances call out for a different approach. Rather than attempt to influence the shadow negotiation directly by holding out incentives and stepping up the pressure—moves that always carry a personal dimension for you and for the person with whom you are negotiating—you can center your moves on the negotiation process itself.

Process-oriented moves, while they do not directly address your interests, do directly affect the hearing those interests get. The agenda, the sequence in which ideas and people are heard, the groundwork you lay ahead of time—all these structural elements influence how receptive others will be to your opinions. When your suggestions surprise or shock, you can almost bank on a negative reaction. If a boss or co-workers think you are trying to manipulate them or surreptitiously gain an advantage, they will see any effort you make as a challenge. Working behind the scenes, indirectly, you can plant the seeds of your ideas so that no one is taken by surprise or put on the defensive. Before an agenda gets fixed in anyone's mind, you can build support for your ideas. You might even be able to engineer consensus so that your agenda frames the discussion.

Anticipate reactions. How you present your ideas can be as important as what you say. To insure that your suggestions get a fair hearing, you must pay attention to the process leading up to their presentation. The insights you glean from scouting information refine your reading of the situation, and that knowledge can be put to work. Once you discover where and how your ideas are likely to encounter opposition and, conversely, what kinds of proposals generally meet with approval, you can shape the process to your advantage.

Over the past year, Marcie's group had taken on several large projects. To staff them, they had recruited talent from other departments and added new hires. Their current quarters were cramped, with most people doubled up in cubicles meant for one person. Despite these crowded conditions, Marcie was not optimistic when the annual negotiations over space were scheduled. If past experience were any guide, a high degree of gamesmanship would govern the discussions. Extra room typically went to those who pushed the hardest or protested the loudest. The previous year Marcie had stated her actual needs and been penalized for her candor. The negotiations proceeded according to a hidden rule: To get what you wanted, you had to exaggerate your needs by at least 30 percent.

Marcie believed that there were real costs attached to this process. The company was growing at a rapid pace, yet with the other group leaders pressing inflated figures on the administrator, she was unable to assess the company's actual space requirements. Several weeks before the scheduled negotiations, Marcie invited the administrator over for a tour of her group's facilities. As they walked around, the administrator could see that the group was bursting at the seams. But, more important, the administrator, Marcie discovered from a chance comment, was tired of the games the other groups played. Not only could she not allocate space fairly and efficiently, she could not plan where future needs were likely to develop.

Sensing the administrator's frustration, Marcie proposed changing the process. Rather than allocate space in a series of discrete negotiations with group heads, why didn't they develop criteria for assessing need? They could come up with a formula that took the guesswork and gamesmanship out of the decision-making process. The administrator embraced the idea with relief. There would be heated arguments over the criteria, but it was a step in the right direction. Without any pressure on Marcie's part, she found herself chairing the committee the administrator created to develop more objective criteria.

Marcie's work behind the scenes allowed her to take control of a process that had previously put her at a disadvantage. The shift in process that she initiated changed the game. Not only had she put herself in a position to bring greater objectivity to the company's space planning, under the new guidelines her group moved to another floor, where it had almost twice as much room.

Plant the seeds of your ideas. At times people simply shut down. They don't listen. Whatever the reason, they screen out certain comments or certain people. Being ignored in a negotiation is not always a question of saying too little or saying it too hesitantly. Bargainers tune out the familiar. If they expect to be pressured, forcefulness loses its impact. They have heard the speech before, or a close variant, and they stop paying attention.

Women in particular risk being silenced in this way. Anxious to promote our case, we might come on loud and strong and find ourselves blocked. By working behind the scenes we can keep the voice we sometimes lose when we press too hard. Once we have planted the seeds of an idea ahead of time, we no longer need to be so heavy-handed during the actual discussion. We can let the seeds germinate. Those seeds remain in the back of everyone's mind. They become part of the agenda without the vigorous promotion that can turn another person off.

Pat was a talker, and an aggressive one, in meetings. In the past, her fellow managers had tuned her out during annual staff reviews—not because she was hesitant but because they felt she pushed too hard. Being heard was no small matter for Pat or for the members of her department. Merit increases reflected the managers' collective assessment of what individual engineers contributed to the firm. They were also widely regarded as signs of whether a particular manager was doing a good job.

This year, Pat vowed, the performance reviews were going to be different. No effort on her part was suddenly going to transform her into a shrinking violet—she was too commanding a personality. She could, however, prepare the ground ahead of time so that she would not feel so compelled to dominate the review sessions. Over many lunches in the weeks before the reviews, she casually asked other managers about openings in their departments. On each occasion she slipped in a mention of her star employees, saying it was too bad they weren't available. They had precisely the skills and attitude the managers needed.

Once the actual reviews started, the other managers had already heard of her stars. That name recognition saved Pat from overselling. By lobbying for team members informally, Pat was able to make herself heard without belaboring her case—an objective that had previously eluded her.

Preliminary work like this allows you to build receptivity where an aggressive or direct approach might offend. Once you have planted the seeds, however firmly attached others are to their own agendas, those seeds cannot help but influence their view of the situation.

Build support behind the scenes. Even when we seem to be in control of the agenda, that control is seldom complete. Individual members of a new product team need to be convinced to go along with a development plan. A majority of the board members of a nonprofit organization must be persuaded before they agree that the funding guidelines must be revised.

Generally these negotiations take place in a meeting where the group makes the decision or in stages through back-and-forth consultations. There is a good deal of room for slippage here, and it is risky to leave issues you care about to a process that you might be unable to control. Hidden agendas can surface unexpectedly. "Group think" can overtake substance so that consensus becomes a matter of who shouts loudest or whose voice customarily dominates. Or you might discover that a decision has been reached without your input.

Lobbying behind the scenes provides a potential antidote to these dangers. You can build consensus before matters come to a head. Backstage efforts provide opportunities to gather momentum behind your agenda. As that support grows, it isolates the blockers, making continued opposition harder and harder for them. Moreover, once agreement has been secured privately, it becomes more difficult (although never impossible) for a supporter to defect publicly.

Lynn, a public health expert in her early forties, left a job in a large teaching hospital to become head of a struggling community hospital in a suburb outside Baltimore. Lynn moved quickly to establish control over the direction the hospital's turnaround would take, but she kept this private agenda to herself. Each department head thought his or her budget should be the last to be cut, and Lynn could not afford to watch months of valuable time being consumed by departmental infighting.

> Before I came on board, I crawled all over the place. Once I got here, I met with key leaders of the board, the medical staff, and management in the first six or eight weeks. I did those all one-on-one. These

sessions are time-consuming, but they are also what I call *clean encounters*. When you are pushing an agenda, it's important that your initial interactions not be contentious.

Lynn's private talks linked the multiple agendas in play with specific people. They provided her with a strategic map. She discovered where she would find support and where she was likely to be blocked.

Lynn paid particular attention to the order in which she approached people in her next round of talks. She began with the most supportive player—the medical chief of staff. Not only had he been instrumental in bringing her to the hospital, he had publicly backed the kinds of changes she envisioned. Together they came to a basic understanding on his role in the hospital's turnaround. Next she met with the vice president of finance and administration, who, Lynn thought, would probably go along with her plan provided she had a voice in its development. Cutbacks would take a heavy toll on the nurses; and before Lynn approached the head of nursing, she worked with the chief of staff and the finance vice president to keep the burden on nursing to a minimum. She saved the head of surgery for last, anticipating that he would be the most obstinate. But by that time she had everybody else on board, and he had little choice but to go along with her ideas.[6]

Lynn's private talks, and the way she gradually built support, got the key players to commit, one by one, to her reading of the agenda before any opposing factions could develop. That danger was real. Had the heads of the various services coalesced, they could have blocked her efforts. Her "clean encounters" fixed the agenda for the hospital's turnaround on her terms. When the various parties considered their options, they did so within the framework she proposed.[7] Lynn's consensus building also positioned her as a fellow collaborator. Having built commitment privately, she did not have to rely on her formal position to dictate terms when the department heads met to work on the budget.

In today's leaner organizations, bargainers frequently find themselves negotiating without direct authority to impose their will on an agreement.[8] When you lack this authority, as Marcie did when she negotiated her group's new space, you can move behind the scenes to foster agreement on objectives so the goals of the negotiation align with your goals. When you are concerned that your interests will be ignored, as Pat's were likely to be during the performance reviews, you can plant the seeds of your ideas so that the other party will be more receptive to them. Even when you do have the authority to control a negotiation, as Lynn did, exercising it preemptively might interfere with a longer-term goal—that of building cooperation and a cohesive team. Behind-the-scenes efforts draw others into the consensus-making process that takes place within any group negotiation. Not only do these "clean encounters" allow you to identify and deal with any resistance before it hardens, they insure that your views shape any agenda that emerges.

Step by Step: Planning a Strategic Campaign

Strategic moves bring your counterpart to the table. Not only do they position you to advantage in the shadow negotiation, they increase your influence over how the issues come to be weighted and decided. But your choice of moves must be made against a realistic appraisal of what you can legitimately expect to take on all at once. The more complex the negotiation, the less likelihood there is that it can be brought to closure overnight. A single strategic move seldom carries the day.

The negotiation can, however, be broken down into segments. What cannot be achieved in one giant step can often be accomplished through a series of strategic moves. Approaching a complicated negotiation in stages and isolating benchmarks give you manageable goals. Not all the resources you need to create incentives or to pressure the other person to pay attention to you are immediately available. They must be marshaled over time by building credibility, support, and respect. Thoughtful and well-planned strategies combine multiple moves that create incentives, apply pressure, and exert control over the process. As your value increases in the shadow negotiation, so does the cost to the other party of not coming to terms over the issues. To illustrate how strategic moves can be used, singly and together, we are going to return to Fiona Sweeney and follow her as she negotiates the change in decision making mandated by her boss.

Fiona's negotiations, if successful, would improve coordination between sales and production. Sales managers, driven by commissions, pursued any and all sales opportunities with little regard for the company's capacity to deliver. In turn, production was blamed for delays and cost overruns. Although the lack of cooperation hurt profits and left customers disgruntled, Fiona soon discovered that the attitudes behind it were firmly entrenched.

> *The formal culture at the company supports consensus decision making. The reality is totally different. Sales dominates everything, and the compensation system encourages short-term, opportunistic behavior. There is a disconnect between the official goals of quality and customer satisfaction and the informal operational realities.*

Sales routinely ignored the company's procedures for coordinating with production and quality control, and neither Fiona's predecessor nor the head of production had ever challenged the sales managers on their decisions.

> *The sales managers had been running the business for a long time. Each was an outstanding businessperson in his own right, strong-minded and competitive, with zero tolerance for weakness. They relished a good fight and were accustomed to winning.*

Fiona viewed her assignment as a staged campaign. She had no authority to order sales and production to cooperate. She was new to the division, and none of the players involved saw any reason to deal with her beyond their perfunctory interactions. Most important, Fiona lacked any power over the purse. As controller, she was not in a position to change compensation. Influence over salaries—whatever form it takes—generally confers early credibility; at the least, it gets everyone's attention.

To encourage sales and production to work with her on improving coordination, she needed to be credible to both. "I turned myself into an asset by filling unmet needs," she says. "These efforts gave me visibility and started my relationships with the various departments off on the right foot."

First, Fiona made adjustments to the billing process that cut the error rate over a three-month period from 7.1 percent to 2.4 percent. The increased billing efficiency raised her standing with all the departments.

Customers were no longer calling the salesmen to complain about erroneous bills, and production had an accurate accounting of its output. The move also positioned her as a potential ally.

Next, she appealed directly to sales and made them aware of her impact on their daily lives where it counted most to them—their expense accounts. She reduced turnaround time on expense-report processing from forty days to three. This was a simple task in computer programming, but its results caught the eye of the entire sales force.

Fiona also needed to raise the costs of business as usual for the sales division. Sales was more than satisfied with the current state of affairs. All the informal reward systems, and many of the formal ones, worked to its benefit. Having brought greater efficiency to the billing systems, Fiona started talking about a bonus system that penalized sales if the department oversold and production could not deliver. She could not carry out this threat, but she could float and merely floated it as a possibility. At the same time she took steps to make the lack of cooperation from sales more broadly known. For over two years the company had been surveying its customers about satisfaction. Nobody paid any attention to the findings until Fiona started posting them on the cafeteria bulletin board. Comments began appearing in the employee e-mail, and it soon became apparent that customer discontent was a major problem, not a figment of Fiona's imagination.

Having planted the idea that something would have to change in the sales division, she mobilized allies in production and quality control. Their departments were directly affected by what sales did. Every time sales made a promise to a customer, production had to adjust its scheduling and quality slipped. Fiona proposed forming an operations subgroup with the heads of quality control and production. "The three of us had different areas of expertise," she says. "Pretty soon a common agenda emerged and we had a real impact in full staff meetings." Together, they began to work to isolate sales in those staff meetings. In one meeting, for example, Fiona proposed that a low priority be assigned to orders that had not been cleared by the operations subgroup. Quality control and production roundly supported the suggestion. Fiona no longer faced the prospect of confronting sales on her own.

When Fiona's boss charged her with negotiating a change in behavior within sales, he more or less dumped the problem in her lap. If she succeeded, fine. If not, he avoided being drawn into a contest of wills with the fiercely independent sales division. But Fiona soon reached an impasse. To make additional headway, she required, if not the general manager's active involvement, at least his visible backing.

To build support with her boss, Fiona kept him apprised of progress on her primary assignment, all the time soliciting his ideas privately. Working closely with him insured that she would not be second-guessing his intentions. As his confidence in her judgment grew, he began to send more tangible signs of his backing.

> Whenever he was out of the office on a trip, he delegated general manager authority to me and required that I approve all exceptions to production specs. This caused howls from sales, but made the point.

Moreover, the general manager started to think that the change in decision making he wanted might actually be possible. He let key people know that he backed Fiona's proposal to base bonuses on profits, not revenues. This change would affect everyone, but especially sales. For the first time sales managers began to question how long they could conduct business as usual.

With the general manager's visible support (and the veiled threat of impending changes), Fiona was positioned to deal directly with sales. She joined the division's quality improvement team. The big project in development was a new pricing and profit model to be used as a sales tool.

> I became the local guru on this model and made myself available to sales for consultation and support. They began to want me to be involved in their decisions.

Fiona's gradual moves brought sales to the table. They now trusted her, but they also realized she had accumulated the resources to enforce changes in the decision-making process if she had to. Only then was she in a position to negotiate those changes with sales. By working incrementally, showing them positive results, she was able to demonstrate the benefits of new systems and how counterproductive

*resistance was for everyone. Increased internal coherence,
communication, and efficiency raised profits and tightened quality
control. Sales actually made more money with improved quality, and
production no longer had the burden of delivering on sales's unrealistic
promises. Customers—and the general manager—were extremely
pleased.*

Strategic moves increase your influence in a negotiation. They work to
bring people to the table and to insure that they take you seriously once
they are there. But influence is not static in a negotiation or from one negotiation to another. Strategic moves begin before any exchange takes
place and do not end when an agreement is reached. Present encounters
exert an impact on the influence you carry over to future negotiations. Parity, once reached, is not always stable, and credibility cannot be taken for
granted. Authority earned in one situation does not transfer automatically
to another. A banker spoke to us of the persistent need to "prove up." With
each promotion, she again had to make strategic moves to establish her
credentials. This proof takes place in the shadow negotiation, where you
manage the perceptions the other person has of you.

As the experiences of the women in this chapter show, you do not have
to be in a great bargaining position starting out. With strategic moves,
marshaled collectively and over time, you can shift the dynamics in your
favor.[9] Strategic moves position you in the shadow negotiation, but staying
positioned is a continuous process.

3

RESISTING CHALLENGES

People have a disconcerting habit in negotiations. They don't stay put—at least not where your strategic moves aim to keep them. There is a simple reason for this. The strategic moves you make provoke reactions. They are, after all, designed to increase your control over the direction the shadow negotiation takes. But you are not the only one engaged in strategic positioning. However much the other party believes that negotiating with you is in her best interests, she still wants to conduct the negotiation on her terms. Rather than sit idly by and let you define the choices available to her, she responds with strategic moves of her own.

This chain of action and reaction characterizes all negotiations. It is the way bargainers communicate with each other. Any strategic move you make aims to present your slant on things. It tells the other party not only where you come down on the issues but also what you think of his or her proposals and attitude. Predictably, people react to these signals.[1] They might challenge your reading of the situation. The company chairman agrees that you deserve to be appointed to the executive committee. But two other top executives are also vying for the position. He would like to tap a woman, and you are the best candidate, but he needs to do some lobbying. Pressuring him just puts him in a bind. Why can't you be patient, a team player? A colleague criticizes you for being manipulative. What you consider an effort to build consensus behind the scenes she characterizes as an attempt to short-circuit open discussion for personal gain.

The strategic responses the other party makes can be probing tests to discover points of weakness or real threats meant to fluster or provoke. More often than not, they come at your expense. To gain the upper hand, the other person emphasizes her abilities or experience and implicitly throws yours into question. To make his proposal look good, he characterizes yours as unrealistic and impractical. She casts doubt on your motives. He hesitates over your qualifications for that new assignment.

Actions like these shift the onus to us. That is their intent. The chairman wants to avoid any discussion of how slowly women are moving into top positions in the company. Rather than address the real problem, he focuses not on the company's poor performance when it comes to promoting women but on a specific woman's pressuring tactics. He plays on the encouragement he has given her in the past in the hope that she will back off on her immediate demands.

It is next to impossible to negotiate through any problem when the other party's moves make you the issue in the shadow negotiation. The mere suggestion that you are controlling, incompetent, selfish, or manipulative clouds the issues. But, even more important, it puts you on the defensive. As long as that suggestion hangs in the air, it plays havoc with the balance between you and the other person. Attention focuses on it and you are forced to defend yourself.

Moves to put you on the defensive, however subtle, change the dynamic in the shadow negotiation. Doubt creeps in and you begin to think you are not in such a good negotiating position after all. On the defensive, you react defensively, governed more by the other person's actions than your needs. Inevitably you lose any edge you might have had. And once you are on the defensive in the shadow negotiation, it is difficult to reclaim the initiative when you talk about the issues. It is better by far to avoid the trap in the first place.

What should you do to counter the other party's challenges? You can simply deny the charge, protesting that you are not pushy or controlling or manipulative. But that response just digs you deeper into a defensive hole. Attention remains on what you are or are not. You can always retaliate in kind—giving as good as you get, tit for tat: "I'm not pushing, you are stalling." But rarely do *countermoves* like these change anyone's mind. They make your position no more secure, and they often escalate the tension. Rhetoric heats, attitudes harden, and the exchanges slip into a cycle

of "I am not" denials and "You are so" rebuttals. More significantly, countermoves can give gender free rein in the shadow negotiation, precisely
the result you don't want. A battle of wills can trigger the urge to put a
woman "in her place."[2]

So where does that leave you? If a counterattack is counterproductive,
still less can you let yourself be backed into a corner. Strategic moves
against you require a response. You must put the other party on notice that
you are not going to stumble blindly into the defensive position he or she
is edging you toward. At the same time, you need to respond in a way that
creates space for an alternative place of your own making.

Rather than ignore the other party's move or retaliate, you *turn* it. You
push back on the move and refuse to go where he or she wants to lead you.
Responsive turns are acts of resistance, not reaction. Turns redirect the negotiation by reframing what is happening.[3] They do not have to be hostile
protests or elaborate explanations. You can simply tell a colleague who
charges you with manipulation, for example, that you were gathering as
much information as you could before the meeting and ask whether she
has anything she wants to contribute.

Turns help parry moves against you and resist attempts to put you in
your place. But they serve more than a defensive purpose. They can recast
the way the other person sees you. As you turn a strategic move, putting
your spin on the situation and the issues, you also resist the image of you
that the other party is trying to impose. That image is meant to put you at
a disadvantage. To bring the shadow negotiation back into balance, you
supply a different reading of you, your issues, and the situation.

Moves and *turns,* as we use them, do not imply unethical practices.
Bargainers test each other all the time. Although they often issue outright
challenges, they are just as likely to try to wear down the other party.
When the advantage of time rests with her, she stalls. If he picks up on
weakness or inexperience, he begins to insinuate that you lack the judgment or the authority to make a decision. She overwhelms with numbers
or other resources. He withholds vital information. All these moves stem
from a quite natural impulse to retain control over the negotiation. Once
you recognize the motivation behind them, you can turn them. Alice Ma-
son used a full repertory of turns when she took over a newly established
department and had to negotiate internally for its fair share of clients.

Alice's new department was the brainchild of the vice president for sales. He wanted a separate sales group to target start-ups in the growing biotech field. To get Alice's department off the ground, $5 million in accounts had to be transferred from national sales. No problems surfaced in the planning meetings. Without a lot of fanfare, Alice and Len Davis, the manager of national sales, established reasonable criteria and a deadline for the transfer. Alice trusted Len. His easygoing personality meshed well with her reserve. She liked hearing his company war stories over coffee. When they went on sales calls or developed a presentation, she always learned a lot.

Then the real negotiation began.

Alice: I've put together a list of possible transfers. You were going to come up with a list. Do you have that? We can see where we overlap.

Len: We've been so busy. I haven't gotten to it yet. But I will. Give me a couple of days.

Repeated phone calls prompted no action from Len. The day before the annual sales meeting, when account assignments were distributed, Len finally gave Alice his list.

Alice: These accounts come to only $2.5 million.

Len: Yeah, I know. But I really don't think your department is ready for any more. Why don't we take this transfer a little slower?

Alice: We all agreed to the time line, the $5 million goal. It's a little late to change the rules now.

Len: Look, I'm doing this for the best. Your people can't handle any more right now.

Alice: My people are really pumped up about working on these accounts. What am I supposed to do with them?

Len: Don't get so upset.

Because the department was new, with few ground rules and no track record, Alice was ripe for testing. Len's moves made it clear to Alice that he thought he could force her to make concessions and accept half the number of accounts she expected. Time was on his side, not hers. She was already hearing grumbling about the delays from her team. When she objected to his parsimonious list, he implied she was being emotional. Len came up with a revised list two weeks later, but it was filled with what Alice suspected were dead accounts.

Len's moves challenge Alice on several fronts. He plays on her sympathy and her team's inexperience. He insinuates that she is not being cooperative when she doesn't go along with his suggestions. But his moves also cast doubts on her skill as a manager, whether she has the right temperament. He tries to position her as someone who takes things personally, who is too emotional and excitable to see the big picture.

Is Len the bad guy here? No. He is doing what negotiators do—trying to maintain his advantage in the shadow negotiation. To give up more accounts than is absolutely necessary is a risky policy for him at this stage. The more accounts he keeps under his supervision, the happier his salesmen will be. One of those accounts might be the next biotech superstar. When he tells Alice that her team is not ready for that many accounts, he is not playing dirty. He's trying to make sure the negotiation goes his way.

Alice must turn Len's moves. She has let him put her on the defensive. "It was clear to everyone that Len didn't take me seriously," she recalls. "He thought it would be pretty easy to overpower me or wear me down." But, as we shall see, Alice has a few turns up her sleeve. As Len watches her turn his moves, one by one, it gradually dawns on him that he's not going to maneuver her into a defensive position. Alice pays attention not only to the strategic moves she must make, but begins to anticipate Len's moves and then turns them before they gain momentum. Once he realizes that he is wasting his time trying to take over the negotiation, the shadow negotiation comes back into alignment and they reach a solution that is fair to them both. But before the negotiation is over, she has used a full repertory of turns.

A Repertory of Turns

Strategic moves against you require a response. Often you don't have the luxury of time to plan the best response, and so it is essential to have some "turns" on hand that you are comfortable using. You can turn the other party's moves in any number of ways.

- **INTERRUPT THE MOVE**

  Interrupting turns break the action. They give you time to get collected and think about how you are going to deal with any attempt to put you on the defensive. More important, by changing the pace interruption allows you to exert control over a critical element in any negotiation— its timing—and to halt any momentum that is working against you.

- **NAME THE MOVE**

  Naming turns make the other party's move visible. They let your counterpart know that you are perfectly aware of what is going on and are unfazed. Once the other party realizes a maneuver is not having the impact intended, he or she generally gives it up.

- **CORRECT THE MOVE**

  Correcting turns offer an alternative explanation for what is going on or at issue in the shadow negotiation. Rather than accept the other party's take as given, you substitute a positive account of your actions for the negative one he or she is promoting to your disadvantage.

- **DIVERT THE MOVE**

  Diverting turns shift the talk away from the personal. We are at our most vulnerable in a negotiation when threatened personally—when our motives or abilities are attacked. You disarm the move by diverting the focus from you as the problem to the problem itself.

Turns differ in directness and intensity. Circumstances generally dictate which will be most effective to use. Past dealings and scouting information often give you ample hints on whether the other person is likely to attempt to put you on the defensive and how.

Interrupt the Move

However alert you are, the other party's moves can catch you by surprise. You expect the negotiation to follow a certain path, and all of a sudden it veers in a different direction. Surprise moves tempt immediate re-sponses, but these are not always the best alternative. Unprepared, you might not be able to come up with the appropriate turn on instant demand and react defensively. You can avoid a defensive countermove by buying time. When the other party's move throws you off balance, take a break.

Interruptions stop the action. They prevent you from being swept up in a momentum that is not going your way. After a break, you and the other person never pick up in the same place psychologically. You have had a chance to recoup and your counterpart no longer enjoys the element of surprise. Interruptions don't have to be long. Sometimes just walking over to a flip chart changes the dynamic. Other times a definite recess or a complete change of pace is in order.

Take a break. Even a few moments of interruption can rob a surprise move of its effectiveness. A hasty response can be reconsidered over a cup of coffee. Papers can turn up missing in a file, requiring a short intermission. A trip to your office often provides enough time to assess the new turn of events.

Charlene had just been appointed head of her company's market review committee. Ellen, another member, had actively campaigned for the job and a residue of bad feeling remained. To start her tenure off on the right note, Charlene invited all the members to a get-together session. They were in the middle of discussing how to proceed when Ellen rushed in. Apologizing for being late, she began to pass out copies of a four-page memo. Skimming the elegantly typed pages, Charlene saw the outlines of a market review strategy. "Ellen might not be chair, but she's certainly acting like she is," Charlene thought. She smiled at Ellen. "What a lot of work," she said, and then picked up her mug. "Anyone else want a refill?"

To a person, the committee members got up and began to congregate by the coffeepot. When they sat back down, Charlene told Ellen that the committee had not made so much progress as Ellen had independently. They had yet to identify the approach they wanted to take, let alone the priorities. Perhaps, Charlene suggested, it would be better to consider Ellen's memo when ideas had been discussed a bit more.

Charlene's interruption accomplished several things. She resisted being rude to a member who had obviously put in a lot of effort. At the same time, she prevented that work from dominating the discussion. Without her interruption, the committee's attention would have been locked on

Ellen's memo. But Charlene's interruption had another, more subtle effect. Because she did not cut Ellen off, but rather tabled discussion of her ideas, she signaled to the other committee members that no one individual would control the sessions.

Call a time-out. At times surprise moves create more than a minor setback. Without warning you find yourself facing new players or discover the game plan has changed. A brief break might not give you enough time to get collected or figure out what to do. Moreover, it might not be dramatic enough to change the situation. You still have to contend with the additional players or the new set of rules. To turn these more serious surprise moves, you might have to suspend the negotiation temporarily, rescheduling to a later date and a different place. This turn not only gives you more time, it creates an opportunity to make sure that the next round in the negotiation takes place under hospitable circumstances. Gina, the retailing entrepreneur from chapter 1 who religiously prepares for any contingency, cut short a major meeting with potential investors when they caught her by surprise.

A mid-winter storm made Gina's flight from Boston both harrowing and late. When she finally landed in Minneapolis, she was tired and rattled. She was thrown even more off stride when she walked into the conference room and faced the entire investment committee. The crowded room, Gina realized, was a good sign. Clearly her company had sparked the committee's interest. Despite this encouraging thought, she found the united front intimidating. Although annoyed with herself for being cowed by such a transparent tactic, she immediately cut short her presentation. "I'm asking you to invest in a concept," she concluded. "To talk terms, you need to know what we are selling. That's more than chairs and sofas. It's a lifestyle. Now that we've had a chance to get acquainted, why don't we meet next month at the store?"

Outnumbered and robbed of any chance to scout information on the additional players, Gina did not feel prepared to field questions. Recognizing the danger, she deliberately interrupted the session. That interruption removed Gina from the inquisitorial spotlight and insured that the next meeting had a setting she could control. The shop, she knew, would show to advantage—and, on her own turf, so would she.

Change the pace. People often use time and momentum strategically. They enforce artificial deadlines to pressure you into accepting a proposal before you can puzzle through the implications. Knowing that you are working against a deadline, they capitalize on your tight schedule to press for concessions, trading promptness for benefits. To prevent your schedule or artificial deadlines from driving the negotiation, you can slow the pace.

Bargainers can deliberately create a sense of urgency. Wait, they imply, and you will lose out on an opportunity. These moves are intended to force a decision. They are employed in corporate boardrooms and rug bazaars. By turning them, you keep control over your decisions rather than let the other party set the timetable.

Jill was transplanting her antiques shop from Connecticut to Greenwich Village. She had her eye on a storefront her real estate agent had listed. She promptly stopped by to meet the owner. He told her the location was great, with a lot of traffic. He was retiring; otherwise he would never leave. Jill was barely out of the store when her cell phone started ringing. It was the real estate agent. The space had stirred a great deal of interest. It would be gone by Monday. All the other prospective buyers were ready to take the space as-is. He did not want her to lose out.

The more the agent pressured Jill, the more suspicious she became. "I like what I see," she finally said, "but I need time to do some more legwork. My architect won't be able to inspect the shop until next week."

That inspection turned up major problems. The space needed to be rewired to be brought up to code and the roof had to be replaced. Those "other buyers" failed to materialize, and Jill negotiated a substantial reduction in the purchase price.

Before you either slow or pick up the pace in a negotiation, you have to satisfy yourself that time is being used as a tactic. You must be relatively certain the deadline is artificial or be willing to live with the consequences if it is not. Jill, for example, gambled that the agent would not be pressing her so hard if he had other buyers in the wings. The risk of buying the building without professional advice offset any possible disappointment in losing it. Consequences in organizations are not always so easy to ignore. Clients or colleagues might resent what they consider stalling or undue pressure.

Alice, not expecting the negotiations with Len to be difficult, used interrupting turns to advantage. She took frequent breaks to check her

*frustration and to put a damper on his temper. The moment Len started
to raise his voice, she got them both coffee. If the break did not restore
his usual affability, she ended the session. She declared a time-out
whenever Len tried to overpower her with numbers. If he arrived at a
meeting with his entourage trailing, she rescheduled so that her team
would be available as well.*

*Increasingly aware of Len's stalling techniques, Alice also took steps
to reestablish her control over the pace of the negotiation. Once Len
tendered his meager list of accounts, he continued to stonewall. She
broke the logjam by updating the sales vice president on their progress.
She sent a factual progress report via e-mail to him and Len. The e-mail
prompted action from Len. After a token resistance, he agreed to talk
about interim targets beyond the $2.5 million on his list.*

Turns require a cool head. That is why interruption is such an important tool. It is not only useful in and of itself, but it allows you time to re-
group and consider what other responses you might have to make.

Name the Move

Naming turns attach a label to the other party's move. Just the act of
naming lets the other person know that the tactic is transparent. As a result,
naming turns deliver two direct messages: They show that you are not naïve
about common negotiation tactics and that the particular ploy is not working. You recognize both the tactic and the reason it is being used against
you—and unsuccessfully, at that. Naming must be carefully executed. The
turn needs to be directed at the behavior, not the people. Otherwise it can
degenerate into name-calling. You want to turn the move, not turn off the
other person.

Naming turns run the gamut from a joking aside to a serious challenge.
But for a label to be effective you have to apply one the other party recognizes and accepts as valid. That realization forces him or her to reevaluate
the behavior. Bargainers are quick to jettison tactics that gain them nothing or show them in a bad light. They also discard tactics that generate unintended effects or get in the way of what they want to accomplish.
Naming turns prompt that process along.

Reveal the move's ineffectiveness. The other party generally intends a move to have an impact. By pointing out a move's ineffectiveness, naming deflates the move. Tactics meant to make you feel defensive are not much good if you don't get defensive. By naming the move, you let the other party know it's not working. However clever or disguised the tactic, you see through it and remain unruffled. Gloria, a media executive, was negotiating television rights to a hot property. After trying for several days to reach the elusive literary agent on the telephone, she finally succeeded. Before she could say hello, the agent started screaming abuse at her, attacking her competence and her experience. She was surprised that he would jeopardize a lucrative deal for his client, but whatever his motivation, she could not let his attitude go unchecked and set the tone for the negotiation. "I called to start talking deal points," she interrupted. "Calm down. Yelling won't help. I won't go away."

Several days later Gloria learned that the agent had attacked her to buy himself time. He did not yet control the television rights to the property. He had gone on the offensive to stall. But Gloria's naming of the situation meant that when they did negotiate, she would not be doing so from a defensive position. Naming, used in this way, puts the conversation back on track. The turn effectively says there are better ways to deal with each other.

Expose the move's inappropriateness. Some moves are out of bounds. By naming questionable moves, you make the other person understand that certain behavior is unacceptable. What's more, the behavior doesn't reflect very well on him or her. Rough tactics sometimes call for tough labels. The label you choose must fit the action. You want the other party to realize how serious you consider the breach. When someone crosses a line, he or she has to know it.

Jen's community health center had been pivotal in restoring pride to an inner-city neighborhood. Money was scarce, and Jen watched her budget like a hawk. When *60 Minutes* first floated tentative plans to schedule a program on inner-city revitalization around the center, Jen was jubilant. The construction union, however, immediately recognized a pressure point. If the network producers got wind of any unresolved labor problems, they might scuttle the program. The threat of picket lines alone would force Jen to make the center's construction projects all-union jobs.

The union officials considered the intimidating moves business as usual. Jen called them blackmail.

I was very angry. The union needed to understand that I was personally
disappointed, that we as an institution were disappointed. I was not
going to downplay that. They had violated a trust I thought we had. I
wanted them to understand that we understood their game, that we
disrespected that game, that I disrespected them and their
shortsightedness. The head guy from the Local, who lives in the area,
had tears in his eyes after I finished talking to him.

By calling the union accountable for its actions, naming its behavior,
Jen turned the move. Caught in an opportunistic play, the union officials
backed down. Jen's naming forced them to recognize that their tactics,
rather than giving them an advantage, had hurt their cause.

Jen's turn worked because her label fit the situation. She knew it and
the union knew it. Success in naming unacceptable behavior depends on
whether the other party recognizes that he or she has crossed a line. If
she considers her actions just part of the normal give-and-take of any negotiation, she won't change her behavior. She will merely see you as an
unsophisticated or inexperienced negotiator, unaccustomed to the rough-
and-tumble of the real world.

Highlight the move's unintended consequences. The naming turns
we have discussed so far show the other party the ineffectiveness or inappropriateness of a move against you. In these situations, the bargainers
know full well what they are trying to do. You just point out that they are
not succeeding or should have thought twice before making the attempt in
the first place. But bargainers are not omniscient. They do not always anticipate the impact of their moves, and their actions sometimes produce
effects they never intended.

With the best intentions in the world, people still make mistakes.
Their moves might have consequences they never planned, and those
consequences can be named. Sometimes, the other person is actually trying to be supportive and pushes you in a direction she wants you to go.
She doesn't bother to discover how you feel about that particular destina-
tion at that particular moment. It never occurs to her that you might be
less than sanguine about the shape this support takes.

Cynthia, a partner in a national consulting firm, had a mentor who felt
compelled to micromanage Cynthia's career. The most senior woman in
the company, she had shepherded Cynthia through several promotions.

She wanted Cynthia to succeed quickly. She kept up the pressure, not realizing that she did not micromanage Cynthia's male colleagues. If they wanted to spend more time with their kids, fine. If they argued that their current assignments should be extended, that was all right, too.

Cynthia, on the other hand, never remained in any assignment long enough to catch her breath or get to know the people. She had just come off an exhilarating and exhausting year when her mentor announced that she had another choice job waiting. "This opening could not have come at a better time," she said. "It's very visible and will really stretch you." Cynthia already felt stretched to the maximum. "I cannot take on new responsibilities and a relocation right now," she thought.

Cynthia was caught in a classic double bind—afraid to say no, yet reluctant to say yes. No one turned down a promotion in her company. The opportunity might not come around again. If she wanted any control over her life, she had to turn her mentor's pressure to accept.

Cynthia could have named her mentor's actions in a number of ways. She could have pointed out that her mentor treated male subordinates differently, but the woman, trying to promote another woman, would never accept that label. Instead, carefully steering clear of the personal consequences of the promotion, Cynthia named the professional implications for her. Her rapid rise had stirred resentment. Her colleagues did not see her so much as a leader but as a protected person. If Cynthia was to take on the leadership role her mentor wanted for her, she needed time for reflection and opportunities to develop relationships with her colleagues. Cynthia's mentor appreciated her thoughtfulness and her candor. She wanted to promote Cynthia, but she also wanted to keep her. She dropped the idea of the promotion, shifting instead to what Cynthia wanted to do next.

Naming turns in situations like these flow from a good faith assumption that the moves are misguided, not malicious. In spelling out those consequences—naming them—these turns enlighten. They allow other people to see the distance between what they think they are doing and what you think they are doing.

Characterize the move as counterproductive. Naming a move can also show the other person that a particular negotiating habit or technique accomplishes nothing and might actually create additional obstacles. Sometimes negotiators make moves that have become second nature to them. These moves are employed by habit, and their usefulness goes unquestioned even when they get in the way of fruitful negotiation. Naming behavior that has the two of you working at cross-purposes encourages you to find better, more effective ways of dealing with each other. Naming turns can be particularly effective in organizations where combative or aggressive negotiating styles stifle more collaborative approaches.

Linda wrote advertising copy in a small agency. Creative, with a fertile imagination, she was good at coming up with catchy ad campaigns. But whenever she presented her ideas to the senior account executive, he immediately began to pick them apart. Linda knew she was not being singled out. He treated everyone this way. Still, that assurance provided little comfort. With her ideas under constant attack, she could never decide whether they were being totally rejected or just needed some refinement. Exasperated, she finally asked the senior account executive if he'd noticed that he always played devil's advocate. From her perspective, a stream of criticism left no room to debate the merits of a proposed campaign. He was surprised at her reaction. No one had ever voiced this complaint before. Didn't she know that he would not bother to criticize an idea if he didn't consider it worth some massaging? No, she said. When he started playing devil's advocate as soon as she handed him her copy, she could only assume that he didn't think much of it.

Once his role in their negotiations was named and Linda's reaction to it had been identified, they were able to see how their behavior interfered with their real task. His blanket criticism gave Linda no way to separate important conceptual comments from the details. Going forward, they agreed to reach consensus on a campaign's concept. Then he would have free rein to criticize as they discussed the execution.

Alice took advantage of opportunities to name Len's stalling maneuvers. One presented itself when he handed her his first list of accounts.

Alice: *These accounts come to only $2.5 million.*

Len: *Yeah, I know. But I really don't think your department is ready for any more. Why don't we take this transfer a little slower?*

Alice: *That's not the problem. (laughs) 'Fess up. You just don't want to give up any more accounts.*

Len: *Not at all. I'm doing this for the best. Your people can't handle any more right now.*

Alice: *Come on, Len. You and I both know that's not the case. These*
         people were handpicked to get the new department off and
         running. That's big on everyone's agenda right now.

In this brief exchange Alice lets Len know that she doesn't accept
what he is saying. Her people aren't green or untrained. He thinks he can
get her to accept fewer accounts if he holds out long enough. In naming
his move, she pointedly reminds him that the new department's success
carries a high priority within the company—and with their boss in
particular.

Naming turns rob the other party's move of its intended impact and
force him or her to reconsider its usefulness. The turn arrests the behavior, pointing to its lack of effect or appropriateness, and can, in the
process, provoke a more substantial change in the way you deal with each
other in the shadow negotiation.

Correct the Move

Negotiators use strategic moves for a purpose. To bring you around to
their view, they throw doubt on anything that supports your perspective.
Subtly and sometimes not so subtly, they challenge the underpinnings of
your demands in the shadow negotiation. They dispute the merits of your
arguments and your ability or right to make them. These moves are meant
to make you wonder whether their rendering is not the real one. What had
previously seemed clear and reasonable no longer appears so obvious.
Maybe, you think, my proposal isn't so great after all. I should have put
more time into it. Maybe this is the wrong time to ask for a raise. With the
budget so tight, I'm being greedy. Maybe, you concede, the other person
has a point. Busy behind the scenes gathering support, you did delay open
discussion. Once the other party persuades you to see what's wrong with
you or your proposal or something you have done, it is an easy slide to get
you to back off on your demands.

These moves often cast you in the role of an unworthy adversary. The
other party exaggerates a weakness here or misinterprets a motive there.
The attempt might be deliberate, but then again it might not. It's simply
easier to downplay the requests of someone who is inexperienced, emo-

tional, or too demanding. You turn these moves by directly addressing the faulty characterization. It does not matter if the unflattering image is consciously imposed or accidentally applied. How the other person sees you conditions how she or he deals with you.

Correcting turns unmask distorted impressions and strip away qualities that are being falsely attributed to you. They revise misinterpreted motives or misunderstood attitudes. All these misperceptions, unless corrected, reinforce a bargainer who wants to whittle away at your demands. Correcting turns are not defensive. They go beyond simple protests and denials. They restore balance to the negotiation by elaborating on just what's right about your rendering and why.

Shift the focus to the positive. Not infrequently the other party jumps to conclusions based on the most cursory of impressions and then acts on them—to your disadvantage. Turns that correct flawed impressions of you begin with the faulty image. You need to ask yourself where it is wrong. Often you can trace the error to inadequate or outdated information. Impressions drawn from previous negotiations might need to be revised. A boss, for example, might need reminding that you have outgrown your apprenticeship role and that his earlier image of you no longer applies.

Correcting turns are particularly useful during job interviews where skepticism exists about your credentials or the appropriateness of your experience. At thirty-eight, Leonore was a senior vice president in charge of human resources at a Texas bank. Frustrated at the way her skills were being underutilized, Leonore began looking for another job. "Nothing frosts me more," she says, "than when people assume, because I am a woman and in human resources, that I don't have any business savvy."

Her first interview started off disastrously. The bank chairman barely gave her time to introduce herself. He then fired questions at her about how she handled problem employees. When he ran out of steam, he complimented Leonore on her "people skills." Unfortunately, he observed, the demands of a commercial bank required more expertise from its human resource managers than an ability to deal with difficult people.

> As soon as I could get a word in edgewise, I did. I answered all the questions he should have asked me. I told him how I reduced teller turnover from 82 percent to 15 percent. Then I proceeded to long-term medical benefits. I explained how I saved the bank $250,000 the first

year and over $1 million the second when I renegotiated the insurance package with the carriers.

Leonore went from being dismissed to being desired by correcting the banker's misguided impressions. Her version of who she was piqued his interest, and *she* began questioning *him* about the job.

Leonore's experience points out how important correcting turns can be when you don't know the other person. "Most people," she argues, "don't understand how to interview."

But that becomes *your* problem once you are in the room. You have to get over the automatic assumption that it is your fault when an interview goes badly. The interviewer might not have a good idea of who you are or what you do. That's correctable.

Correcting turns don't necessarily insure that you get the job or whatever else it is that you want. They can, however, restore balance to the shadow negotiation so that you and the other person can figure out whether some agreement on the issues is possible.

Supply a legitimate motive. Most people want others to consider them fair and ethical in their dealings. Moves that question your motives attack not so much your competence as your values and character. What you consider honest self-interest or a justified objection gets characterized as underhanded, opportunistic, and self-serving. Asking for that raise is labeled as greedy. Pushing to get more people assigned to your team is called shortsighted. Nor do these aspersions need to be explicit. A hint is often enough to damage your confidence and your position. By casting your actions in a bad light, such a move pushes you into defending them. No one wants the other person in a negotiation to think badly of him or her. Barbara found herself in this quandary when another woman implied that she was being insensitive to a working mother.

Barbara, a cross-country track coach in her late twenties, had led her team to the state's annual championships that spring. The athletic director, recognizing the team's potential for the coming season, hired an assistant coach. For the last several years the team had rented a house at the New Jersey shore for preseason workouts. Just before the team was to leave, the new assistant coach proposed that she bring her five-month-old daughter along. Barbara rejected the proposal for what she saw as legitimate reasons. Two coaches had their hands full keeping a group of teenagers in check and focused without one of the coaches' being distracted by a baby. "That will be difficult," Barbara said. "We have to be on our toes all the time."

The assistant coach immediately accused Barbara of putting unnecessary roadblocks in a working mother's way. "I felt terrible," Barbara recalled. "I began to suggest ways we could make it work—hiring a baby-sitter, asking another coach to come along." The assistant coach, impressed by Barbara's willingness to work on a solution, saw that Barbara's response was motivated not by a bias against working mothers but by a concern for the logistical problems. "She finally admitted," Barbara said, "that it was stupid to hire an extra person just so she could go along."

When the other party casts aspersions on your motives, it becomes difficult to stay in the negotiation. You can't help but feel attacked. That is often the purpose behind the move. You don't want to stay in that situation. Rather than retreat, you turn the view around. Barbara, by coming up with ideas, corrected the negative explanation for her decision that the woman put forward. The possible arrangements she suggested not only showed that Barbara was flexible, they offered convincing proof that her original response to the proposal was legitimate.

Counter stereotyped images.   Not all strategic moves can be turned so quickly. Sometimes they require a concerted campaign, particularly when they rest on gendered assumptions. Gender often slips quietly into the shadow negotiation. A woman has different priorities. She has responsibilities at home that make her a less-productive employee, less flexible or available. She's too sympathetic to make hard business decisions. Many women entrepreneurs battle these assumptions when they seek capital to launch or expand a business. They lack business savvy and are too softhearted to make objective, unemotional decisions. Their businesses are "risky," too service oriented. Undercapitalized to begin with, they don't have the collateral to back up a loan. Certain of these objections can be overruled by the facts. The bias behind them must be turned.

Maryanne's West Coast catering business was a success almost the moment she opened the doors.[4] The firm's imaginative menus attracted immediate attention in the press. Within months her operation was being touted in the local media and ranked among the city's top catering services. Maryanne was delighted with the reception. She loved cooking, she loved her clients, and she loved putting together great parties. She soon needed to expand her operation to accommodate her growing list of clients. With a $125,000 loan, which she believed she could easily handle, she could take on more staff and buy additional kitchen equipment.

Despite Maryanne's track record, she quickly ran through her prospective lending sources. Then the last loan officer on her list turned her down. "I cannot approve a loan just because you make the best puff pastry in town." What, Maryanne asked, would change her mind? "A business manager," the loan officer shot back. "I need to be sure you can repay the loan. I don't have that confidence."

Maryanne recognized the reasons behind the rejection. The loan officer did not want to lend money to a cook. She was a risky proposition. Although her cooking got rave reviews, nothing in her loan request suggested she was equally adept at managing money or that the business was solid. She needed to change those impressions. Would the loan officer reconsider, Maryanne asked, if she had proof that her business could comfortably handle the monthly repayment schedule? Forced into a corner, the loan officer had to admit she would.

For the first time, Maryanne asked her largest clients to commit to specific levels of work a year in advance. Demand for her services was high, she argued. Without a commitment, she could not guarantee that she would be available. She managed to secure enough pledges to satisfy the pickiest of lenders that she could cover repayment of a $125,000 loan. Maryanne then set about making her loan request more "professional." With help from a friend, she installed a computerized financial accounting system that she could manage easily. Then she bought some desktop publishing software and redid her loan request, discarding the pretty pictures and replacing them with detailed financial projections.

Her banker began to see Maryanne not as a cook but as a businessperson. The revised loan request went through without a hitch. Instead of defending herself against the unfavorable biases in the banker's lending policies, she turned them, but it took some time.

Len was a master at putting Alice on the defensive. His moves reinforced a simple theme: She did not deserve more accounts; she was too emotional and too inexperienced to handle them. Exasperated, she put

*out a counterproposal to Len. She would accept his list, but only if she
could have thirty days to identify and discard dubious accounts. Len
refused.*

> Len: *You cannot have it both ways. If you want the accounts, you
> have to take some risk.*
>
> Alice: *I'm perfectly willing to take the risk as long as it's based on
> some decent information. And that's not what I'm getting.*
>
> Len: *Okay, okay. How about you take these (quickly ticking some
> items on his sheets with a pencil). And I'll keep these?*

*When Len tells Alice she is not a risk-taker, she does not contradict
him. Rather, she corrects a faulty impression. Her appetite for risk
depends on good information. Her turn takes the personal sting out of
Len's comment; she is willing to take risks, but she is not so naïve as to
take foolish ones. When Alice turns this move, she revises the image of
her as a weak manager that undergirds Len's rationalization for holding
back the accounts.*

Correcting turns help insure that the other party sees you in an accurate yet favorable light. They stop moves the other person might use to justify holding you or your opinions in little regard. In effect, correcting turns restore respect to the shadow negotiation. That respect is a precondition for successful negotiation. Without it, you will have a hard time convincing another person to take you or your needs seriously.

Divert the Move

Emotions run high when you are made the problem—whether the other party's move is based on some imaginary inadequacy or something you did in the past or something you want to do now. You can always take a break to recoup and gain some perspective. You can try to turn the move by correcting the other person's perceptions. But you can also deliberately step back and take the personalities out of the equation for the moment.

Diverting turns shift attention from the people to the problem.[5] Rather than confront a personal challenge directly, you channel the conversation to the problem at hand. In effect, you refuse to admit that you are the problem. The other party can disagree with the ideas in your proposal, but she can no longer make your expertise or competence the issue once you walk her through the intricacies of its logic and supporting documentation. When you suggest ways of being rewarded for a job well done that won't strain the budget, a boss has difficulty keeping up the pretense that you are being greedy. A co-worker, harboring past grievances, might be persuaded to put them aside if you come up with a plan to avoid tensions in the future.

Look ahead, not to past mistakes. Negotiations that have a history can get bogged down in that history. Bad experiences or uneasy relations focus attention on past wrongs instead of future solutions. The discussion faces backward, tempting the bargainers to justify earlier deeds or disclaim misdeeds. You might recognize the part you played in what happened in the past and push for less in the current negotiation. The other person might try to lay all the blame on you. To divert moves of this kind, you acknowledge the past and move on to the present problem.

Relations weren't good between the neighborhood association Susan headed and the town's administration. When Susan went to the mayor's office to talk about the association's annual fair, the mayor launched a volley of objections. He's looking for a scapegoat, she thought. He doesn't want his office to take the blame for last year's fiasco when massive traffic jams gridlocked the neighborhood. He wants to pin it on us. Admittedly, the association had been disorganized, but the administration had also been lax in its police and traffic support. The weather had been beautiful and no one had expected such a huge turnout.

Susan worried that the mayor might punish the association by raising the cost of extra police details or, worse, by refusing to renew its permit for the event. She had to get him talking about the fair, not past mistakes. "You are absolutely right, Mr. Mayor," she said. "No one wants a repeat of last year. That's why I wanted to talk to you before we started our planning. Let's see what we can do to get it right this year." Had Susan not diverted the mayor, she would have spent the next half hour defending the association against the mayor's attacks.

Not only can you be held personally responsible for past events; you can be blamed when a negotiation begins to sour. To prevent hostility from growing over a particular issue, you can divert the discussion and turn to a less-divisive issue. A politician, chair of an influential committee, was one of the few women in any position of power within the state government.

> Whenever we hit a rough spot, the anger and frustration were directed at me. If that started to happen, I shifted gears and took up another item on the agenda.

Often when everyone at the table has managed to agree on less-troublesome points, they are more inclined to tackle the hard issues with an open mind. The progress generates confidence and they stop seeing you as an impediment.

Substitute a better idea. Common moves that women and young people encounter are challenges to their legitimacy or authority. The moves can be subtle: a raised eyebrow that expresses surprise when you introduce yourself; the failure to pick up on an important point you have made; a covert glance at a watch that intimates the other person is really too busy to deal with your issues. No matter how much forethought you have put into establishing your credibility, these unexpected moves can still challenge you.

Allison, a psychologist, was negotiating a contract with a large auto manufacturer to provide workshops on sexual harassment. She arrived for a meeting and was greeted by a new company representative. The woman she had been dealing with had been involved in a serious car accident. Since she was going to be out of commission for several months, the company, anxious to move forward on the sexual harassment seminars for legal reasons, had asked her boss to take over the negotiations.

Allison soon discovered the atmosphere had chilled. The new man, dubious about the harassment seminars in the first place, immediately started revising the contract terms. The company did not need a full-blown course, only enough to kick off an in-house effort. What exactly did he mean by that? Allison inquired. Well, he was not sure. Why didn't they play it by ear? Instead of making a lump-sum payment, they could pay her firm on a workshop-by-workshop basis. Allison objected to this idea. Her firm had designed an entire sequence of workshops. If the company could sample one or two and then cancel the contract, the firm would lose money. "Look," the company negotiator came back, "this is not a big deal. Take it back to your boss. I'm sure it's okay."

With that move, Allison's authority to negotiate the contract evaporated. She restored it with a diverting turn. She did not bother to dispute the inference that the decision was not hers to make. Instead, she put on the table a solution to the payment problem. "Why don't we work out some penalty for cancellation right here? This is not the first time this issue has come up. I've developed a formula that's fair to our clients and to us. Once we get started, I'm sure you will want us to continue. That gets expensive for you if we bill on a flat workshop-by-workshop basis."

Allison's turn accomplished several objectives. She forced the discussion back to the issue—how her firm would be paid and what was fair. But she also established her credentials in a concrete way. She ignored the aspersions cast on her authority and then offered up a demonstration of her ability that robbed them of any weight. She brought her past experience and expertise to bear on a solution. She'd encountered this problem in the past and had dealt with it successfully. Allison's story illustrates an important point: If you want to divert a move away from the personal to the problem, you need to have an idea about how that problem can be solved.

Shift from the personal to the problem. Some moves to undermine your credibility are fairly easy to read and turn. Others are much more complicated. Frequently you negotiate with people who know you or have known you in another guise. Maybe you have just been promoted. In the past, you were a silent observer in negotiations, an assistant taking notes. Now you are leading the team. Or you work in a family-owned business where almost everyone remembers what you looked like with pigtails. These multiple or overlapping roles confuse the other person. Does a colleague suddenly stop seeing you as an assistant once you have been promoted? Does a father cease being a father on the job when the employee happens to be his daughter? Because it is often difficult for people to shift gears, they revert to old habits. Their moves push you back to roles they are comfortable with. Rather than address these constraining moves directly, you can establish credibility in your new role by engaging the other party in the problem at hand.

Trina was thinking about going to work for her father in a family-owned business. "My family is Greek, very close and very traditional. My father is a wonderful man," she stressed, "warm and kind. But he's also very much from the old father-knows-best school. He's a meddler. If I was going to work with him, I had to be convinced he would listen to what I said, let me make my own mistakes, rather than just telling me what he thought I should do."

Trina wanted to join the family firm for several reasons. She could use her education and experience to help the business. Customer service, her specialty, had always been a problem. She could lighten some of the burden her father had been carrying since her uncle's retirement. And she thought she might have more flexibility. She was planning to go back to school to get an M.B.A.

Serious negotiations had just begun when Trina learned she was pregnant. Her father worried that she could not handle a baby, school, and work. (Given his dibs, he would have preferred that she stay home with his future grandchild.) Whenever these concerns surfaced, Trina deflected them by focusing on the business issues: her needs for generous health benefits and a flexible schedule; his concerns about what she should be paid and about possible charges of favoritism from his longtime employees.

By turning the moves that her father made to position her as a daughter, Trina was able to negotiate with him as a prospective employee. He agreed to let her coordinate her hours with her school schedule and do some work at home. In exchange, she accepted a cut in pay. To finish her degree, she would take an unpaid leave for a semester, but the company would reimburse her tuition.

Alice used a diverting turn after Len complained that he was being pressured by his people over the lost commissions.

> Len: *Cut me some slack here. I'm getting a lot of pressure from my people. They don't want their commissions hurt.*
>
> Alice: *No one does. That's the reason behind my group. While we work on the developing accounts, you can concentrate on the established ones. It's an opportunity.*

Alice did not respond to Len's obvious appeal for sympathy. That would have put her in a no-win position in the shadow negotiation. If she took on the role of understanding colleague, she would not be able to push Len on the accounts. If she didn't, she risked coming off as unfeeling and inflexible. Nor could she simply reply in kind—protesting that her team was just as mad as his.

Rather than "cutting him some slack" or launching a counterattack, she directed the talk to features that made the new arrangement an opportunity for his team. Since a possible loss of revenue and not the specific accounts was the real issue for his team, she suggested that she and Len work together on a scheme to ease the transition. The commissions could be phased out instead of coming to an abrupt end. To insure a smooth turnover, management might even be persuaded to compensate both sides for a period of time.

This diverting turn broke the impasse in their negotiations. Len dropped his attempts to wear down Alice and took up her suggestion of a phased transition in the commission structure.

Diverting turns bring everyone's attention back to the issues and prevent you from getting sidetracked by the other person's psychological maneuverings. The shift from the relational elements of the negotiation to the problem can be subtle, perhaps nothing more than a suggestion that it's time to get down to business. It can also precipitate a change in process from one of claims and counterclaims. Originating in a need to divert a personal challenge, the suggestions that such turns produce can take on an energy of their own and yield creative agreements.

A Caveat: Turning Demeaning Moves

Almost to a person, the women we interviewed intuitively understood the dynamic give-and-take of negotiation. They expected to be challenged and tested. They had had their fair share of experiences with the "dirty tricks" of negotiation. Although few had been caught in the cross fire of a good-cop/bad-cop routine or seated with blinding sunlight in their eyes, they had more than a passing acquaintance with bullying or intimidating tactics.

Most advice on negotiation recommends that bargainers ignore such heavy-handed tactics. It is far better, the argument goes, to take the high road and refuse to participate on the same level. This advice ignores a special brand of intimidating moves—those that gave the women we interviewed the most trouble. They wanted to be able to enjoy being women while they negotiated, but that left them vulnerable to disparaging personal remarks. Often they had to do nothing more than look certain ways and they would elicit unsettling comments. Too casual an approach or too great an enjoyment of banter led to sticky situations. It fed demeaning assumptions about "women's wiles."

Throughout the stories in this chapter women have dealt with gender issues. Gendered moves exploit inequalities in power. They play on weakness and uncertainty to enforce subservient or conciliatory roles. But demeaning moves are qualitatively different from run-of-the-mill dirty tricks or the gendered moves you must turn. Demeaning moves call attention to a woman's body, making her the sum of her physical attributes rather than her abilities. They belittle with words—*babe, sweetheart*, or even the occasional *bitch*. They dredge up tired stereotypes that reduce a woman to a member of a group—women—and erase individual distinctions. As a result, demeaning moves carry different implications. The female bargainer bears the brunt of a familiar or denigrating remark. If a woman opts to take the high road and ignores the behavior, she might reinforce the very stereotyped perceptions she needs to turn. No response *is* a response. Unless contested, the label sticks. But if she objects, she leaves herself open to being dismissed as too sensitive, too naïve, or too rigid.[6]

Casual assurances of "Nothing personal" often follow demeaning challenges. If the bargainer reacts, gets angry or flustered, that's *her* problem. There is something wrong with *her*. But these attacks *are* personal. They take place in the shadow negotiation, and their primary targets are the bargainer's self-confidence, her equanimity, her "appropriate" persona. They are meant to keep her from getting out of line or stepping farther out of line.

Demeaning challenges are difficult to deflect because so often they are cloaked in friendly language or compliments. Kicking up a fuss after a bit of flattery seems churlish. Raising an eyebrow at a tasteless joke can make the bargainer appear humorless or mean-spirited. But if a woman leaves these moves on the table, she participates, by her silence, in her own diminishment.

To turn a demeaning move, you have to *disrupt* it. The turn must stop the move cold before it gathers any momentum. Unless demeaning moves are disrupted, they automatically put you in a one-down position and set the tone for the rest of the negotiation. Finding the right balance is tricky. Too much disruption keeps attention on your reaction. The offending party realizes he has managed to rattle or annoy you. Too little disruption, and the attempt at censure goes unnoticed.[7]

Many factors come into play in choosing a response to a demeaning move. You must gauge not only the severity of the challenge but the comfort level you have. In environments where there is little toleration for exploitative behavior you have more leverage, but still must choose from a wide range of possible responses. Turns of this kind are as personal as the moves they counter. Success depends to a great extent on delivery—wit, inflection, an arched eyebrow. A humorous or mocking retort elicits a different reaction than a stinging rebuke. Few negotiators like to look foolish, and an ironic twist or sarcastic comment often exposes the absurdity of demeaning behavior better than a rapier thrust.[8]

One thing is certain. You need to think about how you are going to handle these challenges ahead of time. They *will* come up, at one time or another. Demeaning moves are unnerving precisely because they require instant turns. You seldom have the luxury of taking a break in order to figure out a great comeback, let alone an effective turn. Giving some thought to your possible responses prevents you from being caught off-guard.

Before a major sales presentation, a young accountant hears a stage whisper. "She can run my numbers anytime." That *sub voce* commentary is not a compliment. It is a deliberate move to put the presenter in her place, a woman's place. Having learned from experience to be prepared, the accountant had a retort handy: "Would you repeat that. Yes, you in the red tie. I couldn't hear." Suggestiveness and innuendo, she finds, don't survive repetition. The accountant had other options available as well. Any of the turns we have discussed would work, provided she was prepared to act quickly.

Interrupting a demeaning move.   Moves don't have to be overt to be demeaning. Sometimes they simply relegate you to the sidelines in a negotiation. Not just your comments but your presence become inconsequential. The conversation before a meeting never leaves Saturday's golf tournament, in which you did not play, or the Stanley Cup playoffs, which don't interest you. A dirty joke is told, and then another. What makes these moves so damaging is that they can set the tone for what follows. When actual discussions get under way, people talk through you or over you.

You cannot call a time-out when confronted with a demeaning move. Interruption must stop the action. Interrupting turns are particularly effective against exclusionary tactics. Unless you break an exclusionary pattern, you will continue to be invisible even though you have an important stake in how the negotiations turn out. One of the best stories of interruption we heard came from Dot, head of workouts for a money center bank's bankruptcy department. She used irony, laced with humor, to cut ritualized and exclusionary bonding short. This low-key approach served her well when she was involved in restructuring the debt of a major retail conglomerate. "The combative gamesmanship started before the participants had finished their coffee," Dot recalled. "As the only woman in the room, I became a nobody, a phantom on the sidelines." She listened for a while, then rummaged around in her bottomless pocketbook. With some flourish, she pulled out a bottle of bright red nail polish and started applying lacquer to an already perfect manicure. Silence gradually descended. Dot looked up and smiled.

"Any time you're ready, boys," she said. Her invitation brought the conversation to a halt. The irony was unmistakable. She controlled the money, and *she* was ready. The group got right down to business.

Dot's use of irony to interrupt was effective, but does it work for everybody? Early in a career, without experience or authority, polishing your nails during a staff meeting is likely to be interpreted as poor judgment rather than ironic commentary. Dot's turn cannot be separated from her position. She was a leader in these negotiations. But the general principle holds. The key to interruption is a dramatic or humorous remark that stops the action. Teresa, an intern in a city hospital, interrupted a dispute over a patient's care. She watched herself being shut out as the discussion turned into a duel between the surgical and the medical residents. They fired questions at her for information but otherwise she was invisible. After a few minutes, she broke in. "You guys going to arm-wrestle all night?"

Naming a demeaning move. Interrupting a demeaning move stops the action. In naming the move, you not only call a halt, you also let the other party know that you recognize the move and that it is unacceptable. Naming sets limits. These limits are important to establish. Each woman has her own threshold of tolerance, and the other party needs to be made aware of yours.

Naming offensive or intimidating behavior must leave the performer with no comeback. Otherwise, it can provoke an even stronger retort or prompt a bland "Who me?" response—an incredulous or wounded look, a mystified denial.

Annie, about to negotiate a contract important to her struggling travel agency, knew ahead of time she would be dealing with a tough negotiator. "But, hey," she says, "the contract was worth an hour or two of negotiating with an unpleasant personality."

> With car and hotel commissions as well as airline tickets on the line, Harry, this one man, was all I needed to end my short-term cash flow problem. He had a reputation for being a bully, but I figured I could drop the account later if he was too difficult.

To prevent Harry from gaining the upper hand, Annie planned to keep him focused strictly on the business issues. The strategy worked. Harry liked her proposal. Annie had seen nothing of the hard-nosed Harry she'd heard so much about. Pleased, she relaxed her guard.

> "By the way," he sneaks in just as he is about to leave, "you are rebating three percent of your commission back to me."

Besides being financial suicide and wiping out her profit margin, rebating commissions was illegal. If Annie were caught, her $75,000 performance bond could be revoked and her ticketing plates canceled. Annie remained cool and reminded Harry that rebating was against the law.

> "Wake up, bitch," he says. "Your competitors do it all the time." I just shook my head. I could see he was getting annoyed that he couldn't provoke me.

Caught in the moment, there was no way for Annie to gauge whether Harry was serious about taking a cut off the top or testing her. She knew only that what he was asking was illegal and that he was using offensive comments to intimidate her.

> I am nose to nose with this man, so stressed I'm afraid I'm going to start crying. "Get the hell out of my office," I tell him.
>   The office goes deadly silent. Then Harry's face turns purple, and he begins to twitch. Soon Harry is laughing so hard tears are streaming down his face. I wanted to kill him.

"Babe, you were great," he says gleefully. "Whoever would've figured a little girl like you would have the balls to tell me off?"

This rhetorical question provided Annie with her first opportunity to let Harry know she was on to his game. She named his behavior but did not stop there. Rather than reveal how much his performance offended her, she complimented him on it.

He made a move to give me a hug and I put out a cautionary finger that stopped just short of his chest. "Impressive, Harry. You're very good. You got all the information you wanted. But I passed the test. A repeat is not necessary, okay?"

Annie poked fun at Harry's intimidating moves. Instead of taking what he dished out, remaining a passive target, she "turned" herself into a critic of his behavior. Her message was clear: "I'm on to your game. Don't think you are going to get away with it the next time."

Correcting a demeaning move. Often the demeaning moves most difficult to turn are those that bring negative stereotypes to the surface. Confronting the bias directly only serves to legitimize it. No one readily admits to personal prejudice against working mothers or a belief that women get emotional when the going gets rough. They almost always have examples on hand that buttress their prejudice: "I can't depend on her to be there in a pinch." Rather than counter arguments like these, you expose the bias behind them. You are not the exception to the rule. The rule itself is wrong. In using a correcting turn, you not only set yourself apart from the stereotype, you also prompt the other person to question the stereotype.

Jane's group leader caught her where she was most vulnerable—her dual role as a working mother. When she was in the office, she was there 110 percent, but the time she blocked out for her family was sacrosanct. Everyone in Jane's department knew she came in early and left promptly. One morning she was checking her e-mail and discovered a message from her group leader. Weekly group meetings in engineering would now be held at 5:30 P.M. on Wednesdays. Jane assumed the group leader had forgotten her schedule and dropped by his office to remind him. The weekly gathering was the only time the group got together. If she couldn't attend, she would miss the project updates.

Jane: Late afternoons are not good for me. Can we change to an early morning meeting?

GL: Not necessary. You have to get home to the kids. Just write up your notes.

"Not overlooked," Jane thought, "inessential—not exactly the ideal employee." At that moment Jane did not care whether the head engineer was deliberately promoting that view. She could puzzle through motives later. She needed to set him straight about her commitment to her work before his attitude took root and her fellow engineers picked up on his cue.

Jane: Sure you don't mind?

GL: Of course not. Your kids need you at home.

Jane: Gee, I thought you needed me here, too. Guess not. Back to the kitchen for me? So much for progress.

GL: For Pete's sake, I assumed you'd be more appreciative, one less meeting. We'll go back to the regular time.

Jane used self-deprecating humor to turn a move that headed her toward the "mommy track." Moves like these are among the most difficult to turn. Often they stem from careless or unquestioned assumptions about a woman's priorities and are made unwittingly, without malice. Their effect, however, is not quite so harmless. They work off and perpetuate stereotyped generalizations that immediately put a woman at a disadvantage when she negotiates. Jane's boss was probably not even aware that he was applying a gendered standard. Correcting turns chip away at these attitudes. Generally the other person learns something about bias in the process.

Diverting a demeaning move. Moves that draw attention to physical appearance can be embarrassing or downright annoying. They are also difficult to turn. You don't want to come across as being overly sensitive. On the other hand, you cannot let an inappropriate remark linger, unchecked, in the shadow negotiation. The issue you focus on in diverting demeaning moves is *their* content. Exaggerating that content and showing its absolute irrelevance turns the demeaning move. It would be fruitless to point out that you can look good and think at the same time. The diverting turn comes in demonstrating that looking good has nothing to do with the business at hand and then segueing to the issues.

Grace, an intellectual-property lawyer who could easily pass for a model, has become a master of the strategic one-liner.[9] When Grace went into a meeting to finish up the last details of a contract, both men in the room, one of whom she had not even met yet, immediately referred to her appearance.

> First Jack tells me how stunning I look. Then Frank, the new guy, turns to Jack and says he understands why the negotiations have taken so long. Then he gives me an exaggerated wink. You get jerks like this from time to time. I never let that nonsense go. As soon as the words were out of his mouth, I turned a cold shoulder on him and said to Jack, "He's a real charmer."

Frank's implication was obvious. With a distraction like Grace around, who could blame Jack for not paying attention to business? Grace silenced Frank. Without making a direct reply, she cut him out of the conversation and addressed his partner. The exclusion was calculated. She took the papers out of her briefcase and began discussing them with Jack. If Frank wanted to deal with her, he had to stop his "charming" observations and start talking about the contract.

Demeaning moves must be turned. Left hanging, they undermine you and your ability to negotiate. When you don't respond, you kick yourself later, and that regret can eat away at you. But there is always a risk that any response to a demeaning move will provoke retaliation or amusement. To succeed, disruptive turns have to disrupt the offensive behavior. That means the message must be delivered in a way that its audience understands. Some of our contributors rely on nonverbal signals. A raised eyebrow, an exaggerated sigh, or a roll of the eyes leaves little room for a verbal rebuttal. Just having a comeback makes it easier to take these challenges in stride. Often you don't have to use it. Knowing you have a turn at hand translates to body language and that is often enough to get the message across.

Making Moves, Making Turns

Negotiations are commonly viewed as a set of offers and counteroffers, proposals and counterproposals. They are also a sequence of moves and turns in the shadow negotiation. Everyone wants an edge in a negotiation. Bargainers maneuver constantly to gain an advantage. How you are heard depends on the deliberate moves you take to position yourself and the equally considered turns you use to respond to strategic moves against you. Left unchecked, moves against you tip the balance in the shadow negotiation and make it difficult to promote your interests. If your interests don't get a good hearing, it is unlikely that you will be satisfied with the agreement, either.

Both moves and turns establish your place at the table. They are the tools of an effective advocacy. Moving strategically, you force the other person to take you and your demands seriously. Turning challenges that would undermine you and your demands, you maintain the balance in the shadow negotiation. In the process, you lay the foundation not only for acceptable agreements, but also for creative ones.

PART II

The Promise of Connection: Building a Collaborative Relationship

4

LAYING THE GROUNDWORK

In the 1961 movie *The Hustler,* Paul Newman plays Fast Eddy, a young pool sharp who gets bested by Jackie Gleason's Minnesota Fats. Fast Eddy can handle the cue stick. That's not his problem. He's simply no match for Minnesota Fats's ability to read him. In 1986, Newman reprised the role in *The Color of Money.* Still a wheeler dealer, but now down on his luck, Fast Eddy pins his hopes on a newcomer with a natural talent. Fast Eddy has learned a good bit about pool and life in the intervening years, and he tries to pass on some of this accumulated wisdom to his cocky protégé: "Pool excellence is not about excellent pool. . . . You gotta be a student of human moves. You study the pool moves. I study you. You pick up the check every time."

In a certain sense, Fast Eddy's advice also applies to negotiation. The strategic moves and turns you make all aim to get you where you want to be—and that is not being left with the check. But a singled-minded concentration on your agenda takes you just so far. As Fast Eddy says, "You gotta be a student of human moves." When you are negotiating with a car salesman or trying to sell your condo, the bargaining is pretty straightforward. There is a buyer, there is a seller, and the issue on the table is money. Each party has an incentive to make a deal if the terms are right. The car salesman needs to move inventory to reach his monthly quota; your pickup has developed an ominous rattle. The couple likes your condo, and you want to get settled in your new place. There are limits to how hard or far anyone can push. Neither of you can hold out for a windfall. If the salesman tries to gouge you or won't budge on price, you can always go someplace else. The Yellow Pages list plenty of car dealerships. On the other hand, the car salesman won't cut a deal with you if he is going to lose money, and the couple looking at your condo won't pay more than they consider fair.

The moves and turns you use to advocate for your interests enable you to strike the best bargain possible in these market transactions. But as the bargaining moves further away from marketplace haggling, the shadow negotiation becomes more complicated. Needs and interests are no longer so obvious, and the outlines of a good agreement are not always easy to grasp. The other person's actual statements often tell only half the story. A negotiation over a production schedule can mask a hidden need to look good to the boss or to take time off without admitting to family pressures. In order to negotiate all the issues in play, you must create a collaborative climate where hidden agendas like these can be brought out into the open.

People come together to settle differences, but how they feel about themselves and how they are treated determine how willing they are to work through those differences. Think about what happens when someone makes moves that put you down in the shadow negotiation, when he or she trivializes your needs, dismisses your concerns, or probes only to find an advantage. You feel frustrated, angry, or insulted, definitely not in the mood to communicate candidly. The same thing happens to the other people involved in the negotiation. When they feel undermined or unappreciated, they typically react by trying to turn the conversation, not by participating in a collaborative effort. Inevitably, communication chills and choices are cut off.

You prevent this reaction from taking hold by building a relationship with your counterpart and deliberately linking your self-interest to his or her needs. The sense of connection you can then establish changes the tenor of the shadow negotiation. The effort begins with an open mind— thinking of the person you are negotiating with not as an opponent or as a means to serve your own ends but as someone who can illuminate the situation and has insights that might differ radically from your own. By deliberately narrowing the distance between you and the other side and by opening the lines of communication, you increase the odds of making the person you are negotiating with a partner in a joint endeavor rather than a contestant in a competitive enterprise.

Why Connection Can Be Complicated for Women

We stress the skill required to manage the relational dimension of negotiation because too often empathy or concern for others is treated as an inherited or natural disposition, not an acquired one. It's considered a predilection you either have or don't have. Folk wisdom also tells us that women are inclined to emphasize relational needs and men individual criteria in their dealings with other people. The word *connection* itself constitutes a shorthand of sorts for what many believe defines a woman's special qualities, her way of approaching the world and negotiating her place in it. Ironically, this common assumption produces an unhappy fallout for women when they negotiate. Despite the importance of relational skills in negotiation, a woman practicing connection runs the risk of having her efforts shrugged off as "women's work" or being exploited. Inexorably connection slides toward an association with accommodation. She'll give in, the other party thinks, just to keep the peace. As a result, a woman might discount her own relational skills or others might do the discounting for her.[1]

The notion that connection leads to concession or accommodation blocks real engagement in two ways. Differences never get fully aired or appreciated when one party expects the other to sacrifice her interests or she feels obliged to do so. Alternatively, aware of this risk, even a woman inclined to be collaborative overcompensates when the stakes are high. Afraid of being taken advantage of, she digs in her heels and becomes unnecessarily rigid or inflexible.

Both traps are self-defeating, but there is a simple way to avoid them. We are going to argue the case for a muscular, dynamic kind of relationship building that is inextricably yoked to successful advocacy. Connection and advocacy do not cancel each other out. On the contrary, one does not happen without the other. To build a relationship with the other person, you don't have to forget about your own interests or rein them in. Quite the opposite. You connect in a negotiation by engaging your counterpart, not by giving in to demands just to make him or her feel good.

When someone tries to back you into a corner, playing on your "feminine" sensitivities in the shadow negotiation, you need to turn that move before you can get connected. Avoiding connection and digging in your heels is not the answer, either. It is a defensive response that leaves you on the defensive. It makes no sense to jettison real skills simply because others assume you have them. Why not use those skills to engage your counterpart and move the negotiation to a place where neither of you needs to be on the defensive? If need be, you can always check attempts to convert your interpersonal skills to a liability with a strategic turn.

Getting Ready to Listen to the Other Person

As we prepare for a negotiation, our focus is naturally on ourselves— what we want and what we need to do to better our chances of success. But there is a danger in this single-mindedness. We can become so engrossed in our take on the situation that we lose sight of the person we are negotiating with—except as a means to our ends or as a stumbling block in our way. Once into the negotiation, it is inevitable that we process whatever happens through that filter. A certain deafness sets in. We edit out what we don't want to hear and listen to what is said with a fixed script in mind. We make attribution errors that have us ascribing good intentions to ourselves, but not to the other person. We create self-fulfilling prophecies. Expecting the other party to be overbearing or ineffectual, we interpret his or her behavior as overbearing or ineffectual.[2]

We think nothing of it when playwrights, novelists, and filmmakers use the tension between different points of view to heighten the drama. Consider Iago's asides in *Othello* or the private musings of Hamlet. Each provides a selective lens for the action unfolding and the psychological dynamic. So, too, different perspectives drive a negotiation. Other views and other emotions, equally justified and probably as strongly held as yours, are in play.

Any two people will give a different (sometimes wildly different) account of the same event. Naturally when we tell our stories we are the heroes and heroines. Our story puts our spin on the events, conveniently editing out facts that don't fit. Typically we cast ourselves as virtuous, always doing the right thing. What we want is always reasonable and well deserved. The other person is greedy or stubborn, focused only on the short term. We have done all the heavy lifting, finishing up the proposal or going the extra mile to satisfy a client. The other one is the free rider. But what is true of our stories is also true for the other person's. If you want to influence your counterpart in a negotiation, you need to accept that she is equally convinced of her interpretation. You might disagree with that slant, but it is never wrong in her eyes.

Approaching a negotiation as a compilation of various stories carries a distinct advantage. Stories alert us to the challenge we face in hearing the other person. Each story is told from a specific point of view and never includes every detail. Stories are filled with gaps, laced with contradictions and puzzling inflections. As we listen to the other person, we learn from those gaps and contradictions. What is left unsaid, or is said silently through body language, becomes as important as verbal comments. Stories don't trade in certainties. They deal with "maybe" and "what if," not statements of fact. Because stories admit no rights and wrongs, but depend on different but legitimate points of view, they weave together both the stream of feelings and the stream of thought that meet to make decisions in a negotiation.

Connection, as we use the term, is intimately tied to the idea of storytelling.[3] To listen to the other party and hear what he or she is saying, you must be open to what is being said—to your counterpart's story. Connection, like piano playing, takes practice, and negotiation has its own equivalent for "finger exercises." An exercise in circular questioning can help you regard the other party's actions not as biased, self-serving moves but as valid representations of what she is thinking and feeling at that point in time. The sequence of questions moves through three stages. It starts with you—what the situation looks like from where you are sitting, how you are feeling, how you got there. Then it circles around to the other person's story—how he or she might view the situation and might be feeling. Finally, it considers the ways in which those accounts might be linked.

The purpose of the sequence of questions is to break the hold a hardened viewpoint can have on your thinking during a negotiation. As you consider a situation from various perspectives, you force yourself to entertain other explanations for why people might be acting the way they are. With a more complex story line, it is easier to see how those behaviors are linked. Often common concerns emerge with unexpected clarity,

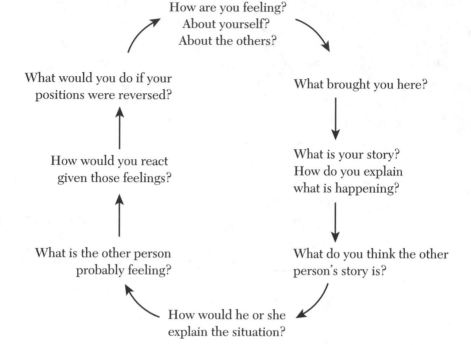

How are you feeling?
About yourself?
About the others?

What would you do if your
positions were reversed?

What brought you here?

How would you react
given those feelings?

What is your story?
How do you explain
what is happening?

What is the other person
probably feeling?

What do you think the other
person's story is?

How would he or she
explain the situation?

while differences in priorities become the building blocks of an agreement.[4]

Conventional wisdom on negotiation has it that negotiators pursue "enlightened" self-interest when they take into account the needs of others. This is the notion of doing good for your counterpart and doing good for yourself. But "enlightened" solutions require enlightenment. Just as effective advocacy begins with you, with a positive attitude, connection emerges from a willingness and a curiosity to hear your counterpart's side of the story. It grows out of a belief that agreement depends on the wider understanding that comes from free exchange. This conviction grounds how you relate to the other party. It forces you to suspend belief or at least resist drawing premature conclusions—about the situation or your counterpart's motivations.

How Circular Questioning Works

Alison Thomas, an account manager in an advertising agency, picked up the telephone. Her new client was on the line. "Look, Alison," he demanded. "What is going on? I've just spent half an hour I don't have talking to your creative director about the television commercials. I thought you were handling the coordination."

Alison temporized, trying to recover lost ground with her client. "Agency policy dictates that all client communication goes through the account executive. Bob, the creative director, was obviously trying to cut me out of the loop."

"I was furious," Alison says. "I immediately headed for the studio to call Bob on his behavior. The account was difficult even before Bob's interference. The client manufactures drills and handyman tools. He's down-to-earth, without an aesthetic bone in his body. From the first, Bob's artsy approach made him nervous." Finding that Bob was away on a shoot, she left a message on his voice mail that she wanted to talk to him ASAP.

Alison, working in a creative but highly competitive environment, kept a wary eye out for encroachments on her turf. She had learned from experience that she needed to react if her authority was challenged or undermined. This time, she realized, it was probably a good thing Bob was out of the office. Otherwise she would have attacked him, touching off a spiral of denials and counteraccusations. To cool down and get to a point where she was collected enough to deal with Bob, Alison went through a systematic re-storying of the events leading up to his phone call to her client. Alison's imagined walk-through of what had happened put her in a positive frame of mind where she no longer saw her relationship with Bob as irreparable.[5]

Step #1: Look at your story. It is important to start this re-storying process with you and your feelings. Sometimes we're relatively neutral, without much at risk. But in high-stakes situations, our emotions can run high. We might be so anxious or angry that we are ready for a fight. We might be so confident that we disregard the danger signals the other party sends. Or we might be so excited about the possibilities that we ignore our counterpart's lack of enthusiasm. These gut reactions color our impressions of any situation and clearly influence how we interpret the other person's actions. Unexamined, they can channel what we do in two ways: we overlook what is missing from our account; and we have no way of testing whether our initial reaction has any merit.

Examining your own story in depth can reveal aspects you have been ignoring or refusing to see. Once you are aware of these missing segments, you have the tools at hand to do some self-imposed editing. Kristen's firm had just received an unexpected assignment from a major client. The new contract was a plum, and she anticipated no problems in assembling the team she wanted. To her surprise, her initial overtures met with one excuse after another. One colleague did not bother with an excuse: "Sorry, Kristen. I've got too much on my plate right now. You'd soak up all my time." Somewhat taken aback, Kristen decided she had better think about what was going on before she reached the bottom of her list of candidates.

Technically and socially adept, Kristen took good care of her clients. Staff members were another matter. Whenever she heard grumblings about how demanding she was, she dismissed them as the general complaints that go along with working flat-out. At first she rationalized the comments away. She set high standards and had zero tolerance for sloppy work. There's nothing wrong with that, she usually concluded. Now she was not so sure.

Kristen went over in her mind the difficult interviews she had had over the course of the last month, the times when she had chewed out a subordinate to get him or her to toe the line, the occasions when she had been abrupt with a colleague. She had an explanation handy for each case, but the list was long, way too long. She could not have had more tough situations than any other department head. "Chances were slim to none that I had inherited all the lemons in the firm or that every other manager precipitated the same confrontational responses." Suddenly it clicked for Kristen. She expected people to pitch in as members of a team, but she never treated them as respected colleagues. She expected collaboration on demand. She didn't negotiate. She issued orders.

Kristen's re-storying of her behavior opened her eyes. She began to question her rationalizations for her demanding behavior. Setting high standards, she saw, did not equate with a dictatorial delivery. By shutting people out, not valuing their opinions or feelings, she cut herself off and gave her co-workers little incentive to work with her even on an exciting assignment. "International consulting on this level is a results-oriented pressure cooker," she says. "At some point I guess I just absorbed a peremptory attitude by osmosis." As she began a second round of negotiations with potential team members, she knew she had to deal with the impressions she had inadvertently created if she wanted their cooperation. She could not change her negotiating style overnight, but she was now aware of the difficulties that her previous approach had generated.

Kristen took a hard look at what she had inadvertently left out of her story, but it is equally important to pay close attention to what you include. Emotional reactions influence your reading of any situation and need to be examined. Alison, for example, admitted how furious she was that Bob had called her client.

> *At first Alison allowed herself the luxury of venting her anger at Bob. He had no right to contact her client directly. He always pushed ideas that were too radical for the client. She covered for him, but now he was going behind her back. He was a stickler, a perfectionist who complained regularly that he didn't have enough time or people. The only thing he cared about was winning another design award. The client's needs, the agency, policies, and procedures—all came a distant second, if they even registered on his radar screen.*
>
> *How did they get into this fix? After Alison got a grip on her feelings about the situation, she began to think about what landed them there. Step by step, she reconstructed the history leading up to Bob's call to the client.*
>
> > *We'd had a meeting—Bob, the client, and me. The client's company was about to launch a national television advertising campaign and he wanted to talk about the first spot. Bob put up storyboards for a snappy video that was meant to capture the sleekness of the new product. My client liked the concept but worried that his customers would be turned off. He was selling power tools, not CDs.*
> >
> > *We met again when the rough tape was finished. Bob was enthusiastic, really pleased, but the client remained dubious. Afterward he told me that he wanted the agency to work up another treatment. I agreed right away. Satisfying the client is our business. Bob, always argumentative, hit the roof when he found out he had ten days to produce another tape.*
>
> *At this point Alison also admitted that she might have anticipated Bob's reaction to her lack of support. "He always digs in his heels when*

someone criticizes his designs." Bob's actions, she felt, forced her to take sides. *"They put me between Bob and the client. The client was lukewarm about Bob's tape and it's my job to keep the client happy. There was no reason for Bob to expect that I'd do anything different."* Alison pulled no punches in her examination. The new account was important to her. She resented Bob's interference. She looked bad to the client and to others in the office.

Connecting with your own story, as Kristen and Alison did, gives you a baseline. From there you are in a better position to separate your version from your counterpart's. Once you are clear on your story—what is missing and what is legitimately included—you can look for what is included in his or her version and what just might be left out.

Step #2: Look at the other person's story. The tendency to get caught in our own perspectives is one of the major barriers to effective negotiation. It's simply too easy to become overly enamored of our own opinions. Operating in a closed world of our own making, we push our own agenda, reiterating the same argument over and over. We explain our reasons and don't ask questions about theirs. Talking but not listening, we fail to pick up cues that what we are saying is not being heard. Over half of the information conveyed in personal interactions and on which we make decisions in a negotiation is nonverbal. Women are, by and large, acute observers of these cues, yet we often fail to use them.

Taking a hard look at how the other person might view a situation often brings these overlooked cues to the surface. More important, as you consider his or her side of the story, you generally have to revise your initial explanation of what is going on. How people view a problem depends on *their* experience, not yours. Although you can never be completely sure ahead of time what that experience might be, you can make educated guesses about it as you prepare for a negotiation.

Josie, a big producer in an insurance company, had weathered a merger and postponed demands for a raise during the upheaval. When yet another new man arrived from headquarters to whip the department into shape, she decided it was time to become more vocal about a raise. Her request provoked a polite but temporizing response from her new boss. Bad experiences in the past inclined her to project them into the future and onto her new boss. Frustrated at being blocked again, she considered his reaction a stalling tactic. Then she began to wonder whether she was actually hearing another version of the same old story. After all, even though her new boss was in a position to refuse her request outright, he had not actually said no. "If I were in this new guy's shoes," Josie thought, "I'd resent being pushed to act precipitously. I'd want some time to assess the problem."

Although Josie was no less annoyed at her new boss's reluctance to move on her raise, she was willing to concede that he might have good reason for his inaction. What she had been quick to write off as stalling might just be prudent management from his point of view. His predecessor had been fired when she could not turn around the drop in employee productivity. By giving him the benefit of the doubt, Josie not only got a higher raise than she requested. She opened the door for her new boss to talk about his plans for the department.

To reconstruct how a situation might appear to the other person, you must pay attention to more than the apparent and logical reasons behind his or her actions. Events precipitate feelings about them, and those feelings are just as important to the other person's story as the plausible explanations you can find for his or her behavior.

> Alison, certain she was fully justified in her reaction to Bob's interference, turned the tables and began to consider Bob's position: "Bob is difficult, but he is also a crackerjack designer. He loved the original tape, and I'm sure it took the wind out of his sails when the client sent him back to the drawing boards."
>
> At this point Alison admitted that Bob probably did not appreciate her failure to back him up with the client: "He was 'high' on his design, already anticipating the awards he would win. I'm sure it put his nose out of joint when I didn't talk it up with the client." Alison, disappointed in Bob's failure to support her, could no longer deny him the same right to disappointment. This realization tempered Alison's self-righteous justification of her own actions. Bob no doubt was as mad as she.

To get inside another person's story, you must suspend your own interpretation. This suspension is particularly important when it comes to motives. You might have cast your counterpart as the culprit, but chances are good that he or she doesn't see the situation that way. When we have a fixed idea in our head about a person's interests and concerns, we cannot help but process everything she or he says and does through that filter. We concentrate on what we think the person should do, not what he or she can or wants to do. We quite naturally assume the other party will act and react the way we would in a similar situation. This is the danger of "mirror-imaging." State Department manuals, for example, urge foreign service professionals to guard against interpreting data solely on the basis of their own experience. If they do, they risk assuming that one course of action is logical and likely only because that is the one they would pursue were they in the same situation.

To imagine the other explanations possible, try to think of the reasons your counterpart might use to justify his or her actions. Since people rarely ascribe negative motives to their actions, this positive emphasis pushes you to think about what the situation looks like from the other person's perspective.

Although Alison was sure she would not have called the client had she been in Bob's shoes, thinking about his reaction to being sent back to the drawing table gave her pause. She began to develop some hypotheses about why he called the client in the first place. She even started to question how she would really have reacted.

> *If I really liked my design, I'd be tempted to give it one last try. I'd know I should clear it through the account manager, but if she weren't available, I'd probably just go ahead. Then again, ten days might not be enough time to produce something decent. Quality might be compromised, and I'd want the client to know that.*

> *Pursuing this train of thought forced Alison to concede that Bob just might have believed he was acting in the client's best interest by contacting him directly.*

> *Maybe he thought I was new on the account and needed some help. Maybe he really believed that tape was terrific, the best design the art department could turn out. Maybe, since drills and machine tools are a guy thing, he thought he was a better judge than I. Maybe he was under the gun, feeling the time pressure. Maybe he tried to reach me and couldn't get through, but I doubt that.*

Thinking about possible answers to these questions, Alison began to suspect that Bob could have acted in good faith—at least in his eyes. His actions suddenly took on a different character. Maybe he was trying to help Alison, not to undercut her with the client.

When our actions bump against those of someone else in a negotiation, it is all too tempting to question the other person's motives. Just as there are always two sides to every story, there can be similarly benign explanations for the motivations behind the other party's actions. Lingering suspicions about his or her motives make it next to impossible to get to those underlying reasons. Until and unless events offer proof to the contrary, it is best to assume that your counterpart is acting in good faith and is not out to undercut you. Otherwise you shut down communication and prevent any real understanding from emerging.

Step #3: Look for links between the stories. These final questions in the sequence help you understand the extent to which the other person's behavior might be prompted by your actions. The other party might be reacting to how *you* are treating him or her, rather than pursuing some malevolent or unreasonable plan. Marjorie, who oversees joint ventures for a large pharmaceutical firm, kept a wary eye on a struggling marketing initiative in South America. Based on her numbers and financial modeling, she saw further deterioration ahead. Additional funding, she decided, was not warranted until the political and economic climate in the region improved. She began to push the head of operations in South America hard on cutting back. "Dick believed the currency crunch was a temporary setback," she says. "Although he agreed that revenues would be slow to materialize, he pointed out that we had invested significant sums in order to build distribution channels in the region. These would be put at risk were we to scale back."

Marjorie believed Dick was being less than candid about his real reasons for opposing the cuts. "Dick handled only South America. He didn't want his budget sliced. I, on the other hand, had overall responsibility for these distribution agreements and I, not Dick, would be held accountable for poor performance." At first Marjorie pressed her case on the grounds of corporate profitability. "Then I realized that Dick was taking a longer look. Withdrawal during a crisis would jeopardize carefully nurtured relationships throughout South America." Until they actually put these different perspectives on the table, they were at an impasse. Once Marjorie revised her initial assumption that Dick was resisting the cuts solely to protect his power base, she could appreciate his long-term strategic reasons. Together they worked out a compromise. Rather than make across-the-board cuts, they slowed some aspects of the program to minimize the threat to earnings but maintained a budget level that would not imperil future work in the region.

This kind of disciplined look at a situation from various angles enables you to view the actions people take in a negotiation along an array of possible explanations. Because actions produce reactions, they are linked and those linkages are important to uncover.

> *Alison's circular questioning led her to see the connections between the role each participant played in the negotiation. Bob, the client, and she all contributed to the way in which events unfolded. With that understanding, she shifted from seeing herself as the aggrieved party to recognizing that everyone was implicated in what happened. Having looked for patterns of behavior and the reasons for them, she was able to understand that those patterns were determined by the premises and suppositions that constituted her map of the world and what she could only imagine Bob's or the client's to be.*

Narratives like Alison's are implicitly ambiguous. When Alison says "Bob *is* argumentative. He *is* undercutting me," she casts him in a single dimension. Bob's definition is open to neither debate nor interpretation. He *is*. When she starts to move to the realm of "maybe," into a narrative way of thinking, she uncovers various explanations not only for Bob's actions but also for her contribution to them. She has shifted from a distancing detachment, a focus on what he did and laying blame, to viewing the event itself as a product of their interdependence.

Working through the discipline of circular questioning, concocting plausible stories forces you to probe your initial reactions. As you turn your assumptions inside out and attribute positive motives to someone's behavior, it becomes much more difficult to hold on to erroneous and self-serving impressions. You have to find more charitable explanations for the other person's actions. You have to tell another story.

Soon you reach the stage of maybe—maybe he means something else, maybe she has another reason for what she's doing. When you think about the good reasons for your counterpart's actions, sensible accounts are possible for what he does or what she says. From there, it is a short transition to "what if"—What if I did something else? What if I gave her the benefit of the doubt and responded more positively? A single "what if" always contains the promise of additional options, other ways the plot you construct together can play out. How you solve your differences links with how you treat each other. Instead of concentrating on your own concerns and actions, you start to view the problem as a joint one, one that connects you both and for which you are both responsible.

> *Because Alison took time out to get in a connected frame of mind, she did not greet Bob with an attack or a lecture when they next met.*
>
> Alison: *You must have been disappointed about the first tape.*
> Bob: *Disappointed doesn't begin to describe it. I was furious. That's why I called the client—to give it one last shot.*
> Alison: *That's what I figured, but it took some effort to get me there. Next time, let's talk first, okay?*
>
> *Alison went on to recount the criticism she had taken over the phone from the client. Rather than bristle at the implied censure, as Bob usually did with Alison, he turned uncharacteristically sympathetic. Although he stopped far short of an apology, he agreed to run any problems he had with a client through Alison. That was enough for her.*

Connecting with Others

Good relationships do not occur in a burst of goodwill at the negotiating table. Atmospheres, attitudes, and habits often operate in the opposite direction. The question is not one of communication per se, but of the kind of communication that takes place. When people negotiate, they tend to hold their cards close to the vest. Caught in a strategic communication game, they do not always say what they mean or mean what they say. Often they remain silent on what matters most to them as differences in status and role or past experiences put a damper on candor.

Efforts to connect with your counterpart encourage more open participation. The goal is to get people to share their experience with you so that you are not running blind on your own impressions. To negotiate on more than the purchase price of a car or the selling price of a condo, you need to understand the rationale your counterparts might have for the stands they are taking. But unless they have some signal, some confidence, that they are being heard, that you appreciate their concerns, they will be reluctant to share them with you. When the person you are negotiating with hears the communication going only one way, when all you are doing is telling and selling, he or she typically reacts by withdrawing or by making a defensive move or an offensive turn. No one has a chance to recognize the mutual concerns that might exist. For those to emerge, you have to draw out the other side's story. It is not just information you are after. You want to build rapport and trust so that, together, you can engage in a dialogue. Many negotiations start out with opposing sides squared off. When you connect with the other person, you alter this dynamic. Being open to hearing him or her is a first step. The next challenge is to turn that positive attitude into action.

5

ENGAGING YOUR COUNTERPART

It's easy to brainstorm about a problem—even a difficult one—once it's shared. The rub comes in finding ways to get to that point. For collaboration to take hold, your counterpart has to *want* to work with you. Reaching the point where the other person feels comfortable sharing her perspectives takes concrete encouragement. You have to be prepared not only to talk about your demands but to draw out hers.

The rewards of collaboration are great. In a truly collaborative negotiation, the participants engage in an open exchange, not just in parallel telling and selling. The mutuality of the interaction changes the negotiation over issues. As we listen for the reasons behind the other person's concerns, we learn from what we hear. Often that learning is reciprocal, and as everyone understands the other's perspective more fully, the issues begin to take on different dimensions. The relationship worked out in the shadow negotiation can also change. The respect implicit in the give-and-take builds trust. When the going gets rough, instead of getting tough, we are more likely to pull together than apart.

Usually people have solid reasons for taking the stands they do in a negotiation. They are not being difficult just for the sake of being difficult. They dig in their heels, fearing they will lose face if they don't. They reject proposals out of hand not as a tactical maneuver but because that particular compromise does not come close to meeting their needs. What we interpret as recalcitrance or gamesmanship might be prompted not by the other party's stubbornness or competitiveness but by the conviction that we are not willing to compromise or listen.

However important it is to uncover these hidden fears or perceptions, as negotiators we often get locked into habits that work against collaboration. Efforts that appear mutual on the surface are anything but when we pay attention to the other party's reactions only to test how far we can push. Collaboration does not get far when the give-and-take remains narrowly focused on individual demands. The negotiation becomes a balancing act. We probe the other party's reactions to discover the minimum we must give up to insure that he or she does not go away mad and we still get what we want. These relational efforts might increase the odds that our demands will be heard and met, but mutual needs don't have much chance to surface. Nothing is so transparent in a negotiation as an effort to be "nice" in order to manipulate the outcome.

Even when we are genuinely interested in the other person's thinking and feelings, he or she might question our sincerity. Negotiators don't automatically assume that expressed concern about their concerns is real. It takes some convincing, some active demonstration that goes beyond the perfunctory or the expedient, to override these doubts. You have to *show* the other person that you appreciate his or her point of view. There is a level of proof involved here. It is not enough simply to *think* you are being empathetic. Those thoughts must be translated into actions, and that task can be difficult. Sometimes the other party puts us on guard and our defenses go up. The negotiation's outcome can be so important to us that its consequences for our counterpart slip out of focus. When his or her point of view pales in comparison to our worries, it takes a disciplined effort to draw it out.

Brenda Jacklin found herself in just such a place when Alec, her boss, pressed her to sign a noncompete agreement. Convinced that Alec would misinterpret any lack of firmness on her part as a willingness to just go along, Brenda presented a solid and uncompromising front. Anxieties about her situation blocked out any concerns Alec had about his.

Before the dispute arose, Brenda was on top of the world. At thirty-six, her future with Westcott and Price, a nationwide outplacement firm, looked rosy. Her group had just had a phenomenal year. Brenda was responsible for over 30 percent of the Chicago office's revenues. Clients liked to do business with her. She was fun, outgoing and enthusiastic. They could count on her to listen hard and deliver what they needed.

Inside W & P's sleek offices, problems generally landed on Brenda's desk. "In my previous incarnation, I was a practicing therapist," she explains. "My roots are in a nurturing profession, and I've sort of fallen into the role of office sounding board." Brenda's training in her "first career" surfaced particularly in her dealings with Alec, who ran the Chicago office. Both Alec and Brenda are smart and ambitious, but the similarities end there. Brenda is soft-spoken, elegant, and always immaculate. Alec, on the other hand, is aloof and gruff, with a hair-trigger temper. Uneasy with people, he generally closets himself in his office. Brenda is the only member of his team he turns to for advice.

That spring Alec came to Brenda and again asked her to sign a "non-compete" agreement. The head office had recently made the agreement a requirement for all senior staff. Brenda, a single parent, was the sole holdout in the Chicago office.

Alec: Brenda, you cannot put this off any longer.

Brenda: Well, I don't know (laughing).

Alec: It's company policy, and you know it. I'm taking a lot of heat. Headquarters doesn't want anybody in management without one.

Brenda: They'll recover when they look at our results from last quarter.

Alec: Not this time. There's no more wiggle room.

Brenda: Alec, you know there's always wiggle room when you're producing the results we are.

Alec: I'll leave a copy on your desk. No more stalling.

On the surface, Brenda humors Alec, but the signals she sends in the shadow negotiation underscore the strong hand she thinks she has. She skips over Alec's complaint about being pressured by the head office. Her track record, she implies, robs his ultimatum and the head office's of any force.

Brenda had good reasons for taking a hard line. Signing, in her mind, gained nothing. It would put her firmly under Alec's thumb and sacrifice her leverage with him: "Once my John Hancock's on the dotted line, Alec can do pretty much what he wants. I lose all influence. If I leave, I cannot work for a competitor for a year. I cannot sell so much as a hot dog to my clients."

Brenda worried that Alec would try to bulldoze her or play on her sympathies: "Alec has two speeds when he negotiates with me. He tries to take over the talk or he acts out his emotions. He huffs and puffs so I'll feel sorry for him." Brenda, disinclined to be pushed in either direction, decided to find out exactly what rights she had. The agreement, according to her litigator friend Nick, fell well within industry standards. "But that's no reason you shouldn't be compensated for signing," he advised. "Hold out and Alec will sweeten the incentives." Nick's advice reassured Brenda. As a rule, she avoided confrontation and did not quite trust her usual negotiating style in this situation. Alec, she suspected, would be "argumentative at first, he always is," but he'd live with her refusal once he realized how adamant she was.

When Alec discovered she had consulted an attorney, he did not read her move as a show of strength or even as a prudent step in getting informed. He was livid. Brenda recalled that his broad face turned redder than she had ever seen it.

Alec: How could you get an attorney involved in this? What's he know about this office?

Brenda: Alec, if our positions were reversed, wouldn't you?

Alec: Hell, no. Look what you are doing to me. I got written up for running interference for you.

Brenda: Hold on. Look what you're doing to me. You're boxing me in with no protection in return.

Alec: I'm not going to discuss that now. I warned you two weeks ago—no more stalling. Until we get this resolved, you are off the executive committee. You cannot have it both ways. You cannot participate in confidential discussions and not sign. Those are the rules. Everybody else is playing by them.

Neither Brenda nor Alec expected this negotiation to escalate so quickly. Nick's advice had sounded good, but it had backfired. "Hanging tough," as he put it, was not the answer. It would cost Brenda her seat on the executive committee and possibly her job.

A company policy put both Alec and Brenda in a bind. In order to connect on their mutual problem, one of them had to take the first step in breaking the stalemate. With neither of them listening, Brenda realized, they cut off any route to compromise. She would end up with exactly the outcome she wanted to avoid along with a residue of bad feeling between them.

Brenda took deliberate steps to reconnect with Alec and his concerns. Concentrating only on what she wanted, she had not picked up on Alec's signals, as she normally would have done. If she could not figure out what Alec was thinking and feeling, she saw little hope of coming out of the negotiations with her job intact and their relationship back in balance. Brenda, in effect, reclaimed those relational skills she had temporarily put aside and reversed the negotiation's course. Through a series of connective overtures that we chronicle throughout this chapter, she moved them away from confrontational posturing. No longer seeing each other as adversaries, they could work together constructively on the problems the noncompete agreement caused them both.

Connecting overtures draw us to a place where mutual solutions can be found. All too often, especially in tense negotiations, we fail to hear what the other party is saying. Many techniques have been developed to prevent us from falling victim to this common habit. Active listening—a practice that involves paraphrasing what others say and using open-ended questions—helps. Although techniques like these are useful, they remain only techniques unless you genuinely believe there is something to be gained from hearing more about the other person's point of view.

Appreciation is the key to drawing out a counterpart's concerns.[1] Despite the confessional trend in our society and daily exposés in the press, few of us are inclined to reveal much in a negotiation. The costs are too high. Any information we let slip, we think, might be used against us. But the reservation goes deeper. As we share our perspectives and feelings, we expose something of ourselves. When they are disregarded, we feel diminished. Something meaningful to us, it seems, carries little weight. Appreciation lowers the costs of communicating by explicitly expressing the value you place on the other person's perspective.

Appreciation is tied up in notions of "hidden" value. An old drawing, a fine chest of drawers, a discarded toy in your grandmother's attic all appreciate when someone recognizes their enhanced value. Appreciation is not limited to assigning concrete value to tangibles, however. It is also linked to a sensitivity to impressions and feelings. When you appreciate the other party's concerns, his situation or the "face" he presents to the world, you open the negotiation to the nuanced perceptions that *this* person brings. Appreciation conveys the importance you place on these differing perspectives and the opinions, ideas, and feelings that shape them.

Just as you must position yourself positively in the shadow negotiation in order to be heard, you must also take steps to position your counterparts so they can tell their side of the story. By showing appreciation—for their situation, feelings, and ideas—you encourage them to elaborate, to fill in the gaps in your understanding.

- **APPRECIATE THE OTHER PERSON'S SITUATION**
  Your counterpart has a better sense of her situation than you can ever hope to have. By openly soliciting her views, you validate them (and her). You show her that they are important to you and to how the negotiation comes out.

- **APPRECIATE THE OTHER PERSON'S FEELINGS**
  How your counterpart feels about you and the negotiation often drives his behavior. Those feelings are communicated through nonverbal cues as well as actual comments. Pick up on them and acknowledge the emotions the other party carries into a negotiation.

- **APPRECIATE THE OTHER PERSON'S IDEAS**
  If the other party puts out an idea, build on that contribution. Just holding the idea up for consideration shows her that you value what she has to say even though you might not agree.

- **APPRECIATE THE OTHER PERSON'S FACE**
  Give your counterpart room to maneuver. No one likes to be backed into a corner with no visible or acceptable means of retreat.

Appreciation needs to be made explicit. Few of us would accept lightly the charge that we are insensitive to a situation or someone's feelings. But no matter how convinced we are that we appreciate our counterpart's predicament, unless we make her aware of that appreciation doubts linger about the value those opinions or perspectives carry. So long as those doubts remain, the other party hesitates to tell her side of the story. Appreciation validates that story. When a bargainer's story is valued, when he or she is valued, a more complex account emerges.

Appreciation does more than produce useful information, however. It creates the context for mutual exchange. The tempo and the character of the conversation change. Subtly, sometimes imperceptibly, the negotiation moves away from defensive arguments and counterarguments to an inclusive discussion where everyone feels free to talk candidly about what they need from the negotiation.

Appreciate the Other Person's Situation

You can safely assume that your counterpart knows more about his or her situation than you do. Anthropologists have long been alert to the "local knowledge" that distinguishes one group of people from another. It is made up of customs and rituals and language, all those things that are simply accepted as part of the fabric of a culture and give it meaning.[2] Individuals have their own particular brand of "local knowledge," and one of your primary goals as a negotiator is to tap into it. The same words, the same actions, can carry quite distinct meanings for you and your counterpart. It is those meanings you are after. Those meanings help you understand the demands that he or she might be making.

How people see a problem depends on their experience. A dancer knows her world in a different way than the research physicist. A marketing specialist's slant on a new R&D initiative might diverge dramatically from that of the project's engineer. These differences in perception matter when you negotiate.

Encourage the other person to elaborate. Everyone has his or her story to tell. You cannot disprove it, although the person might come to revise it on his or her own. Just as important, you can only conjecture about the person's perspective unless he or she talks about it. To negotiate with people, you have to understand why they feel the way they do, not just how you think they feel.

This understanding is not easy to come by. The way we start a negotiation, our opening gambits, can shut down the conversation. By talking too much, we deny the other person an equal opportunity and ourselves the benefit of his or her "local knowledge." Even when we listen and question, pointed probing can scuttle communication so that the other person's story never emerges. Unless we communicate a need to learn more, actively encourage others to elaborate on their views, the discussion will continue to run along parallel tracks. Appreciation, at this basic level, offers the other person reassurance. It says it is safe for him or her to be expansive. Not only are his or her insights valued; the process and the outcome of the negotiation hinge on their elaboration.

Roberta, marketing director for a chain of foreign language centers, more often than not encounters hostility when she first negotiates with center directors over corporate marketing plans. "The tension between marketing and teaching, between the local centers and corporate head-quarters, is a constant in my work," she says. "Managers in the field generally come from backgrounds in education. To many, marketing smacks of commercialism. It's a pollutant, a danger to the quality of teaching and programming."

Not much about Roberta is intimidating. Barely over five feet tall, she's relaxed and keeps her calculator carefully hidden. But however casual her dress and warm her greeting, the center managers view her as an adversary when she arrives on-site. Anyone from the corporate office, they assume, will force them to compromise standards so that the bottom line looks good. "They absolutely do not think marketing is something they *should* care about," Roberta says.

One week Roberta called at a center in the Southwest where the manager had not been using the new English as a Second Language (ESL) program developed at the head office. As soon as Roberta started to talk about marketing the program, the manager bristled. Rather than follow up on this reaction, Roberta asked if they could tour the facility. "I was there to help, but first I needed to get to the why—what about the program caused the problems for her." As they walked around, Roberta learned about the center and what was going on in the community. Only when they returned to the office did Roberta take up the subject of the ESL tapes again.

> First off, the manager brought up her budget. With funds tight, she resented having to contribute to a marketing function that she couldn't use. When I pressed her on why, she told me something I hadn't noticed: Not a single Mexican appeared on the tapes, and her center worked primarily with Mexican immigrants.

Roberta, by drawing out the manager's story, discovered the complicated ethnic issues she dealt with on a daily basis. In turn, the manager learned that the ESL program could help her reach her community if it was revised along the lines she suggested. Until then the manager had remained silent, convinced that the corporate office would not be responsive to criticism from her. This negotiation, a common one between staff and line, established the ground rules for a working relationship. Problems that came up in the field affected both of them. But they each had something to contribute to the solution. They had to work together.

Respect the other person's objections. All too often you face a negotiating situation where the other party sees only negatives. Ironically, appreciating those negatives can turn the conversation around. Blaming someone *for* the situation chills any discussion *of* it. People can work on a joint problem. They generally don't feel so cooperative when that problem is defined as them. By steering the talk away from personalities to the issues, you make it possible even for difficult people to talk about what in the particular situation causes them trouble. A woman generally acknowledged to be impossible to deal with was blocking Donna, the CFO of an HMO on Long Island: "She could have doubled for a teacher I had in grade school—rigid, inflexible. Everything had a place, and that was where she said it should be."

The joint endeavor Donna was proposing was in everyone's best interests. Donna's HMO had a new health center located at the airport and staffed by doctors who were not busy; the woman's insurance company supplied health coverage to airport employees and could increase enrollment. However rational or obvious the dovetailing of interests appeared on its face, both sides had to experience that mutuality.

Helen had been dragging her feet on doing anything to support us. I called her up, and she started right in. They needed this report and that report, all these other data. I felt like screaming. Instead I just said, "Fine, I'll get it to you this afternoon." Then I set up a meeting.

Donna orchestrated that meeting so that Helen would not be on the defensive. She started laying the groundwork for collaboration by preparing her own staff. Everyone had negative vibrations about working with this woman.

There was real history there. I knew it would be easy to overreact during the initial talks. Helen is legendary in the industry for stonewalling new ideas. The challenge was to be patient and not let any animosity surface.

Brainstorming with her people about Helen's good reasons for objecting to the plan, Donna shifted their focus to how the situation might look to Helen. Everyone soon agreed that the major stumbling block was Helen's tendency to evaluate any suggestion in terms of the additional work involved. "She is," Donna said, "a person who will always, but always, see the glass as half empty." Any change was bound to make her life miserable and stretch her already overworked department.

Donna opened the talks by appreciating Helen's situation. By admitting right up front that they were asking Helen's department to do more work, Donna respected Helen's objections. She legitimized them, attempting neither to override nor to trivialize her real concerns.

Once we named this issue, brought it out into the open, she began to talk about the havoc the new program would cause in her department. We countered with concrete suggestions for evening out the burden.

How you treat people at the beginning of a negotiation often determines how willing they are to work with you. Bad feelings left over from previous encounters can chill the negotiation next time around. Donna met Helen as a manager dealing with a difficult problem, not as a difficult woman. That positive signal provided Helen with an opportunity to explain the headaches the joint venture could generate for her. Once she sensed the extent to which Donna appreciated and had anticipated those difficulties, she shifted gears. Instead of raising further objections, she began to talk about possible solutions.

Even the idea of a noncompete agreement worried Brenda. She was afraid to relinquish so much control over her life. She could not afford to be forced out of her field for a year if things went wrong at the firm. Preoccupied with her misgivings, Brenda ignored Alec's concerns. To come to any understanding of why Alec was taking such a hard line with her, she first had to break through the growing distrust between them. She asked about the one complaint Alec had actually voiced.

Brenda: *What do you mean you were written up?*
Alec: *Just that.*
Brenda: *C'mon. It's more than that.*
Alec: *Corporate gave me an ultimatum. I stalled. End of story.*
Brenda: *Obviously it's not, Alec. You must have been furious.*

Brenda's probing coaxed from Alec his side of the story. To his mind, she had blown an administrative detail, a requirement of the job, all out of proportion. As far as he was concerned, the noncompete was a nonissue, a matter of company policy. So far he had been able to placate the head office, but the situation was now beyond his control. He couldn't understand why she seemed so intent on putting him in a difficult position. Corporate had given him little flexibility. If he made an exception for Brenda, the head office would wonder about his ability to manage his people. Besides, he thought she was overreacting. That accusation, grudgingly slipped into the conversation, broke the logjam. It surfaced the misunderstandings each had of the stakes involved.

Negotiators have complex concerns behind their interests. Time pressures, conflicting responsibilities, financial worries, physical or mental fatigue, fear—all contribute to their perspectives. To the extent that you can bring worries like these out in the open, you clear the air. The difficulties you are both experiencing, although different, can provide a bridge to connection. You are in the situation together.

Appreciate the Other Person's Feelings

The concerns negotiators have don't boil down to their perspectives on the issues alone or to their take on the situation. Like Alec and Brenda, they are driven to their positions as much by their emotional reactions as by their objective concerns. Often it is impossible to separate the two, yet emotions supposedly have no place in negotiations.[3] Keeping one's cool is the name of the game. Emotional displays can be and are feigned for strategic effect. Actually getting emotional is another story. "Calm down, don't get so emotional" is not something anyone wants to hear. For women particularly it can be a not-so-subtle put-down.

In dismissing emotional messages or frowning on them, we miss out on important ways in which people communicate. We cut ourselves off from valuable insights into someone's experience. That information is useful, of course, but something else can happen when people share emotional reactions. Emotions reveal a person in a new dimension. When we reciprocate, the exchange can build a sense of connection.

Pay attention to the undercurrents. Emotional reactions can be expressed in many ways—by silence, by nonverbal cues, by cloaked signals. Sometimes people assume others will be sensitive to their feelings and then condemn them for being "thickheaded" or callous when they are not. After a negotiation takes a sudden turn for the worse, there is a common refrain: "She should have known how I would feel. I shouldn't have to tell her."

Everyone in a negotiation has concerns besides the demands they verbalize. By drawing out the reasons they feel the way they do, you come to a better understanding of what is going on for them. More important, you let them know that their feelings matter. This appreciation does not oblige you to give in to their demands. Responsiveness conveys a quite specific meaning: Any agreement will take their feelings and yours into account. By making them aware that you empathize with their reactions, you build the rapport necessary to work on the problem together.

Marsha, program director for a state agency, managed an internal supervisory staff in the state capital and a network of social workers based in major cities. Although she drew on a decade of experience as a field-worker to develop the state's pioneering quick-response program, she was now viewed by those in the field as a bureaucrat. "To their way of thinking," she says, "field-workers represent the 'front line.' They look down on those of us in administration. We are parasitic paper pushers, effectively cushioned from any harsh realities or hard work." Resentment from the field came to a head over the reporting requirements the agency imposed for the quick-response program.

> One of the field-workers stomped into my office and started blasting me about a new policy before I could say hello. She was primed for a fight and began ranting about why certain of the clearances and procedures were totally impractical in the field.

Marsha just sat there, nodding occasionally. In the back of her mind, she sensed something else was going on. No one gets that upset about paperwork, however onerous or superfluous. Aware that the woman had just come off a horrendous court case, Marsha asked her about it. The woman talked about the child, how she felt she had let him down, not intervened early enough. After a few minutes, the woman took out a Kleenex, blew her nose, and resumed her criticism of the procedures.

Marsha built connection with the field-worker by making it legitimate for her to express her regrets about the little boy. That appreciation bridged to the field-worker's complaints about the additional procedures. Not all these objections were reasonable, at least not from where Marsha sat. In fact, two of the procedures would have helped in the little boy's case. But because of the shared emotions, Marsha and the field-worker were no longer "us" and "them." They could talk about cases where the new protocols might be useful and those where they might be redundant or onerous.

Pick up on nonverbal cues. A good ear can alert you to emotional undercurrents. It also helps to keep a good eye out. We reveal more about ourselves than we ever put into words. Hidden agendas are usually not verbalized in a negotiation. Our counterparts signal important clues to their feelings and reactions with facial expression and body language too. When you pick up on these signals, you let the other party know that you are paying attention with all your senses. The cues you pick up can also prevent you from escalating the tensions inadvertently.

Andrea, an admissions officer at a university in the South, was having difficulty with one department. The professors there short-circuited the admissions process by interviewing and admitting candidates on their own. As a result, admissions was stuck with incomplete or inaccurate files and cut out of the loop when the department's admissions standards were determined. Andrea needed to put new procedures in place.

Andrea, not much older than the undergraduates, armed herself for the meeting with the department members. Knowing she would be at a disadvantage by virtue of her age, experience, and academic credentials, she designed two forms. These, she believed, would solve the problem if the department filled them out for each student interviewed. As soon as she arrived, Andrea sensed the impatience in the room. The rigid postures, the perfunctory greetings, and a lack of eye contact warned her to hold off on producing her forms.

It was a good call. The meeting started off with a litany of complaints from the department members about administrative paperwork. "The only answer the administration has," the chairman said, "is another form to fill out in triplicate. We started interviewing candidates on our own to avoid that." Andrea, conscious of the forms burning a hole in her briefcase, never brought them out. Alert to facial expressions and body language, she jettisoned a plan that would have polarized the talks from the get-go. Instead of supplying the professors with additional paperwork, Andrea requested that the department secretary notify her by e-mail of any upcoming interviews with prospective students so admissions could follow up.

Andrea took the professors' emotional temperature, but her appreciation remained as silent as the cues they sent. You don't have to probe feelings to demonstrate an appreciation for them. You can respond to them by changing your approach.

Brenda did just that as she watched Alec's face turn red. Alec's reaction is a prime example of what can happen in a negotiation when one party feels unappreciated. Alec construed Brenda's recalcitrance over the noncompete agreement as disloyalty, her involving a lawyer as a breach of trust that crossed some unwritten line in their relationship. Having gone to bat for her, he was left hanging out to dry.

    Alec: *You caused me major headaches with the head office. I don't like being written up.*

Brenda: *Well, I don't particularly like being tossed off the executive committee, either.*

Alec: *What was I supposed to do? You were talking to a lawyer. Lawyers sue. That's how they make their living. How was I to know you weren't thinking about leaving?*

Brenda: *Well, if that's what went through your mind, I can certainly see why you'd want me off the executive committee. Alec, I honestly did not have a clue that you were taking such heat on this.*

To respond to Alec's feelings, Brenda had to listen to the silence, what he left unsaid. Alec felt betrayed, although he would never admit it. Once she showed a concern for his feelings—those expressed and those unacknowledged—they each had a better grasp on the other's "local knowledge," that complex intersection that makes us who we are.

Appreciating the other side's feelings, however expressed, shows that you are paying attention. Those feelings in themselves can open up a dialogue—they can be discussed. As you understand more, you might be forced to revise radically your assumptions about the other party's motivations and the reasons behind a particular set of demands.

Appreciate the Other Person's Ideas

It does not take much to shut people down in negotiations. The other person puts out an idea and watches it sink like a rock. The suggestion might be sketchy or so tentatively offered we fail to grasp its possibilities, but we discard it nevertheless. The rejection does not even have to be verbalized. A shrug of the shoulders or a hasty diversion to another topic is a sufficient signal. This rush to judgment affects a negotiation in two ways. Most obviously, it limits the ideas on the table. A suggestion that is ultimately rejected can spark other ideas. Equally important, people usually take it as a personal rebuff when their ideas are skipped over or ignored. Not only do they get offended; they are much less likely to expose themselves further. Women especially know what it is like to have an idea dropped, then appropriated by someone else or ignored altogether. There is a wonderful cartoon that made the rounds a while back. The conference room is filled. Everyone looks attentive, but the caption reads: "Mr. Smith, can you repeat what Ms. Jones said so we can remember it?"

Respond to the other person's ideas. No matter how casually an idea is thrown out, it deserves consideration. You want to encourage the other party to share ideas. Showing appreciation for an idea, for the gesture that the other person makes in putting it forth, does not bind you to it. You can invent options without deciding on them. Neither a yea nor a nay, consideration says, "That's interesting, let's explore it." The idea is held up for discussion, looked at from various angles, weighed. Picking up on another's suggestion shows respect not just for the idea but for the person doing the suggesting. That respect is often reciprocated, and everyone becomes more open to considering multiple possibilities, regardless of who puts them forth.

In the most difficult of situations, Betty learned how shared ideas can lead to connection. No parent in her child-abuse program approached discipline in quite the same way. They did, however, have quite definite opinions and were not shy about voicing them. Many resented the court-ordered intrusion of people like Betty into their personal affairs.

Counseling sessions with parents were complicated for Betty. She was younger than most of the parents and had no children of her own. She had also been raised in a household where physical punishment was never used. Although living in Los Angeles, she was a Yankee from a privileged background. To downplay these differences and to get the parents communicating, she began her sessions by asking each parent to share with the others what trouble his or her kids had gotten into that week and how he or she had punished them.

Workshops with parents were extraordinarily difficult. We'd be talking about alternative ways of disciplining and a parent would state flat-out: "I hit my kid. That's what my parents did. I'd probably be in jail if they'd lightened up. Kids need to know who's boss." Telling the parents they were wrong would have gotten us nowhere. The parents would hit the door and have to be forced back for another session. I needed to encourage them, to acknowledge how difficult parenting was, and to create possibilities for them to see other alternatives. I'd ask them to think about the benefits of spanking. But then I'd ask them to consider the advantages of other ways of disciplining, too.

Once the parents started talking, differences soon appeared, breaking down the barrier between Betty and "them." Using their own anecdotal accounts, she could help them see that a beating was not their only recourse.

Betty suspended judgment when disapproval was a natural reaction. Without that suspension, other alternatives would never have been considered. She supported the parents, neither criticizing nor accepting their behavior, and kept them connected by focusing on the task—becoming better parents. Now in medical school, Betty applies the same technique in her group tutorial. Every Monday morning the group meets to decide how to tackle the week's assigned case. "The twenty members usually voice twenty opinions. To me," Betty says, "this is negotiation—finding a way through the disagreements."

> Some members of the group try to impose their views, cut off discussion: "This is the way I see it, and these are the reasons." Pretty soon we have a war going on. It's better to say: "That suggestion is good for this or that reason, but what if we looked at it this way?" When suggestions are offered like that, no one has to go to the wall for his or her views.

Betty's appreciative interventions, with the parents and with her fellow students, help the groups rethink their ideas in a connected way. By summarizing the benefits of a particular solution and linking it to other suggestions, she reinforces the individual group member's contribution but also keeps discussion open to other alternatives.

Link the other person's ideas with yours. Betty's approach is similar to what linguist Deborah Tannen calls cooperative overlapping.[4] In many conversations, opinions or ideas are heard sequentially with everybody competing to be heard. By contrast, when cooperative overlapping structures the conversation, opinions are considered in relation to one another and get revised as the participants make new contributions. Each person builds on what went before. Everyone is both an empathetic critic of other people's ideas and a participant with his or her own opinions.[5] However definite these ideas might be at the beginning, they evolve through the exchange and commentary. The process is one of constant looping back, deliberately soliciting ideas from others, including them in the conversation, revising as you go along. In this sense it is quite different from brainstorming, where people invent options, throw out ideas, without making a decision. In an appreciative conversation those options and ideas do not remain distinct. Choices are not kept separate, to be selected or discarded. One idea builds on another.

Nancy, director of managed care for a community health center, began to explore administrative steps to control costs. Her interest picked up when she noticed a rise in patient complaints about billing. Nancy soon found out that a computer glitch was the culprit. A simple problem, she thought, until she met with George, the resident in-house expert on information systems: "He was incredibly hostile. As soon as I said there was a minor problem, he shot back a sarcastic rejoinder. My comment told him just how little I knew about computer programming."

George, a perfectionist, was not going to change the system just because she asked. If there was a problem, as Nancy claimed, he wanted complete documentation on the contracts. He clicked off all the data he would need to track down the problem. "What a great idea," Nancy replied. "Perhaps we could develop a form that includes everything you need and won't be too hard for my people to complete." George acknowledged that the suggestion had some merit and probably wouldn't take much effort. Still, he cautioned, he would want to do a test run on one department before making sweeping changes. Nancy, who was just beginning to get a glimmer of the difficulties her "glitch" might produce, immediately agreed.

Both learned something about the other in the process. George was pleasantly surprised at Nancy's flexibility and her willingness to admit that she did not have the answers. Nancy, in turn, was grateful to George for preventing her from tripping over her misguided impression that the difficulty was relatively minor and could be easily remedied. By actively soliciting your counterpart for ideas and taking them seriously, you give both of you something to build on. Those ideas become explicitly linked to your needs and evolve as they are explored.

Brenda and Alec's negotiation could have continued to be conducted in either/or terms, pitting his authority against her will. Alec was the boss, and a boss with a natural bent to take over any discussion. Brenda created room for mutual commentary by teasing out an idea embedded in Alec's remarks. She had, however, not lost sight of her objective. She still did not want to relinquish so much control over her life without some compensating protection. The way in which she and Alec worked out that adjustment, however, had to fit with his notion of what was possible. She created the opening for him to put an idea on the table.

> Brenda: *Alec, why did you stall the front office instead of just telling me about the pressure you were under?*
>
> Alec: *I thought you'd be more cooperative. We've handled bigger problems before.*
>
> Brenda: *Sign and figure the details out later?*
>
> Alec: *That's about it. Once the pressure was off.*
>
> Brenda: *All I want is some protection. I worry about what would happen if, for some reason, I had to leave the firm.*
>
> Alec: *If that's all you are worried about—some protection during the noncompete period—then we can work something out.*

Brenda's responsive intervention shifted the negotiation's focus. By taking up Alec's tentative suggestion that the arrangements were fluid, she made it possible for them to move on and discuss just how fluid.

When we introduce more than one way to deal with a problem, pick up on other ideas, we shift the negotiation from a yes-no, up-down decision to a process that weighs which ideas work best for everyone. Appreciating the other party's suggestions, building on them, we break down the resistance to new ideas. With multiple possibilities, rather than two mutually exclusive ones, we increase our chances of reaching agreement.

Appreciate the Other Person's Face

Image is a major concern for all of us when we negotiate. How we look to ourselves and to others who matter to us often counts as much as the particulars of the deals we make. In fact, these are seldom separate. "Face," a concept popularized by sociologist Erving Goffman, captures what we value about ourselves and the qualities we want others to see in us. Negotiators go to great lengths to preserve their face. They stick to their guns against poor odds simply to avoid losing face with those who are counting on them.[6]

Show respect for the other person's position. To connect in a negotiation, we need to be protective of everyone's face, not just our own. It's pretty easy to read what people think is important and what they value about themselves. If our demands tread on the other party's self-image—in front of a boss, a colleague, or even privately with us—they probably won't be accepted. Being sensitive to a counterpart's face does more than prevent resistance from developing. It lays the groundwork for trust. It says, in effect, that you respect what she is trying to accomplish and will not do anything to embarrass or undermine her, even if you can. This appreciation concedes nothing and often is the only way to move the negotiation forward.

Sensitivity to another woman's "face" saved a negotiation for Selma, a senior foundation administrator. The woman, drafted from academia to head the foundation's new initiative on women's health, had an impressive list of publications but had never run a large-scale program. Selma, on the other hand, had managed the financial side of the multimillion-dollar endowment for over a decade.

During negotiations over program goals and funding, the new program director continually rejected Selma's ideas. They drifted into a routine. Selma would make a suggestion. Before she got out the last sentence, the program director would be vetoing the idea. "This woman," Selma thought, "is bound and determined to resist me at every turn."

Finally it clicked for Selma. "The woman had never run a major foundation program. This was her way of establishing her authority. She thought if she looked to me for advice, somehow she would be admitting that she wasn't qualified. I didn't see it that way, but that didn't matter. She did." From that point on, Selma began to make suggestions differently. Rather than put forward a single idea, she would offer an array of possibilities. This presentation underscored the extent to which the final say rested with the program director. Authority was an important part of the director's self-image. The need to assert her position waned when she no longer sensed a threat to her status. She gradually became more receptive to working collaboratively with Selma on the program's grant selections and their funding.

Make it easy for the other person to retreat. Sometimes the people we are negotiating with back themselves into a corner. They dig in their heels and stubbornly cling to positions. They make comments they don't mean and do things they regret. All our antennae tell us that they want to reconsider but see no way of doing that without appearing weak or indecisive. In these circumstances, protecting the other person's face means providing him or her with a way to retreat gracefully.

Lois was a senior researcher on a major study at a large university. Three years into the study, she and her fellow researchers were having trouble getting their original subjects to come to follow-up interviews on campus. When Lois took her difficulties to the woman in charge of the study, she recommended that the researchers use home visits to conduct the follow-up interviews.

The new system worked. Follow-up rates increased markedly. There was a snag, however. Lois and the other researchers were constantly on the road and covering the extra travel expenses themselves. Lois, who considered reimbursement of these out-of-pocket expenses part of the study's obligations, went to see the study's head again.

> After discussing the good results our home visits were getting, I mentioned that we had forgotten to talk about the extra costs. The researchers needed, of course, to be reimbursed for gas and sometimes for an overnight stay. Before anyone got further in the hole, I wanted to clear up the matter.
>
> The study director suddenly tensed. Her hands were tied. Home visits were not included in the original study budget. The grant came through a federal agency, and she could not authorize any additional money.

Lois appealed to the director's sense of fairness. The researchers, all graduate students, should not have to bear the additional costs. The new system should never have been put in place, she said, before the reimbursement issues had been straightened out.

Lois suddenly realized she was putting the study director in an untenable position. If Lois had been responsible for implementing the new system, the idea itself had come from the director. "Look," she said, "I realize you are in a bind. Could you talk to the university's grant administrator? He might know some loopholes in the federal guidelines or have some other sources of funding."

Lois did two things here that saved the director's face. She essentially inserted an objective third party as an intermediary into the negotiation. The study director could discuss "bending" the rules with a senior administrator in ways she could not with a postdoctoral assistant. The director never had to admit that her original suggestion was premature or ill-advised. Lois also removed herself from the final solution, telling the director that she knew the problem would be worked out fairly. "The researchers were reimbursed for all their expenses by month's end," Lois says, "but I never knew where the money came from."

> *"Face" played a critical role in Brenda's negotiation with Alec over the noncompete agreement. Brenda was backing him into a corner. Her continued objections to signing the agreement not only caused him to look bad to his superiors, getting him "written up," they also left him exposed in his own office. In fact, he might have threatened to remove her from the executive committee in part to let the rest of the staff know that he was still in charge. As Brenda negotiated the actual terms of the noncompete, she paid particular attention to Alec's face. Having been burned once, he was not about to accept any arrangement that would subject him to the same danger all over again.*

> Brenda: *I'll check around with some of my friends. These agreements are difficult for single parents. There are bound to be some creative solutions out there that the head office would appreciate.*
>
> Alec: *That'd be great. We're having more and more problems with these agreements. The head office likes to shoot the messenger.*

> *Brenda's suggestion created room for Alec to maneuver. At the same time, it informed him quite explicitly that any terms he negotiated with Brenda would respect his standing with the head office.*

The cooperation needed to reach a good agreement doesn't have much chance of developing when the other party senses he or she is being backed into a corner. The prospect of compromise then seems like a retreat or an embarrassing surrender. Overtures that demonstrate a respect for the other person's "face" provide the room necessary for him or her to back away without cost and with dignity intact. They do not, however, constitute a signal that we are backing down.

> *Brenda and Alec's negotiation had a good outcome for both of them. Brenda signed the noncompete agreement. In return, Alec made sure that she had a "golden parachute" that guaranteed her salary for a year if she left the company for any reason. In addition, they agreed that if he decided to sell his stake in the franchise, she would have the right of first refusal. That Brenda wanted to negotiate this right assuaged Alec's doubts about her commitment to the business going forward. That Alec granted it reassured Brenda about that future.*

Limits on Getting Connected

For collaboration to happen, the connection needs to go both ways. Negotiators do not get connected by making concessions or by accommodating the other side for the sake of peace. Nor do they connect with everyone and at the same level of intensity. It takes time and energy to build a relationship. There are limits to how willing someone is to go the extra mile, to devote the time as well as the emotional resources required in collaboration. Not everyone wants to bother. Sometimes people are limited by their rusty or undeveloped interpersonal skills, other times by their lack of interest. Not everyone can operate in a collaborative mode. The need to win, to beat down the opposition, is too ingrained to be overcome by even skillfully managed appreciative overtures. And sometimes the situation itself works against collaboration, yielding no compelling reasons to make the effort. In other words, efforts at appreciation do not always result in a collaborative relationship, and it's important to know when to back off.

Resistant personalities. For a sense of engagement to develop that goes beyond superficial comfort or attentiveness, there has to be some reciprocity. Whether and to what extent a mutually respectful give-and-take can be nurtured is often difficult to judge. But for collaboration to have a chance, you have to begin a negotiation assuming that it is at least a possibility. If and when you discover that the other party is playing a different game, you can shift course to protect yourself. Harriet, a partner in a West Coast firm that invests in early-stage Internet companies, leans heavily in the direction of the collaborative in her negotiations. She also knows when and where to draw the line. Harriet, who has turned fifty, works in a field of aggressive deal making dominated by male entrepreneurs in their thirties. "To put it bluntly," she states, "sometimes I stick out like a sore thumb."

Early on Harriet recognized she could not and would not "play by the usual rules." In part, this decision was pragmatic: "I would be a sham; people would see right through me in a New York minute. But I get results—good companies, happy partners."

Trust, Harriet believes, is the glue that holds deals together. She works hard on establishing relationships. "It is a joke in the office. My fellow investors bag a hot prospect. I add to our family of companies." Harriet's collaborative approach does not always succeed. One negotiation crystallizes in her mind the difficulties she can encounter.

> We'd invested heavily in a small company as a joint venture partner. When its software suddenly took off, the founder wanted to renegotiate the terms of the original agreement. Otherwise he would buy out our interests—and not for a very good price given the market. The only way I could see to make him comfortable with the deal was for him to think I cared about him personally. I courted him. I tried to be there for him. I went to hear him give a lecture. I flew to Washington to listen to his testimony during a congressional hearing on the Internet.

Despite her courtship, the deal started unraveling. Harriet's boss cautioned her against being overly invested in the relationship—or, as he put it, "spending emotional capital." Translating, Harriet took that warning to mean too much connection was unhealthy. Her involvement might be skewing her judgment.

As the entrepreneur stepped up the pressure on Harriet to cave in, Harriet redoubled her efforts to save the venture. In rapid escalation, they reached a point of no return. Harriet did throw in the towel, but not in the way he anticipated. She gave up on connection. When he embarrassed her in public and in comments to her attorney, she took him to court for reneging on the original contract. Nothing else was going to prevail over his need to best her and dominate the negotiations.

A tough bargainer, Harriet works through a collective "we" that demands parity at the table. This is part of the groundwork laid by strategic moves and turns. Connection, by contrast, demands a certain reciprocity from the other side. Finding none, Harriet took the only option left available to her.

Difficult situations. Sometimes the power imbalances are so great in a negotiation that they cannot be overcome with deft strategic moves and turns. Being responsive to the other side might be the only game in town. In these situations, acts of appreciation are used tactically, not so much to engage the other party in mutual exchange as to get a hearing. In other words, appreciative overtures become the tools of advocacy rather than of relationship building.

Jackie is an intensive care nurse at a major teaching hospital. Daily she confronts hierarchical relationships that work against her being heard when she negotiates with senior physicians and residents about the postoperative care of patients.

> One of my chief responsibilities as a critical care nurse is to advocate for the patient. A lot of players are involved in caring for critically ill patients. They look after a specific aspect of the patient's care, and each has definite ideas about how the care should be handled. Negotiating among these differences is the most exhausting part of my job.

Everyone in critical care is pressed for time. How Jackie phrases her concerns and times her approach determines how her suggestions are received.

> I had a recent case where I was convinced the patient needed a transfusion. Each time I moved him, his blood pressure dropped, and he was uncomfortable. Medication would ease his discomfort, but it would also cause his pressure to drop. We needed to get the patient stabilized, not just for his own good, but to move him off the ICU. Transfusion seemed the only route.

The surgeon, however, opposed transfusion. "He shot me down but good when I suggested it," the resident informed Jackie. This history made it doubly difficult for Jackie to bring up the issue with the surgeon.

> I knew I'd only get a few minutes with the surgeon to get my story out.
> I needed to engage him in a conversation explicitly and succinctly
> about the transfusion. I caught him on the way to the Coke machine.
> I told him I was confused and wondered why he'd ruled out a
> transfusion.

The surgeon and Jackie had a mutual concern—the health of the patient. They were both implicated in that outcome. To the extent that she
understood the surgeon's hesitation to transfuse, the better off the patient
would be.

> While he was waiting for the Coke can to drop, he told me the patient
> himself was opposed to transfusion, and he wanted to hold off as long
> as possible. I then voiced my concerns, and he listened, between
> swallows. He still wanted to wait, but we agreed on a plan of action. If
> the patient's blood pressure continued to fall over the next four hours,
> he would be transfused. This was a great outcome for me.

Low person in the medical hierarchy, a nurse negotiating with a car-
diac surgeon, Jackie responded to those dynamics and, in turn, made it
easy for the surgeon to respond to her concerns. That was probably the
only way he would listen. Timing and phrasing were as important to her
success as her actual proposal on how to handle the transfusion.

Jackie had to accommodate the surgeon to be heard. It was his decision
to make. Did the surgeon see Jackie differently after their interaction?
Would he respect her opinion more on their next encounter? Perhaps, but
only perhaps. Limits on mutual engagement were woven into the relationship she had with the surgeon and the one he had with her.

In unequal situations like these, appreciative efforts can be used to
support your interests. They aim not so much to promote collaboration as
to parry differences in status. Cindy, executive director of a shelter that
provides a safe haven from domestic violence, depends primarily on public sources to keep the doors open. The shelter, without a high-profile
constituency behind it, is not high on the Texas legislature's agenda. Responsiveness and appreciation frame the way she advocates for herself
and for her center.

When I meet with the state senators, I am literally begging. I'll do whatever it takes. The "good ole boys" like to see me as a sweet young thing who couldn't threaten anybody. I flatter them, help with their fund-raising, and play up to their egos. I wear soft, feminine clothes, not suits. I'm not crazy about this, but if they knew what I was really thinking, I wouldn't get a nickel for the center.

Cindy recognizes the extent to which she is stepping into a stereotype and pragmatically weighs the cost. Her actions are consciously instrumental. She believes in what she is doing and uses the means at her disposal—including the advantages of being young, attractive, and female. In effect, she becomes a female female-impersonator to get what she wants.[7] She approaches the senators with feminine deference not to build mutual relationships with them, but to loosen their grip on the state's coffers.

Connection has been called the weapon of the weak. Admittedly, when real inequalities exist in a negotiation, it is difficult to talk about true connection. The bargainer with the least power is almost always the one who pays the most attention to the other person's feelings and opinions. There is little reciprocity. Jackie and Cindy, for example, both monitor the other side and then use responsiveness to get what they want. Despite this uneasy relation between connection and power, connection can actually create power in negotiation, but it is a shared power, and women can have an advantage here. Because we so often juggle multiple and conflicting roles, we can be flexible in our decision making. We think little of changing course on a dime. As arbiters in family conflicts, we soon discover there is seldom one "right" decision and can be comfortable with the ambiguity inherent in different stories. And because we tend to be interested in other people's stories, we frequently have a great deal of practice in listening with a keen ear.

Whatever the reason, these orientations add up to a valuable set of skills—an appreciation of multiplicity, an ability to listen, a capacity to suspend judgment. Without them, dialogue and discovery are next to impossible. One of the unfortunate side effects of the debate on gender is that it has made some women self-conscious about using these skills. They come, supposedly, from tainted origins and set women apart. Understanding how appreciative efforts can be interpreted or exploited does not mean they are not extremely valuable. They just have to be used with your eyes wide open. The benefits are too great to miss.

Connection takes place primarily in the shadow negotiation. It involves you in a process of making the other person feel appreciated in all his or her complexity. Negotiators cannot be reduced to their issues alone. How they feel and how we feel influence how we work together. When people sense that their opinions and perspectives are valued, they are poised to learn from each other. In a collaborative dialogue, where connection has been made, arguments and counterarguments become forms of collective reflection. Mutual rapport, once established, multiplies the chances of finding a creative solution to the problem. But it takes work to engage your counterpart so that a shared purpose can emerge.

6

GETTING COLLABORATION TO WORK

Negotiations fall into predictable patterns that we encounter all too often. First there is the forest-and-the-trees scenario, in which symptoms of a problem are mistaken for its root cause. We go around and around on trivial matters, blaming each other for delays or a failure to follow through. However involved or heated the talks become, we get stuck in grooves and never explore together the reasons for the delay or the inability to deliver. The root of our conflict remains hidden or disguised, and it's a lose-lose situation. Because the underlying issues are not addressed, everyone feels somewhat disappointed. We have not really gotten to the heart of the matter or even been able to let off steam and air our differences.

Then there is the dance of concessions that produces competing monologues. Each of us comes to the table with our interests clearly defined and with fixed arguments in mind. Suspecting that any disclosure might jeopardize our case, we hold back and give away as little as possible. We whittle away at each other's demands until eventually we settle on a compromise, usually somewhere in the middle. This process, too, leaves everyone dissatisfied, wondering if perhaps we have given up too much.

Dissatisfaction like this rarely produces good or lasting agreements. "The clever thing to do," advised Mary Parker Follett, considered by some to be the mother of negotiation theory, "is not to let the negotiation drift toward two mutually exclusive alternatives—your way or my way." An either/or approach almost always leads to partial and disappointing results. There is a more promising, although admittedly more difficult alternative. You can take steps to insure that the negotiation conversation unfolds as a collaborative dialogue rather than an adversarial contest. The negotiation then becomes a continuous process of *relating* and *revaluing*. As you and the other person connect with each other, you both become aware of the gaps in your assumptions and have the means at hand to reassess them. Disagreements, rather than leading to a hardening of attitudes, form the basis for further inquiry.

Once engaged in a collaborative dialogue, it's often possible to generate solutions that would never have occurred to anyone independently. The reason for this is simple. When bargainers put their cards on the table, face the real issue, and bring everything into the open, they relate to each other differently. As Follett wisely pointed out, "I never react to you but to you-plus-me; or to be more accurate, it is I-plus-you reacting to you-plus-me. . . . In the very process of meeting, we both become something different," more receptive to that unknown that the other party knows. When we come to trust each other, we can engage in dialogue instead of talking *at* each other. As we learn from the exchange, the boundaries of set arguments become elastic.[1]

But the barriers against achieving that trust are considerable. We don't naturally trust the other party. We wonder whether, in revealing too much, we give him or her an edge against us. If, for example, she knows precisely what salary we are aiming for, she might discount our figure and offer less. In fact, the uncertainty of negotiations—we can never predict exactly what the other person wants or expects or might use against us—prompts caution even when we are not actually worried about being exploited. So we face a dilemma, one that makes those familiar and dissatisfying patterns into which negotiations fall all the more understandable.[2]

It takes active steering to reach a place where you and your counterpart experience mutual trust and rapport. To be candid with each other, people have to be confident that everyone is operating in good faith. They also have to be convinced that a less-adversarial process can produce better results for them. Once they are comfortable expressing their concerns, secure that what they reveal will not be turned against them, they feel freer to discuss divisive issues. With conflict no longer avoided or suppressed, it is not so hard to work together on joint solutions. As everyone hears about what the others want, individual interests gain greater clarity through the dialogue and at the same time the linkages between those interests become more obvious. Both the problem and an individual's perspective on his or her stake in it evolve through the conversation. Bit by bit, incrementally, trust builds. The relationship that is formed through dialogue reinforces everyone's confidence that the problem can be solved together and our notions of what is possible expand.

Only recently have we become aware of how important the "invisible" work of trust building is to negotiation.[3] Without that effort, a commitment to a joint solution has little opportunity to develop and solutions will remain, in one way or another, dissatisfying. It takes work to change the perceptions that people bring to negotiation. It takes work to keep a dialogue going when the other party's only inclination is to put demands on the table and press for a deal. It takes work to get everyone to own his or her part of the problem. The invisible work of negotiation creates that "you-plus-me" that Follett talked about. Dialogue doesn't just happen. Trust and respect have to be nurtured before others feel safe in speaking their mind or want to bother. That takes some effort.

- ### • WORK TO MAKE ROOM FOR RELATIONSHIP BUILDING
  You have to give collaboration room to grow. There are several ways to foster an atmosphere in which trust and rapport can build. The simple act of making other people comfortable goes a long way toward insuring that they will not be left guessing about how they will be treated. Carving out time for informal rituals like sharing a meal or a coffee break provides those often-pivotal moments when you and your counterpart can get to know each other apart from your "official" roles. And, most important, by deliberately encouraging opportunities where experiences can be shared, you create the possibility of finding a common thread and a common language—a basis for actually communicating with each other.

- ### • WORK TO ENCOURAGE PARTICIPATION
  To get a collaborative dialogue off on the right foot and keep it there, you must take steps to draw the other parties into the process. That means making sure that all the participants have the same information.

It also means constant backtracking to check that everyone has a common sense of what has been achieved so far and can move forward on the basis of shared assumptions.

• **WORK TO KEEP THE DIALOGUE GOING**

At times it is difficult to keep the conversation going. But as long as you continue talking there is a chance to come together. It takes time for trust and rapport to be established and for the other person's story to emerge. It takes time for people to adjust to seeing things differently. The steps you take to keep the dialogue going provide that time.

• **WORK TO GET EVERYONE TO "OWN" THE PROBLEM**

For the other person to have a real stake in working with you, he or she must recognize that the problem itself is a mutual one. The work you do to create a shared history and to link your issues with the other person's makes joint ownership more likely. Only when your counterpart buys into the problem with you can you explore mutual solutions.

When negotiators connect and become more candid, they often discover that the problem they were worrying about is not the root conflict but a symptom of it. But any collaboration requires a good deal of effort. We humans are a suspicious lot when it comes to negotiation. Most of our models push in the other direction—toward strategic analysis that emphasizes differences rather than points of mutual concern.

Collaboration Is Not Easy

Kate Griscomb has faced multiple challenges in getting collaboration to work. Kate, who was an English major in college and has no formal technical training, plies her marketing skills in a high-tech company in Silicon Valley. Friction has been more the norm than the exception in the relations between marketing and the engineers in R&D.

The thirty-something mother of two characterizes the company culture as "pretty low-key and nonconfrontational." Policy appears to be made by walking around, talking, catching people on the run. "The place is an informal, quirky democracy where people tend to settle in for the duration," Kate says. "People stick around for a long time, and they know they are going to bump into each other later."

All is not so calm under the surface, however. Priorities have a way of being set at the top and filtering down, and R&D propels the company. Marketing seldom gets equal airtime. As soon as Kate was put in charge of launching an innovative medical software, she noticed a pronounced uptick in the friction between marketing and R&D. "This tension is not without cause," she says. Marketing decisions focus on the client, but in R&D the schedule rather than client satisfaction drives the decisions.

I'm always the bad news lady, screwing up the engineers' schedules. Everyone knows we could have a better product. But why should the engineers put their schedules at risk when that's what they are being measured on?

Kate envisions her role as being the client's voice in internal decision making, of bringing the client into the debate, but the responsiveness she can offer the client depends upon the engineers in R&D. Wearing two hats, advocating for the linkage between the client's concerns and the company's goals, she trips alarms at two points. The first resistance comes from obvious and to-be-expected turf issues. Who has the final say, R&D or marketing? The second is less visible and stems from the ambiguity of her role. The engineers in R&D wonder whose side she's really on—the company's or the client's, whose case she constantly pleads.

The issues are complex on both fronts. "This place has zero tolerance for discrimination. It doesn't matter whether it smacks of racism, or sexism, or ethnic prejudice." That said, Kate still points to problems.

Until recently women were few and far between in R&D. Most of us are clustered in marketing and investor relations. The engineers in R&D just don't think someone from marketing can understand their problems. It's impossible to parse out whether that's because we are women or because we lack the technical training.

Lessening the tension between marketing and R&D is Kate's number-one priority. As we shall see, the connected way in which she goes about that project has interesting ramifications for the entire company.

Work to Make Room for Relationship Building

How we think about a negotiation affects the solution we are liable to come up with. Mental models tend to shape our actions. If we approach a negotiation as an adversarial or competitive contest, we think in terms of winners or losers. Bargaining over the price of a car or a condo, we know the game and what is required of us. Our role is clear—we are either a buyer or a seller—and we play out a familiar script. Usually we don't care if we ever encounter the other party again. But this script is next to useless if our negotiation involves longer-term relationships or more complicated problems. We cannot perform as disinterested buyers or sellers. We need to engage our counterpart in a different process, one where we both acknowledge the stakes and the promise. That engagement, in turn, depends on reaching a certain comfort level with each other. Right from the start of a negotiation you can work to put the other person at ease.

Creating a comfortable space. When people are ill at ease with each other, suspicious of the other's motives, or intent on pursuing specific agendas, their exchange is constricted. A space—physical and psychological—must be structured that makes them comfortable. Negotiations, even among the most amicable players, can be charged with emotion and anxiety. Large sums of money, reputations, futures, and relationships are often on the line. To get a productive dialogue going, you first have to create an atmosphere in which friendly meanings attach to words and actions.[4]

The setting of a negotiation—both physical and psychological—has a subtle and sometimes not-so-subtle impact on its process. Any setting can be manipulated to lessen awkwardness or increase tension. Where a meeting is held sends a signal about control. Seating people in low chairs or across a wide expanse of desk sets the stage for an attempt to dominate. Sitting everyone in comfortable love seats conveys welcome. The same goes for psychological settings. When no one occupies the metaphorical head of the table, differences in status are downplayed.

Making people comfortable—physically and psychologically—establishes a baseline for behavior. At an elementary level, it lets people know how you operate and how they can expect to be treated. When they realize they won't be forced to sit with a symbolic sun in their eyes or left to squirm in the outer office, mutual respect becomes a given. This is not a question of whether you have the clout to make them cool their heels for half an hour. It's about the kind of negotiation you want to have. When your gestures show that you notice things about them and are willing to accommodate them, they signal your regard for them as people.

Marisa, a successful real estate developer in her late thirties, pays particular attention to setting—in part, she says, because she is a "people person," but also to distance herself from the reputation for ruthless bargaining that follows many real estate developers: "I want anyone I'm doing business with to know that we are not all unscrupulous."

> People come in expecting me to be out to dupe them. I have to try to overcome this prejudice, and it's not easy. One of our new tenants, a fashion photographer, wanted to paint his loft purple, but he started out making all sorts of outrageous demands. These were just a screen to protect his real interest. He came on strong because he thought I'd automatically fight him on every point. You cannot get to the heart of things, to what others really want, unless they feel comfortable with you.

Earlier in her career Marisa admits that she frequently wanted to "cut to the chase, get right down to business." Oscar Wilde called experience the "name everyone gives to [her] mistakes," and it is experience that has taught Marisa to be much more sensitive to who is sitting across the table. Marisa generally starts out with the power balance tipped in her favor, but she deliberately creates a perception of equal footing.

> Are they sensitive to the courtesy of being called Mr. or Mrs.? Or distrustful of too much formality? Are they fastidious about their dress? If they are, I use the conference room instead of my messy office. Are they a forest or a tree person? Do they start with the big picture or the details? With the foresters I'll draw up an outline and not pin down too much.

By working to make the other person comfortable, you offer tangible proof of how you prefer to do business and lay the groundwork for the kind of negotiation you want to have. Marisa, for example, usually begins a negotiation knowing she is in control and takes steps to neutralize the negative impact differences in status can have on the negotiation conversation. Her actions are symbolic gestures of inclusion.

> *Kate's efforts to put the engineers in R&D at ease with her take another direction. She goes out of her way to meet the engineers on their turf. More separates the corporate offices, where Kate works, and the R&D lab than the two hundred yards of landscaped brick pathway between the two buildings. The engineers keep erratic schedules, often working into early morning and coming in late. Breakfast meetings in the marketing department's fancy conference rooms they write off as corporate power trips.*
>
> *Whenever Kate has something important to discuss, she does not schedule a meeting or pick up the phone. She walks over to the lab. Not only are the engineers more comfortable, she has a chance to see what is going on. They are a graphic bunch, and she picks up useful information from the cryptic messages and charts pasted on the walls and workstation dividers. These change daily and let her know when things are going well, when she can push, and when she should hold off a day or so on a new wrinkle.*

Establishing a "comfort zone" means doing more than paying attention to the seating arrangements and the supply of Danish. Whereas a strategic move might have you emphasizing differences, particularly those that highlight your control or status, connected actions seek to minimize them and draw the other person into a dialogue. You want to assure him or her that there is no need to be defensive or wary. The fewer elements of surprise the better. Defensive guards are not so likely to come up when others have some idea of what you are about and what they will encounter.

Creating space for rituals. Rituals bind people together. Some are ceremonial occasions, with all the trappings of pomp and circumstance. Others provide quite unstructured and informal places for people to interact. From time to time, most people have a real need to doff their masks, to set aside the emblems of status and ceremony. The informal rituals of daily life—breaking bread, a softball game, or just schmoozing—answer to this need. They are times carved out of busy lives when people can meet simply as human beings unmediated by their differences. By mutual consent, defined roles get suspended temporarily in the shared experience of enjoying one another's company.[5] As Virginia Woolf's Mrs. Dalloway puts it, dinner parties are a time to risk "one's own little point of view" for that "immeasurable delight in coming together," a time to "create" rather than "manipulate," to "combine" instead of separate.

The settings of informal rituals are places where dialogue dominates, where people can get to know one another beyond their professional or public personas. In formal negotiations, the exchange is constricted as people worry about what they might give away. Ritual occasions are more open. Not only do people speak differently in such situations, they also provide more details about themselves. For many years in the garment industry, negotiators for management and labor would have a dinner right before collective bargaining began. Precisely because no one minimized the hazards ahead, they wanted a chance to encounter each other on a human level before the hard bargaining started. When they later met across the negotiating table, they had an enhanced sense of whom they were facing.

These kinds of informal rituals foster connection. A highly placed elected official we'll call Susan was brought up in a household where food automatically appeared as soon as any "big" issues came up or someone was out of sorts. The habit, she says, is almost imprinted on her DNA. Even in her professional life, she brings out food whenever she feels the need for a warming-up period or when things get tense.

> When we were hammering out the judicial reform, we were working around the clock. On Saturday mornings, I'd get coffee and doughnuts for everyone. I wasn't trying to be manipulative. By having lunch brought in or taking a break, you get to know one another very differently. It doesn't matter what the food is. So tell me about your daughter. She's going to be a vet? In my experience, those confidences change the dynamic in the room. Not 100 percent. But they help.

They help by filling in the blanks, casting people in a rounder dimension. We've all taken part in the sometimes frantic "do you know" game played at the start of a negotiation with relative strangers. Informal rituals provide a more leisurely way of finding these points of connection.

In Susan's peregrinations around Capitol Hill and political caucuses, she has observed a dramatic fault line in the way some female professionals view connecting rituals. For some, the occasions are a natural extension of how they deal with people, and they enjoy them. Others are more ambivalent. They balk at participating because of the caretaking obligations these occasions can impose. Susan doesn't find this reaction so surprising. Women, after all, have been in the kitchen for a lot longer than they've been in the boardroom. But, she warns, women can shoot themselves in the foot by stepping so warily. To illustrate she points to a small working group she chairs.

> We start the meetings at 12:30 with lunch. The men are always there, right on time. But the women often come late. They're too busy or they don't eat lunch. It drives me crazy.
>
> One guy had just taken his thirty-something daughter on a golfing weekend for four days. He was all excited to tell us what he had done with her. A woman who has too much to do and skips lunch doesn't hear about the golf trip. She's probably the same age as the guy's daughter, and they would have a ton of places to connect. Later, if they disagreed, it would be a very different kind of disagreement, but she doesn't bother.

Susan's "professional" is all business. Her demeanor signals to everyone that she is basically uninterested in them as people. Asserting her independence from the group, she insures that if any informal linkages are made, they won't involve her.

> One of these women arrives with yellow pad in hand. She's always late and she's always got a list of ten or fifteen issues. All she wants is to get through those items and then go on to the important things she has to do. She gets visibly annoyed if there is any personal chat. Everybody wants to get the deal done, but most realize the going won't be smooth unless each has a sense of where the other people are coming from. That's even more important when things get rough. She misses all that.

What is specifically missing is not just the time spent in schmoozing or at lunch. It is a willingness to suspend roles, to set aside the professional persona and to meet people without the buffer of a title or a particular piece of work that needs to get out the door.

Kate, recognizing the chill in her working relationship with the engineers, looks for occasions when she can take off her marketer's hat and interact with them more casually. The engineers are a tight group, brought together in part by their common rituals and in part by their idiosyncrasies. They share a particular addiction to junk food, a fondness for practical jokes, and a work ethic that merges with play.

Each summer the "nerds" organize a lunchtime Olympics. People from all departments—from the mailroom to the CEO's office—get assigned to teams and play volleyball, softball, and Frisbee. Whenever she can, Kate now joins in. "I've gotten to be a real killer with the Frisbee, but that is beside the point. The object is to have fun." Kate has also started dropping in on the engineers' monthly "martyr reward" ceremony, at which they hand out a plaque for the department member voted most sleep deprived over the past four weeks.

Ritual occasions like these provide opportunities for people to let down their hair and see each other in different settings. Rapport cannot help but build as they step outside their usual roles and come to understand each other better. When, for example, Kate joined the engineers at play, she began to have a much better sense of the constant strain under which they worked and their need for an outlet.

Creating space for storytelling. It is commonplace during breaks for negotiators to connect with each other outside their roles. But rituals that enable us to know each other better do not have to take place "off line." People can come together over the problem or the task at hand. Prompting opportunities for the other person to tell his or her story helps that coming together.

A good many factors motivate people when they negotiate. They can throw themselves behind an issue or remain lukewarm for personal reasons. An outcome can be good for the company in the long run but bad for their careers in the short term. They can cushion their demands in order to protect a relationship or care only about short-term results. If we think about interests analytically, almost as an objective third-party observer, shutting out all but the rational or obvious, we can perhaps identify these factors, but only perhaps. When people swap stories about their situations, however, they fill in informational gaps and give the facts color, a context, and a history. Bargainers cannot recognize shared interests unless they can talk to each other and be understood. Stories provide the means of finding a common language and common values.

Interests and values need to be distinguished in negotiations. They are often taken to be the same thing, but they are not. Interests are what we want and need. They can be translated with relative ease into a currency we can trade. Values, on the other hand, cannot be traded or compromised, and yet they often define what a negotiator holds most dear. When we discover something about the other person's value system, we open a window on what drives his or her decisions. Differences in interests we can bargain over; differences in values require another order of understanding before we can work through them. We face this clash between values and interests in many communities. When a developer comes to call, conservationists concerned about urban sprawl and the bird habitat are not usually receptive to any proposal, no matter how lucrative. Union officials, on the other hand, often care more about jobs than birds or an increase in blacktop.

Storytelling, when woven into a negotiation's fabric, provides a means for the participants to express not only their interests but their values as well. As understandings become less superficial, they are better able and more willing to tackle the difficult issues dividing them.

Storytelling is not the norm in negotiations. You must incorporate opportunities for it or else generally all you will hear is a list of the other party's demands.

Tamara grew up in a small eastern European town where children are weaned on folktales. Now a health care consultant in Cleveland, she works for the city's major teaching hospital. Over the past few years, Tamara has watched the area hospitals consolidate. Strategic partnering has real advantages. But, she cautions, wagging an admonishing finger, bigger is not necessarily better. "My mother used to remind us all the time that you cannot make soup from a stone. However good a potential merger looks on paper, in operation it can be a disaster." When Dr. Black, the head of her hospital, sounded her out on the possibility of a merger with City Hospital, she was skeptical. "The whole idea," she says with a throaty laugh, "reeked of problems."

The only thing the two institutions had in common was generic. The way they practiced medicine and delivered services diverged at every conceivable point. City provided a safety net for the urban poor. Located in a blighted downtown area, its plant was antiquated, its staff dedicated to service. Tamara's teaching hospital, by contrast, prided itself on its research and its state-of-the-art facility. The differentials in pay were substantial across the board. Dr. Black was strong-willed and opinionated. The head of City matched him in stubbornness. They were, Tamara suspected, likely candidates to battle over turf.

When an excited Dr. Black outlined a broad-brush proposal, Tamara politely suggested he take several steps backward. "Slow down," she advised. "There are synergies here because our institutions have almost nothing in common. We don't overlap, but we don't talk the same language either. How can we negotiate a merger and have it be successful?"

We started, instead, by convening small groups of administrators and senior physicians from various services at both institutions. Merger, even the concept, was never mentioned. These sessions were billed as get-togethers to discuss health care reform. Participants were specifically encouraged to talk about their history, what worked and what didn't. At first, you'd have thought they all walked on water. Gradually they opened up.

When the possibility of a merger was eventually raised, the turf issues and disparities in mission and practice remained, but the participants' suspicions had, at the very least, been blunted. "It doesn't matter what you are involved in," Tamara maintains, "you still have to speak the same language." People, even busy doctors, she finds, discover they can communicate more directly through stories. "It's not too different from swapping war stories." They are able to build on similar experiences or the odd anecdote.

Sometimes others listen to stories with a jaundiced ear at first. They hear them as self-serving accounts or question the motives behind them. Bias is pretty much read into the tale. That is, in part, the function of storytelling. It puts on the table, or at least allows to surface in shadowy form, the negative personal assumptions people are making about each other. Understanding derives as much from airing these negative attitudes as from learning more about specific wants or needs.

In the initial stages of Kate's negotiations with R&D, the client, while more than familiar to her, was a relatively unknown commodity to the engineers. With major responsibility for marketing the new product, Kate spent most of her time translating the client's demands to the engineers.

> When I came to the engineers, I was usually asking for something that would throw a monkey wrench into their schedule. The request might make the product better or the customer happy, but it screwed up the engineers' timing.

Meetings to decide which "bells and whistles" on the client's demand list would actually be included in the product quickly split into opposing camps. "The marketing people did not understand why R&D couldn't just give the client what it wanted. The engineers kept saying no way. Suddenly," Kate says, "it hit me."

> I was so focused on my customers' concerns, I had started to sound like a broken record, not appreciating the incredible pressures R&D was under. We are measured against schedules in marketing, too, but we have more flexibility. If marketing gets caught in a time crunch, we can let some of the pieces go. Engineering doesn't have that luxury. A more formal sequence is involved in designing a product and working out the bugs. When they get surprises, which almost always happens, those blips ripple through the entire project, causing delays and headaches.

With this realization, Kate reversed direction. Instead of pressing her concerns in the lab, she began to push the engineers out into the field. At a trial site, the engineers could talk directly with a client without her serving as a conduit or a buffer. To help solve "her" problem, Kate converted what were two-way disputes—between R&D and marketing—into three-way discussions involving the engineers, herself, and the client. She brought the client's story into her negotiations with the engineers.

As soon as the engineers had a chance to listen to the customer, they started to understand it wasn't a question of bells and whistles versus their schedules, but what trade-offs had to be made. "When they came back from these visits," Kate says, "we were singing the same song, maybe not at the same volume yet, but we were getting close."

Difficulties still arise—and often. But because the engineers have

*come face-to-face with the client and its dilemmas, they no longer see
Kate as a source of their troubles. She's someone with whom they share
a problem that has to be puzzled through.*

Making room for relationship building is a prerequisite for a collaborative negotiation. The other party must feel comfortable with you before he or she begins to accept that your commitment to a mutual solution is genuine. Part of connection's invisible work is to create opportunities for rapport to grow—whether you are sharing a coffee break or swapping stories. Work of this kind makes it clear to the other person you want the negotiation to be a collaborative one.

Work to Encourage Participation

Negotiations can get confusing. Sometimes no one knows where they are in the process or how they got there. Confusion like this breeds suspicion or is just plain disheartening. Making sure everyone is equally informed keeps them engaged. When people all have the same cut at the information, they are much more likely to trust the process and their fellow participants. Equal access to information goes a long way toward convincing people that nothing underhanded is taking place.

Negotiations can also be chaotic, especially when things move quickly or take unexpected turns. If people leave a negotiation session and discover later that what was agreed upon was not at all their understanding, they feel duped or see themselves as the victims of a dirty trick. By circling back and reviewing the progress, you avoid misunderstandings about what has been said and what has been accomplished.

These connective steps build commitment to the process, but they also affect the content of the discussion. Everyone starts in the same place, inside the circle. Once individuals are drawn in as active participants, they become vested in the process and have a different stake in its success. The exchange becomes freer and more collaborative.

Information performs many functions in a negotiation. It can be a source of power or a defense against attack. It can also be the means of bringing people together. Sharing information is an act of trust. It tells everyone that there is nothing hidden. Sarah manages the information flow in her negotiations like a zealot. "When someone suspects he or she is not getting the whole story," she says, "participation becomes guarded." Sarah practices corporate law in a high-powered New York firm where she specializes in putting together complex mergers and acquisitions. Although she deals only in friendly takeovers, time pressures are excruciating and tempers fray easily. "The kitchen," she says, "can get pretty hot. You don't want somebody flying off the handle or forging ahead when you haven't reached any real consensus."

Two points, she finds, are critical in any session: how it begins and how it ends. At both moments, she takes deliberate steps to make sure everyone is operating from the same assumptions. Before a marathon conference call gets under way, she calls a time-out.

> Can we spend just a minute now that everyone is hooked in and see where Jim thinks this thing is coming out? Where Marcia thinks it's coming out? Where Al thinks it's coming out? I guarantee those are all different right now, and we need to be on the same page.

All parties know they are getting the whole story. "This softens the ride when the negotiation is bumpy. Once they know they don't have to be suspicious," she says, "there is nothing that brings people together faster than a shared sense of imminent disaster."

Keeping everyone in the fold and making sure the process is moving are not easy tasks. When talks begin to stall, Sarah communicates her concern immediately. With what she calls "reality checks," she lets all the key players know that progress has bogged down, but she is scrupulous about not attaching any blame.

> If these guys start screaming at each other about who is slowing things down, they will never be able to work together once we put the deal to bed. They're still in the courtship phase, and it takes a certain amount of patience. We'll get on the same page eventually. We might be a couple of chapters behind, but I'd rather spend a little more time. You cannot assume anything, particularly consensus.

If all the participants need to start from the same working assumptions, they also need to come away from each session with the same notion of where they are. At the end of every session Sarah circles back, checking that everyone has the same impressions of what has been agreed upon. This practice reveals cracks in the consensus and at the same time reinforces what has been accomplished.

Sarah's information loop relates to a single deal. Kate's, on the other hand, is ongoing with the engineers. Anxious to involve them more actively in initial contract negotiations—where price and schedule are worked out—she has begun e-mailing the group as soon as the client requests a proposal. Rather than inundate the engineers with detail, she keeps these updates brief—what the client will be looking for and when. By alerting the engineers, she improves her chances of getting their complaints and suggestions before and not after the fact.

Keeping the other parties involved increases their commitment to the process. If they seem confused, check in with them and give them an update. If they appear left out, make sure they realize they have as much information as anyone else does. And when the process bogs down, highlight the progress so that everyone focuses on it rather than on the temporary setbacks. Even daunting problems seem solvable when everyone is equally engaged.

Work to Keep the Dialogue Going

In real estate, location is everything. In negotiations, some people think, timing is everything. When Ann Douglas studied labor negotiations back in the early 1960s, she noticed that everyone seemed to agree when the time had come to settle.[6] At that moment the tone and tenor of the negotiation changed. People spoke faster. They didn't break for meals. Everyone focused on reaching a settlement, and generally they did reach one.

The longer we stay in a negotiation, the more likely agreement becomes. Sometimes the participants just wear each other down and grasp at any out to escape. Or, having expended so much time and energy, they consider it ridiculous to come away with nothing. The dilemma is somewhat akin to being put on hold on the telephone. The recording tells you calls are answered in the order they are received. You stay on the line but agonize about when to hang up. The longer you are kept on hold, listening to Muzak, the surer you are that someone will pick up soon.[7] A similar conflict arises in negotiations. Do we continue to hang on or should we cut our losses? The longer we stay in the negotiation, the more that calculus shifts. Quitting becomes less and less attractive as an option. But time operates in positive ways as well.

Giving the relationship time to develop. Good working relationships are not built in a day. We can start out as wary adversaries, honestly believing that we have no other choice. But as long as we keep talking, there is always the possibility that our feelings about each other will change—and along with them our take on the issues. What seems unreasonable at one point in a negotiation can be accepted without question at another. Given some time, relationships can develop that shift everyone's view of the issues. For Diane issues became nonissues.

Diane, a research biologist with a business degree, saw opportunity knocking when Howard approached her to join his struggling biotech firm. Too eccentric and too opinionated to fit into a corporate mold, Diane liked the idea of working with Howard. Equally appealing was the prospect of a smaller place where she could exercise more direct control. Big, bold, and in a hurry, Diane is high energy from her corkscrew curls to her staccato sentences.

> Large corporations are not right for me. There are too many layers in the decision making. Particularly in biotech, the drug conglomerates can become the tail that wags the dog. Howard's small company seemed ideal. What's more, he needed me, or someone like me, desperately.

Diane had worked with Howard before, both when she was a marketing vice president at a large pharmaceutical company and, later, when she went out on her own as a consultant. "As a scientist, Howard bordered on brilliant. As a businessman, however, he was a complete washout. From one month to the next, he had no idea whether there would be money in the till to cover the rent," she recalls.

After taking a hard look at the company's revenue stream, the products on the assembly line, and those in development, Diane was convinced she could reverse the flow of red ink and raise some working capital. "But," she quickly points out, "if I was going to take the risk of a turnaround, I wanted some of the rewards up front."

Diane's demands were stiff but well within industry standards: the title of CEO, a 10 percent equity position in the company, and an annual salary of $100,000. "Howard freaked," she says. "What really sent him ballistic was the equity. I just couldn't understand his reaction. If I left within four years, he'd get the stock back anyway."

After several intense discussions, Diane began to get a clearer picture of Howard's concerns as opposed to the objections that he actually voiced.

> Money was not important to Howard. He was paying himself a pittance, less than anyone else was taking home and only a quarter of what I was requesting. The only thing that mattered to him was the success of the firm. But he was in total denial. He could not admit that the company was going in the drink. He needed a business partner, but he was afraid to give up any control.

The issue of stock was personal for Howard. To raise working capital, Diane planned to tap the venture capital markets. VC investments come with a hefty price tag—generally they take a 50 percent slice of the company and a seat on the board. Even if the turnaround were successful, Howard faced losing control of the company he founded. Nor was he anxious to surrender his title to a newcomer.

> After a few sessions I realized that I would have to backpedal. Working as a consultant for someone was not the same as being his or her partner. I was still an outsider to Howard.

Diane shifted her target salary and dropped the equity demand altogether, deferring the difference as a future bonus. "Unless I could scrape together sufficient working capital to fund our expansion, the stock was worthless anyway. The company would fold."

The most important revision in Diane's demands had nothing to do with dollars and cents or ownership. She asked that Howard set aside lunches on Fridays to talk about where they were headed.

> Howard was all set to have both of us write up a memo before each meeting. I quickly squelched that idea. I was afraid if we reduced everything to writing, we'd become captive of those ideas. I wanted these sessions to be more fluid, more a weighing of strategic possibilities.

Diane's request prevented parallel monologues from developing. After a rocky start, Howard and she realized how complementary their talents were. Neither wanted to build a company and surrender control to their financing source. Considering venture capital money too costly, Diane turned to her own networks and managed to raise all the necessary working capital through contacts in the scientific community.

No longer viewing herself as Howard's lifeline, bailing him out of a dismal situation, Diane thought of herself as his partner. The perspective, now mutual, changed over time. Diane did not have to negotiate to catch up to her original demands. Before she began looking for a second round of financing, Howard voluntarily met them. "He no longer worried about losing control," Diane says, "or about my jumping ship."

Diane and Howard began their contract negotiations in a rather traditional manner—with proposals and counterproposals. Together, they developed a new story for the company and how they could work with each other. After that, the outstanding contract issues resolved themselves. Giving each other time, neither of them lost anything along the way, and in the end they both gained.

Stories need time to come out. Relationships need time to develop. By probing and pushing, you can discover where agreement might be possible and on what terms. You can also discover the differences are irreconcilable, but in that case nothing is lost. Talks would have terminated anyway.

Using lulls to work back channels. Sometimes the moment is not ripe for agreement. Diplomats and trade delegates speculate on this question all the time: When is it possible to negotiate? The theory is that until the other side needs to negotiate it won't engage in serious talks and any effort to prompt action is wasted. That theory is only half right. You might not be able to come to agreement until the time is right, but you can keep the lines of communication open so that when everyone does get serious you don't have a lot of catching up to do. This caveat holds for our everyday negotiations as well. When Francesca began negotiating a pivotal joint venture for her firm, the climate was chilly at best. But she kept her communication channels open and eventually the outlines of a deal became visible to all.

Francesca heads strategic development for a software firm. Recently her firm decided it would grow by acquiring promising applications rather than developing them in-house from scratch. Francesca targeted a small start-up that had designed state-of-the-art software that enabled working women to control their kitchens from their office computers. The CEO gave Francesca the go-ahead, but the in-house director of research was less than enthusiastic. He constantly questioned the product's commercial viability. "Officially he maintained that the market was not large enough to justify the cost and the effort. Off the record, everyone knew he was opposed to any application his department had not developed internally."

Francesca retreated from actively promoting the acquisition. Instead, she began to work back channel with the software designers at the start-up and with industry analysts. Gradually she drew the director of research into these discussions. This gradual approach paid off. The data Francesca had assembled, with the active help of analysts and investment bankers, all pointed to the application's potential. It could easily become a big winner. The director of research began to see that acquisitions like the one Francesca proposed, far from curtailing his department's authority, would actually give it a larger playing field. As soon as he started talking about how much they should pay for the acquisition, they were ready to get down to serious business and negotiate terms with the start-up.

Kate compares the process of maintaining an ongoing dialogue to taking a step into the unknown. When you are not quite sure where you are going, you have to trust each other: "It was actually easier, in some ways, dealing with R&D when we were on opposite sides of the fence. We each knew exactly what to expect."

Dialogue opens up possibilities, but even when people trust each other, they can find it hard to let go of old attitudes and step into the unfamiliar. Frequently you find yourself forced to push in new directions when those old attitudes block you. And most people need time to recognize the benefits of changing old habits or established procedures.

Once Kate and the engineers really started talking, she realized that she was not the only one with a blind spot. Their boss, she concluded, was pretty much oblivious to the problems. As head of R&D, he was a force in the industry and one of the most confrontational negotiators in the company. Whenever Kate negotiated with him, it was always difficult. "He's funny and dynamic," Kate says. "Personally I like him very much. But we can reach a Mexican standoff with my being forceful and his being even more aggressive."

Because the new cooperation between marketing and R&D was so important and so fragile, Kate started inviting engineers on the development team to her meetings with their boss. For the first time, the head of R&D began to hear rumblings from "his" engineers, not from marketing, about the sacrosanct schedule. Privately, he considered his guys the best in the business and pushed them. They were perfectionists, and they delivered, usually on time. But now he began to wonder. Schedules were useful yardsticks, tangible and convenient, but were they the only measurement—or even the right one—for R&D? Things, Kate realized, were getting ripe for negotiation.

Given time, difficulties that once seemed insurmountable can disappear. Problems evolve into other problems. Even when significant differences remain, a growing rapport allows you to talk through them. Just keeping a dialogue going means that change remains a possibility.

Work to Get Everyone to "Own" the Problem

When we advocate for ourselves, we make strategic moves to give the other party ample reason to take our demands seriously. These "carrots" and "sticks" might bring our counterpart to the table ready to negotiate with us. The risk remains, however, that we will fall into those old adversarial patterns common in negotiation. If we want the negotiation to take a different direction—one in which collaboration and commitment to solving the problem together dominate—we need a process that puts our relationship with the other person on another footing. We need to take that additional step—toward discovering where and how we need each other. Only then can problems become joint challenges to be worked out together. With this step we admit that one side is not responsible for precipitating a crisis nor able to solve it alone.

Looking for links in the problem's history. Typically when we sit down to negotiate, everyone involved has an individual take on the problem and the best solution, and these can diverge radically. The distance in these viewpoints widens when the problem itself is the result of something we have done in the past. Blaming substitutes for dialogue as we try to lay responsibility for the problem on the other party, and he or she just as readily assumes it's our fault. It's tough to have a collaborative discussion when accusations are flying back and forth, even unspoken ones. To break this blaming cycle, it helps to reconstruct the history of the problem. Once we are clear on how sometimes inadvertent and quite innocent actions contributed to the present difficulties, we can begin to look beneath the convenient explanations, those hasty assumptions that pull against our seeing the problem as a common one we can work on together.

Helen, a systems whiz who works for a large accounting firm, had her work cut out for her when she ran up cost overruns on a consulting assignment. In order to renegotiate her firm's fee, she had to bring the client around to admitting they had both contributed to the overruns. The conflict could be resolved satisfactorily only if they both "owned" the problem. "I'm not a bean counter," she says. "And at first I ducked the issue. I don't like to talk about fees. Besides, I was mad."

> When we priced the contract, our figure was based on promises of all kinds of in-house assistance. This help never materialized. I had to assign extra people to the project, which put us over budget, and even then we could not finish on schedule.

Annoyed by the lack of support, Helen plowed ahead.

> The company's point person was a hard-nosed numbers guy who considered cost containment close to godliness. I knew getting paid for the additional staff was going to be a big problem.

The project's first phase involved a diagnosis of the company's existing computer systems and recommendations for future software. Helen's analysis was comprehensive, but when it came time to present her recommendations, they were sketchy at best.

The VP liked the proposal, at least as far as it went. He took no responsibility for the cost overruns. Helen was the expert. She had priced her team's services and would have to live with that figure.

> He was angry. He was not about to take ownership of the overrun issue or discuss an extension of the contract. He said his own staff could have done the work for less money in half the time.

Minutes into the meeting Helen realized two things. First, for him to see the situation in a different light, she would have to reorient the discussion, move it away from fixing blame for the overruns. Second, to be heard, everything she said or asked needed to be consistent with his view of himself as a savvy administrator in control of costs. That was the "face" he presented to others. Helen started by telling the story of the project from the beginning, using circular questions to draw him in.

> At key points as I was describing my understanding of what had happened, I asked if he agreed with my account. When we got to the promised support from his staff, I wondered what he would have done had he been in my position. Although he bawled me out for not letting him know what was going on, he was starting to see my dilemma. Then I asked whether the original promise of assistance was reasonable, given his staff's heavy workload.

Working through the project's history, they came to a shared understanding of how one action set off a comparable reaction. The cost overruns were neither her fault nor his. Both parties had acted in good faith. His people were busy, but the assignment was also more complicated than Helen had anticipated. Admission of mutual responsibility required both to take joint ownership of the problem. That acknowledgment pushed them toward a joint solution. They extended the contract, with more realistic cost parameters, and agreed to split the overrun charges. Common problems call for common solutions.

Posing questions that encourage the other person to rethink the problem. All too often in negotiations we don't put in the work that enables our counterpart to see the problem as a joint one. We tell her what is wrong and expect her to be persuaded by the elegance of our arguments. We take up a lot of space trying to convince him we are right and give him (and ourselves) little room to learn and reflect on the situation. As a result, the real problem gets defined within restricted and limiting boundaries. Kim pushed those limits in a negotiation with her boss about procedures in their community hospital. By posing deftly couched questions, Kim encouraged her boss to confront a problem that the boss was studiously avoiding.

New insurance guidelines mandated that the hospital could not collect fees even for minor procedures unless an attending physician was present. Kim's boss consistently turned a blind eye when these guidelines were ignored. Kim, in turn, worried that an audit would turn up the violation. The hospital's reimbursements would be cut and she would be blamed. Despite Kim's warnings, her boss remained unfazed.

> The violations were both unsafe and illegal, but the guidelines put my boss in a tough spot. She was under pressure to keep costs down and at the same time was faced with regulations that made that impossible. Our expenses for medical staff would skyrocket under the new guidelines.

The negotiations between Kim and her boss were poised for deterioration. Kim thought her boss was tolerating illegal, unsafe procedures. Her boss, on the other hand, dismissed Kim's concerns as nit-picking and self-serving. "To her," Kim says, "the chances of an audit were slim, and the increased costs made the risk worth taking." Rather than continue to press her boss on the disaster an audit would cause, in a "tell and sell manner," Kim began to pose questions rather than state facts.

> I started by asking her to assess the risks with me. Neither of us considered the probability of being audited particularly high. We agreed on that. But what would happen if we were wrong? What would be the consequences? As we went through them, we also agreed that they looked pretty bad. Not only would we be denied reimbursements, we would be savaged in the press and lose public confidence.

Kim's boss did not change her mind about the real problem overnight. She asked Kim to gather information on how the guidelines were implemented at other hospitals. That small step was a beginning. Gradually they began to look at the problem together, as one that affected them both but in different ways, and one for which they had to come up with a workable solution.

> *Kate knew from the start that she wanted to renegotiate the terms on which she and the engineers in R&D dealt with each other. Besides casting her as the bad news lady, the adversarial bickering accomplished*

nothing. What started as an effort on Kate's part to open a dialogue with R&D turned into a thorough rethinking of departmental relationships and standards for performance.

As Kate and the engineers began to experience the problem from each other's perspectives, they came to realize they had been focusing on the wrong thing. The source of their difficulty was not the client, or marketing, or R&D. Within their company's seemingly easygoing environment, they uncovered a core inflexibility that caused trouble for everyone. Internal standards and rigid performance criteria made it impossible not to leave someone dissatisfied, usually the client and marketing. As long as the engineers were evaluated on output time, responsiveness to client demands would suffer. The head of R&D, after listening to Kate and his engineers, broadened the limited conversations to a company-wide debate. What was good performance? How should they measure it?

The people you negotiate with seldom experience an epiphany and suddenly own a problem with you. It takes work to bring them along with you so that they recognize their part. A sense of interdependence cannot be forced on them. It must emerge from a deeper understanding that you are both implicated in the problem and must work on its solution together.

Cumbersome and time-consuming, collaborative negotiations create a context where mutual concerns can emerge. When people connect in a negotiation, they relate to each other differently. Because they can appreciate each other's situations and concerns, trust can build.

How the conversation is conducted is as important as *what* the conversation is about. Collaborative agreement making moves beyond the sometimes one-sided strategic exchange of information. Each action, each comment, has mutual implications that must be appreciated. Expecting cooperation, not domination or a forced compromise, bargainers can be more open in their exchange. Differences can be considered from various vantage points, not battled over. With more mutuality built into the discussion, understandings deepen and open up multiple paths to agreement. That's what the invisible work of relationship building makes happen in a negotiation.

PART III

Putting It All Together: Balancing Advocacy and Connection

7

CRAFTING AGREEMENTS

Advocacy and connection go hand in hand. If effective advocacy enables you to claim a place at the table and garners credibility for you and your demands, the relational skills of connection define the engagement that takes place. You cannot ignore either, but where you put the emphasis varies from one negotiation to the next and within a single negotiation. The balance struck is often a matter of personal preference, and bargainers tilt in one direction or another. Experience has taught some of the women in our stories to press hard for what they want and not give an inch, while others depend primarily on their ability to connect. Seldom, however, does any negotiation present a stark either/or choice between advocacy and connection.

The shadow negotiation is where masked attitudes and hidden agendas play out. The personal dynamic established there is defined by which strategic moves and connecting overtures you choose to use. But there is also an interaction between the shadow negotiation and the negotiation over the issues. This interplay affects the balance between advocacy and connection that you strike regardless of whether you personally lean in one direction or the other.

How advocacy and connection come to be blended does not depend solely on the person doing the mixing. Different circumstances and different issues demand different combinations. When you are haggling with a used-car dealer the mix will not be the same as the one you want when you are trying to negotiate changes in your department. The issues or problems involved impose their own discipline on your choice. So far we have focused on the impact that advocacy and connection have on the shadow negotiation. Now we want to turn our attention to the ways that the problem at issue affects your advocacy and relationship building.

When the actual issues in dispute are considered, agreement making is typically framed in one of two ways: as a contest to be won or lost or as a search for joint gains.[1] In win-lose negotiations, bargainers split up or distribute a resource. Usually a single resource is at stake, and money is involved in one form or another. Most of these negotiations end with some compromise. No one loses out entirely or wins everything.

This kind of bargaining is categorized as win-lose because the more one side wins the more the other loses and vice versa. When we buy a car, haggle for a rug in a bazaar, maybe even negotiate a salary, we are operating within this framework. We prefer to call the model not win-lose but *pushing*. As a label, "pushing" captures what actually happens in the negotiation. Each party wants to leave the table with the biggest share of the resources—whether that is the asking price for a house or the requested raise or an extra week of vacation. Since the resources to be divided are fixed, you want to push your agenda so that the final division goes your way. As a result, the balance in both the shadow negotiation and the negotiation over issues leans heavily toward the use of strategic moves and turns. You use the tools of effective advocacy to pressure the other party to make more concessions than he or she had intended.

Even in these "pushing" kinds of negotiations, there can be hidden costs in relying only on the tools of advocacy. You might go into a bargaining session knowing the price you are willing to pay or be paid and the costs associated with victory. But winning, getting the best deal, depends on how *best* is defined. The full price on the table is often not limited to a single resource such as money. Other currencies can be at stake—opportunity, goodwill, time, or the quality of a relationship. As a matter of fact, one of the mistakes negotiators consistently make is to assume that they are dealing with a "fixed pie" and that their only challenge is to figure out how to split it.

When negotiation is defined as a search for joint gains, connective skills become more important. Joint gains come from making trade-offs that benefit everybody and leave as little behind as possible. In the para-ble of the two oranges we told in the introductory chapter, for example, the expanded solution becomes not the rind or the juice but the whole or-ange. Neither the rind nor the juice goes to waste, and the needs of both sisters are met. *Packaging* is the term we use to describe this type of nego-tiation. Rather than push for what you want, you try to discover the differ-ent interests in play—rind or juice—and make a trade based on those differences. In other words, you come up with package deals. Discovering interests and needs requires that you connect at some level with the other person.

Based on our interviews with women negotiators, we think there is a third type of negotiation—one we call *mutual inquiry*.[2] Mutual inquiry builds explicitly on the open relationships and trust forged in the shadow negotiation. Pushing and packaging do not require fundamental changes in the relationship between bargainers for an agreement to be reached. Mutual inquiry initiates such change. As an empowered advocate, you are a full participant in the inquiry, and your invisible work of connection en-courages the other person's full participation. As communication becomes more open, appreciation for one another's concerns deepens. This in-creased understanding makes it possible to see where individual interests intersect with common concerns. When bargainers engage in mutual in-quiry, they may reevaluate what they want. In the process, they often re-define the problem itself.

There is nothing that automatically makes a negotiation one type or another. Buying a car appears to require only pushing. You want the best model for the lowest price. But things get more complicated once you have another car to trade in and financing options to consider. The visit to the car dealer now calls for some packaging. Negotiations with close col-leagues gravitate to mutual inquiry. Yet when time is short and decisions must be made, pushing usually takes over.

Most negotiations can be carried out in different ways. There are choices in which kind of process to pursue—pushing, packaging, or mu-tual inquiry—and in the balance you strike between advocacy and con-nection. Of course, the decision is not totally up to you. The other person might have a very different process in mind and shift in another direction. Then it might be necessary for you to recalibrate that balance.

Pushing

Pushing is the strategy you need when you find yourself in a win-lose negotiation. You and the person you are negotiating with are adversaries. You are adversaries not because of how you feel about each other but because of the structure of the negotiation. When two parties are bargaining over a single commodity such as money or time, what one wins the other loses, and there is little you can do to change that. When you are negotiating a contract and the only issue under discussion is price, inevitably someone is going to come out ahead of the game—or think the other party has. That's true even if the resource in question is split down the middle. Everyone involved can still feel okay about the outcome, but no individual bargainer can ever be sure that she or he couldn't have done better.

In pushing, you try to cut the best deal possible for yourself, recognizing that all the while your opponent will be doing the same thing. The tactical maneuvering begins with opening offers. These camouflage real desires. No one wants to be the first to put his or her cards on the table, and people almost always ask for more than they actually need. In the back of your mind, you might settle for a 5 percent raise, but you start with 8 percent. Once that 5 percent figure gets on the table, it is the most you can hope to achieve. Starting high (or low, depending on whether you are a seller or a buyer) gives you an opportunity to learn more about what the other side wants without giving away much information about your own bottom line.

Opening offers lead to counteroffers and a series of concessions that typically get smaller until you reach a point where compromise is possible. After you have made your opening offer, you try to be as persuasive as you can about the merits of your position and stress the reasons why the other side's demands are excessive. You make your concessions slowly and reluctantly, all the time exaggerating their value. You treat any concessions the other side offers as trivial and in no way a match for what you have put on the table. Power tactics, such as bluffs and threats, are common. Throughout the negotiation, you want to play your cards pretty close to the vest. If the other party learns what you are really looking for, she or he might use that information to extract even more concessions from you. Although compromise is inevitable in this kind of negotiation, you want to make sure you aren't the one doing all the compromising.

Pushing and the tools of advocacy. It is important to understand the rules of pushing. Otherwise you can end up with less than you deserve. Jessica, an architect, mastered the art of pushing to negotiate the best deal possible for her clients with a contractor. Jessica's clients in this commission were leasing new space for their art gallery. The three floors the gallery would occupy had been gutted down to the studs. As part of the lease, the landlord had already agreed to absorb certain costs under what's called a build-out allowance. The more work Jessica got the contractor to include in the build-out allowance, the more money her clients would have left to spend on the interior finishes.

Jessica preferred to rely on a small group of contractors whose work and word she trusted, but she had no choice in this negotiation. The contractor was married to the building owner's sister and came with the deal. She got her first hint that the negotiation would be adversarial when she overheard the contractor and his super joking: "No worries here, boss. Architect's not any bigger than a roll of drawings."

After reviewing Jessica's drawings, the contractor came up with a long list of items he categorized as extras that her clients would have to pay for. Jessica flatly refused. Her clients had signed the letter of intent on the basis of the landlord's verbal representations that those items would be included. The contractor protested. He didn't know anything about the landlord's promises. He certainly wasn't a party to them. Given the close relationship between the owner and the contractor, Jessica didn't trust his protestations at all: "I'd checked him out with other architects. Once I relented on any issue, it would be like opening Pandora's box. He'd push for concessions across the board."

Jessica remained firm. If that work wasn't included, she warned, her clients would think about rekindling negotiations with the owner of a building down the street. She also pushed the contractor hard on the cost of the finish work. By cutting out the padding on the "extras," she believed, they could easily reduce the construction costs by $14,000. The contractor resisted, pressing for concessions on each line item. He claimed the contract was already too thin. Fourteen thousand was impossible. Maybe he could squeeze out $5,000, but it was a long shot. Jessica, who was prepared for a prolonged battle, basically outlasted the contractor. She knew he needed to keep his crews busy, and this was a slow season. After two hours of haggling, all he said was, "Okay, but I'm not going to do a corner bead."

This negotiation—over a contract price—required pushing, and Jessica deployed all the tools of effective advocacy. Going into the talks, she knew exactly where she had leverage. Thoroughly prepared, she used her information strategically. Well aware that the contractor would not want his crews idle, she held him to the owner's previous promises. She let the contractor know she and her clients had an alternative—leasing a building down the street. That signal raised the stakes for him if he continued to resist her terms.

But what about connection? What role, if any, does it play in these "pushing" negotiations? It turns out it can have a major one. Jessica looked good to her clients. She had negotiated a great price. But she had to watch the contractor like a hawk. She could not trust him not to cut corners. "That extra supervision time was the trade-off I made when I pushed only on price." The contractor's reputation and his behavior tilted Jessica toward using forceful moves and turns: "Making concessions on price was not going to get a first-rate job out of this man. Hanging tough on the price was the best protection I could give my clients."

Blending in connection.   It is possible to push in a connected way. You can advocate for your interests forcefully and still promote them so that it is easy for the other party to acquiesce. Barbara used connected pushing in a situation where price (or money) was also the issue. She negotiated a good severance agreement by showing the hospital administrators exactly how they could give her what she wanted.

The community hospital where Barbara worked was downsizing, but for public relations reasons wanted to keep the number of nurses it laid off low. Barbara, an assistant vice president for nursing, looked at the downsizing as an opportunity. She had been thinking about going to graduate school. Rather than wait to be laid off, she agreed to resign, provided she received a lump-sum payment that would cover a year's expenses at school. But she knew that the lump sum she requested would set a dangerous precedent for the hospital. The administrators, she sensed, would worry that other nurses would demand the same deal. The hospital countered Barbara's proposal with an offer that halved her request and was roughly equivalent to what it would pay for outplacement services.

Knowing that the hospital needed to characterize any lump-sum payment in a way that did not create a precedent, Barbara proposed that the missing half be paid as a tuition reimbursement, a standard program for which she would be eligible if she remained on staff and did not leave voluntarily. Barbara was a clear winner here. She got exactly what she wanted. At the same time, she made the solution painless, even attractive, for the hospital administrators. They paid her more than they first intended, but the figure did not go beyond their liabilities had she remained. Equally important, the solution allowed them to avoid bad publicity and sidestep a disastrous precedent.

Pushing has a taint associated with it. Most commentary on negotiation mentions pushing tactics with a warning attached: Unscrupulous people might use them against us. But being able to push effectively is an important skill for all negotiators. Despite whatever collaborative inclination we may have, some deals, by their very nature, require pushing, and some people drive us to push simply to protect our interests.

Packaging

In pushing, you stake out a specific position on an issue. For example, you demand a 10 percent raise. But you might be motivated to make that demand by a whole host of reasons. You might want recognition for a job well done, your child care costs might be escalating, or you might feel you are losing ground to others who are paid more. Different interests such as these provide the raw materials for packaging. By focusing on them, you broaden the discussion from a single issue. The idea is to create more bargaining room than generally exists when everyone sticks to fixed positions. You might not be able to get that 10 percent raise, but there might be other good ways to compensate you and make up the difference—a bonus, a new office, a new title, more time off.

Gains are realized because the people involved in the negotiation are different and have different wants, needs, and goals. Some things matter a great deal to one negotiator but not to another. Preferences, capabilities, experience, and beliefs vary greatly. These differences can be converted into currencies of exchange and traded.[3] They can be used to construct options that sweeten the deal for the other party and satisfy you at the same time. If, for instance, something is important to Susan but doesn't really matter to Carol, Carol might be willing to give it up in return for something she really wants.

Mary Parker Follett gives us a nice example of how interests can be explored to come up with a creative package deal. She was sitting in Harvard's cavernous Widener Library, and someone had left the window open. The breeze was welcome, but it blew her papers all around. The solution? "We opened the window in the next room, where no one was sitting. This was not a compromise. . . . We both got what we really wanted. I did not want a closed room, I simply did not want the North wind to blow directly on me; likewise the other occupant did not want that particular window open, he merely wanted more air in the room."[4]

Packaging like this converts a negotiation from an adversarial contest over a single issue to a problem-solving activity. As different interests emerge, the prospects for new arrangements increase. Rather than fight it out over a single issue, bargainers work through various solutions until they come up with one that meets most, if not all, of their needs. The stark alternative of the window closed or open gives rise to the solution of opening another window. Communications skills come to the fore as negotiators explore how their interests can be meshed in a package deal. Follett's solution hinged on the discovery that her Widener companion objected to a stuffy room but was basically indifferent on how to increase the ventilation.

Tilting toward connection in packaging. The problem solving implicit in packaging works to the advantage of bargainers who dislike confrontation and are more comfortable using their ability to connect with people to work out a good solution. It is also the strategy of choice when pushing is out of the question, when the cost of alienating the other person is too high. Janet manages the systems group for a large pharmaceutical company. Because her group supplies an internal support function, selling its services to the firm's many departments, negotiations over payment for those services are ripe for haggling over time and money. Janet struggles against being held captive to departmental calls for low pricing and fast implementation schedules. The department heads want the best system for the least cost and they want it yesterday.

Janet's negotiations could easily turn into pushing contests but for one thing: Janet's group provides a service to the company. She must maintain the group's profitability, but she cannot leave any dissatisfaction in her wake. To avoid this pitfall, Janet has become adept at developing creative packages in her dealings with the department heads. In fact, she has built her reputation throughout the company on her ability to make constructive trade-offs.

A good illustration comes from a negotiation over the updating of a unit's inventory system. Ted, the unit head, submitted a proposal to Janet's group, and over the course of several preliminary sessions Ted and Janet scoped out the work. They were now ready to begin the real negotiations over pricing and scheduling. Ted needed the system up and running as soon as possible but was under pressure to keep costs down. Janet, of course, wanted her group to be paid a fair price for its services and would prefer more time. Her group was already stretched. As Janet and Ted discussed the project, their different priorities surfaced. Janet immediately recognized the makings of a trade. Since time was crucial to Ted and resources were limited for her, she suggested that Ted's unit pay a premium to get the system up sooner. With additional resources, Janet could assign more software engineers to the project. She knew some of her staff would welcome the overtime. But Janet did not stop there. She proposed that Ted's people do some of the routine preparation to keep the additional costs as low as possible.

In the end Ted chose Janet's first option. He agreed to allocate more funds to get the system up and running. Janet, in turn, committed two engineers to the project during the design phase so that the system was ready to go on-line in three months. They would then return to normal operations during implementation.

Package deals like these trade on differences in interests. The challenge in packaging is to peel back those interests layer by layer. The information you discover enables you to continue to float options that satisfy you and the other party. Ted, for example, cared more about having the inventory system in place than the marginal costs incurred in speeding the design work. The trick in packaging is to access this kind of information and incorporate it into your thinking. In negotiations like these, effective advocacy gets your point across, but it is the connection skills you use that allow you to discover the specific packaging that the other party finds acceptable.

The discovery process, however, can be a challenge. Sometimes the other person is reluctant to reveal much about her interests. If she assumes she is engaged in an adversarial, win-lose game, she is going to disclose as little as possible. Direct questions about what she wants can provoke a hostile response: "Why do you want to know?" Sometimes the other person is not sure about what he wants or what would satisfy him, and vigorous probing would only back him into a position he does not really prefer.

People's interests are complex, interweaving personal and career concerns. Usually they are reluctant to talk about them. When pressed, they often respond with a generalization: "We want to do what is best for the organization" or "I just want to be treated fairly." These amorphous statements are of little help in coming up with good package solutions. Because they are open to misinterpretation, they can actually hamper any understanding of what each side really wants. It is important to be as specific as possible in your probing of interests. You can ask general questions at first to break the ice. But answers to questions such as "Why are you interested in this issue?" or "What are your major areas of concern?" or "What are the key things you need from an agreement?" probably won't reveal much.

Global questions are usually less helpful than more targeted ones. "What about this particular option works for you?" produces a more focused response than "Why do you want this agreement?" Less-direct methods are just as useful, particularly when the other person seems suspicious about the inquiry to begin with. Propose various scenarios and get her to respond to them. Parsing those responses together often reveals the interests she cares about and the ones she is willing to trade.

Using advocacy in packaging. The skills of connection are needed to uncover the differences in interest you use to put together creative trades; they can also alter the bargainers' relationship so that various options are considered and not immediately rejected. Although these skills are of enormous value in coming up with a creative package, the demand for effective advocacy does not diminish in packaging. Even a clever package deal can be difficult to sell, and the other party must be convinced that a particular package meets her needs.

Sue Ellen had just been appointed executive director of the Center for Cross-Cultural Communications. This was the college's first experience with such a program, and no one in the administration had a clear idea of what Sue Ellen should be paid. Sue Ellen, on the other hand, went to her first meeting with the new provost prepared to push hard for a specific salary level.

My colleagues and I had put a great deal of thought and planning into launching the center. Our financial worries were behind us. I knew we

were about to get a huge grant from a foundation, although the terms
had not been finalized. I was really excited about the center's future. At
my first meeting with the provost, my optimism just bubbled over. While
I talked, the provost sat there—emanating skepticism. She simply did
not believe a word I said. I could picture vividly the thoughts behind that
impassive face. I was exaggerating, attempting to put one over on her.
No one in his or her right mind would award that much money to a new
program. The university would end up financing the whole thing.

At that moment any negotiation about salary was risky for Sue Ellen.
She quickly realized that it would result in a bad deal for her. She tabled
any effort to negotiate her salary and went to work without settling the
money issues with the provost. Her friends thought she was crazy, but Sue
Ellen believed she would do better in the long run if she proved to the
provost that the center would be a success and that she would be a big
part of that success.

Sue Ellen's ability to offer the provost a package deal, in effect, hinged
on her credibility. Because the provost needed to have confidence in Sue
Ellen's leadership, Sue Ellen moved strategically to demonstrate that the
center would add to the college's prestige and that her contribution was
pivotal to its success.

Everything I did—the lunches I had with her, the ways I raised funds,
sought out projects—was aimed at proving what a good thing the center
was. How terrific I was. She wasn't going to pay me what I wanted to be
paid until I gave her an incentive—and that incentive was proof that I
could make the center a success. I also made it clear that I was not
going to work for longer than three months without an agreement on my
salary. At the same time, I made it my business to get key people at the
university to tell her about me. She was new, I wasn't, and these people
carried a lot of weight.

Once the foundation grant came through, the provost's skepticism
began to dissolve. Sue Ellen's advocacy allowed her to explore with the
provost how the center's goals complemented the mission of the college.

Sue Ellen used what she learned about the provost's priorities to formulate options on how she might be paid. Under one package, she pro-

posed a low base salary and a sliding scale tied to the grants she received and the fieldwork and training programs she conducted. Under the other, she would be paid a higher salary that included a fixed fee for fieldwork and training. Sue Ellen would have been happy with either option. She was not worried about putting some of her salary at risk. She knew she could attract research projects and build attendance for her training sessions.

Later the provost told Sue Ellen that the choice of two payment schemes helped her focus on which would work best for the college. She elected to go for the sliding scale. If the programs materialized, there would be additional revenues to pay Sue Ellen. If not, the college had limited its financial commitment.

Blending advocacy and connection in packaging. Packaging like Sue Ellen's is a form of problem solving that builds options from differences in interests and priorities. But just coming up with a package deal does not insure that the other party will agree to it. The elegance of the solution alone may not be persuasive enough. Even creative suggestions can encounter resistance, and this point brings us back to the shadow negotiation. Unless the other person recognizes the benefits of making a deal, even ingenious solutions fall on deaf ears. For a package deal to be considered, you must hold out incentives—as an advocate—and at the same time—as a connected negotiator—create a climate in which the proposed idea is heard as an option that improves the outcome for the other side.[5]

The essence of packaging is to uncover as much as you can about the other party's situation so that you can come up with creative ways of meeting both your interests. Although this objective seems obvious, it is not always easy to achieve. No matter how clever you have been, you still have to deal, at some point, with what's included in the package and what's left out. In other words, packaging calls on both effective advocacy and connecting skills, and the balance can differ.

Elyse discovered just how finely advocacy and connection needed to be meshed when she was asked to take over a section of the magazine where she worked but was offered no additional help. She agreed to assume the added responsibilities for the next issue, subject to an important proviso. At the end of the month, she and the publisher would revisit the staff question.

The meeting with the publisher turned into a masterful balancing act between advocacy and connection. Elyse first concentrated on how difficult the past month had been. Having been a longtime contributing editor, Elyse suddenly found herself in charge of a separate department and with all the added responsibility that entailed. She had to decide which stories to run with what artwork, check that the ad revenues were sufficient, and make sure everything was ready by press time. She had too few resources at her disposal, and the publisher had grossly underestimated the time she would have to spend coordinating the various functions. To continue, she insisted, she needed at least two additional staff members.

Then she switched tracks. She started to appreciate the publisher's situation: "The editor-in-chief had died suddenly, and the publisher was in a real bind." The magazine was rudderless on the editorial side, and the publisher was keeping a sharp eye on costs, fearing a drop in readership. "When I told him we all missed the editor," Elyse says, "but he probably more than anyone, he began to open up." The publisher recognized full well that everyone was overloaded but did not want to take on additional people at a time when subscriptions might drop precipitously. "Would I settle, he asked, for some part-time help in-house and maybe outsourcing the rest of the work?" The deal was a good one for Elyse and the publisher.

In each of these examples of packaging, a different balance is struck between advocacy and connection. Where the emphasis falls colors the shadow negotiation and, in turn, defines the agreement eventually reached. Strategic moves and turns keep your interests front and center. Basic to pushing, they continue to be important in packaging. You are, in effect, an advocate of various packages. But it is through the exercise of your relational skills that you fashion the package with the best chance of being accepted.

Mutual Inquiry

Negotiations involve at least two people, so they are by definition a mutual experience. But how the process is actually experienced is not necessarily mutual. In pushing and packaging, responsibility rests with individuals to make demands or propose deals. In pushing, the burden falls primarily on advocacy as one side states a position and the other responds. The bargaining goes back and forth until some compromise or stalemate is reached. Self-interest also drives packaging. The negotiator in search of joint gains finds out as much as possible about the other side's interests so that she can enhance the package deal if further inducements are necessary. Package deals, if well constructed, leave everyone better off, even though some people may not do as well as others. In packaging, the balance between advocacy and connection is more even than in pushing. Connection facilitates but does not dominate.

With mutual inquiry the balance shifts to connection. Inquiry in the context of mutuality is more than trying to solicit useful information about the other party's interests or bottom line. The process is fluid as those involved listen together, learn together, and make their agreements together. The learning that occurs transforms the dynamics at work. The focus moves from individual advocacy to mutual engagement. Interests and problems acquire greater definition through open discussion. Even when bargainers come to the table with fixed notions about where their interests lie, as they engage in mutual inquiry they can rapidly revise those notions and see the problem in a totally different light. Solutions can then be worked out together, not proposed by individual participants to be either rejected, countered, or accepted by the others.

The need for effective advocacy does not disappear in mutual inquiry. You cannot engage in mutual inquiry unless you hold up your side of "mutual." But mutual inquiry moves beyond an instrumental concern for the other party, beyond enlightened self-interest. There is an expectation that everyone in the negotiation will be influenced by the others and be available emotionally as well as analytically. Mutual inquiry negotiations are fluid precisely because the participants expect to learn from and be influenced by the other person's perspectives. And, knowing more, they often change their minds—not only about what would be an acceptable agreement but also about the problem that needs resolving.

Mutual inquiry builds explicitly from the relationships we develop as we negotiate. The process is rooted in the belief that there is only so much you can discover about another person's wants, needs, or feelings without that person's active participation. Questions are asked in ways that make it easy for people to talk about their situations, to tell their stories. Opinions are expressed not as categorical statements but as part of an ongoing dialogue that presents ideas for consideration and further probing. For many, only by talking through their needs and interests in a supportive context do they come to know what those interests really are.

Carrie headed public relations for a large mutual fund in Boston—until she was fired. This experience convinced Carrie that her financial and mental well-being depended on being in control and independent.

> The real slap was that they fired me two months before my pension would fully vest. I promised myself that I would never again put myself in a position where someone else could mess up my bonus by a whim or kick me out without a single complaint ever being filed.

There was a silver lining to her dismissal, however. She immediately started her own firm, taking several clients with her. But being fired left an indelible mark. She wanted to be in control and vowed never to let an organization or other people have that kind of power over her. This determination shaped all the strategic decisions about her company. Then came a phone call from her major client. "Carrie," he said, "I'm paying you so much, you should be working for me full-time. I want you to think about that before we meet next week."

Carrie sweated out the week. "I cannot do this," she thought. "I won't feel safe having just one client. That's as bad as being at the mercy of a corporation." Never before had Carrie discussed her motivations or reservations with a client. Whatever the cost, she simply produced what the client demanded. But this was not a matter of getting a client exposure in the *Wall Street Journal* or *Barron's*. This situation was personal, and this particular client had given her a big boost when she most needed it. She felt she owed him an explanation for her refusal.

> I told him everything. My history with the corporation, how unfairly I had been treated. I told him I simply could not put all my eggs in one basket ever again.

He nodded, then was silent for a while.

> "I didn't realize," he said finally. "I probably should have. Even if I could force this issue, which I clearly cannot, you'd be miserable. What really bothers me is that everyone knows how much I'm paying you. I need them at least to think I'm your most important client. How do we do that?"

Rather than severing the relationship, her client offered an unexpected solution.

> Did I think I could put in a separate phone line for him? I felt like asking him how high he wanted me to jump.

Carrie's fears about being captive to one client blocked her ability to see any possibility of a creative agreement. It also muddied her reading of her client's motivations. "I saw the outcome in black or white. He wanted more control. If I didn't go along with what he asked, I was out. I didn't realize how much he valued my services." By letting her client in on her story, Carrie made her problem his. From a proposal (his) that could be either accepted or rejected (by her), they reached a place where there wasn't any his or hers.

The negotiation not only transformed Carrie's relationship with her most important client, it changed the way she dealt with other clients.

> For me, the most difficult part of starting my own business was negotiating the fees. Beforehand, I would decide in my head what services were needed and what the fee should be. Then I would practice in front of a mirror until I didn't think I was looking guilty.
>
> I would then announce my fee and not budge. Sometimes I would get the clients, other times I would lose them. This negotiation changed all that. I am much less inclined to impose a set arrangement.

Carrie now designs her fee arrangements collaboratively, even with new clients. As they come to a better understanding of what they expect from each other, they can build an agreement that is tailored to the sort of relationship they envision.

In the strategic game of pushing and packaging, most people are reluctant to ask for help or reveal too much. If they show where they are vulnerable, they believe, they will be inviting someone to take advantage of them. That premise works in certain situations. You probably don't want to tip your hand to a car dealer or a prospective buyer for your condo. But the premise doesn't hold as a general rule. Many people, women in particular, consider asking for help and giving it basic to how they do their work and support each other. Mutual inquiry builds on this instinctive helpfulness.[6] It's okay to admit you need help. It's okay to give help. It is also a given in mutual inquiry that people have different contributions to make to the negotiation. Even the language changes. "How can I help?" is a very different question than "What are you looking for?"

A shared sense of responsibility and involvement grows when people feel they can contribute to solving a problem and not just produce or react to a solution. Their relationship changes and that affects how they see the problem they need to solve. It is in this way that problems—and, ultimately, outcomes—come to be transformed by mutual inquiry.

Midcourse Corrections

What happens in the shadow negotiation always intersects with the way bargainers discuss specific issues, and those issues in turn impact the tenor of the shadow negotiation. However clearheaded bargainers try to be in assessing a problem and evaluating proposals, their own as well as those of others, they do not always succeed. They bring to the negotiation biases and feelings, memories of what has worked for them in the past and what has been less successful. These feelings can mask or distort the discussion of the issues. Sometimes the real issues never surface; they are disguised in other terms.

We all know how important it is to prepare for a negotiation. We think through every possible scenario that comes to mind. But we are not omniscient and the other side can have a surprise or two in store for us. We go into a negotiation expecting a rational discussion and find ourselves in the midst of emotional turmoil. We prepare for a tough encounter only to find the other person distinctly amenable and open to new approaches. Successful negotiation requires a certain amount of flexibility. In other words, you have to be ready to change course when the situation dictates.

From packaging to pushing. Hidden agendas lurk in the shadow negotiation. These agendas are quite distinct, but no less powerful than admitted interests, however astutely those might be probed. When gender is the hidden agenda, efforts at packaging or mutual inquiry can be rebuffed for apparent but nondiscussable reasons. Under these circumstances, a negotiator can be forced to switch to a pushing strategy. These undiscussables derailed Sharon's attempt to reach a mutual agreement when she pursued the job of principal for an upper school.

Sharon had been head of a girls' school, K through 12, for four years when it merged with a boys' school. She was the only sitting school head who was going to continue on after the merger. The trustees had selected an outside person to be headmaster. "The decision," in Sharon's opinion, "was exactly the one the trustees should have made." That appointment was not the issue in dispute between Sharon and the board. Sharon wanted to head the upper school, while the trustees were pressing her to take over the middle school. She knew, as did the trustees, that "in our society prestige goes with older kids."

For the merger to succeed, Sharon believed, it had to be a true merger rather than an absorption of the girls' school. Quite apart from her personal stake in the issue, her appointment as head of the upper school would make a symbolic statement. Focused on what was best for the school, Sharon calmly tried to turn the board's challenges back to that central issue.

> The board members raised all kinds of objections that had nothing to do with education. I'd assure them I was quite capable of stopping a fight between two teenage boys and then try to move the discussion back to the educational and institutional issues. I understood something about what they were feeling. They were worried that appointing a woman would diminish the school's prestige. I tried to be flexible. I offered to accept a contract for two years. Then we would be able to test my performance. They rejected that proposal and the other ideas I put to them.

Even though Sharon did not agree with the reasons underlying the trustees' objections, she tried to address their fears through the options she presented to the board. Despite her persistence and widespread support among alumnae and faculty, Sharon was gradually being backed into a corner.

> Only when I realized that the trustees were dead set against me for no clear reasons that they would state did I stop trying to engage them. After that I just kept restating my position, clearly.

Fatigue, stress, and frustration began to take a toll.

They continued to call me at home at all hours of the night, trying to
persuade me not to go after the job. While all this was going on, I was
still running the school. One night I was so tired, I felt like just saying,
Fine I'll take the middle school. Then my husband cautioned me. It was
the smartest advice I've ever been given: "Make them say the words.
Don't give it to them. Make them say the words. That you cannot have
that job." Ultimately, it worked. I got the job.

When push came to shove, the trustees could not verbalize their true
reasons. They had framed the negotiation as a power struggle with a gendered leitmotif, but no one wanted to admit it publicly. Over the course of
the negotiation, the trustees' continual rejection of Sharon's proposals
forced her to push back, harder and harder. At the outset, she experi-
mented with creative packages and made connected overtures to ease the
discussion toward mutual inquiry. But as the position of the trustees hardened, she did not hesitate to hold firm and push her own agenda. That deliberate choice is what effective advocacy is all about.

From pushing to mutual inquiry.   Midcourse corrections can as easily
lead in the other direction — from an emphasis on pushing to a discovery
of mutuality. Bringing more voices into the negotiation precipitated a fundamental change in Lori's dealings with her firm's most important customer.

Lori's promotion to the hospital account was a mixed blessing. When
Lori settled into her new job, she discovered her company had rarely
emerged from contract negotiations with the hospital with a favorable fee
schedule. The hospital management constantly whittled away at the profit
margin, her firm always on the losing end. The relationship was intrinsi-
cally adversarial. When the contract came up for renewal, Lori realized
that redirecting this dynamic would be difficult. The health care environment was competitive, highly political, and prone to constant change. She
had one advantage.

On a day-to-day basis, my relationships on the floors and with the
various departments were good. Traditional boundaries separating
customer and vendor were largely absent. The hospital's operation was

decentralized, cross-functional. There weren't many strict lines of
authority and so I could wander around and see what was happening.

The team in charge of negotiating the new contract for the hospital
was not nearly so cordial. Although satisfied with the quality and level of
service Lori's firm provided, members of the team concentrated on ex-
tracting further price concessions. Lori resisted. She could not reduce
charges further without seriously damaging her company's bottom line.

Lori set out to move the discussion away from the single issue of price.
At first she focused on showing the team the added value in her firm's services. With several carefully executed strategic moves, she began to foster
coalitions with her day-to-day contacts in the various departments while
at the same time making sure that as many influential people as possible
knew about the renewal agreement. But a peculiar thing happened as Lori
began to walk the halls, talking to people on the floors and in their offices.
Because the organization was so decentralized, no one outside top management had much of a sense of how everything fit together. On the floors,
they only knew the problems they had. As she made her rounds, Lori got
her departmental contacts to open up.

After I had a feel for each department's needs, I would follow up with a
written report outlining their difficulties and possible ways of working
together to solve them.

What started out as a search for a package deal, as an effort to shift the
negotiation away from a fixation on price and pushing, turned into something very different when Lori consolidated her department write-ups.
Her information gathering had already sparked debate within the departments. Complaints that "there must be a better way to do this systems
stuff" now became common. Lori's consolidated report brought unrecognized needs out into the open and provided a context for expanding discussions across departments.

Previously isolated because of the hospital's decentralized decision
making and organization, each department saw a given problem as peculiar to it and as something it had to solve on its own. Once Lori's report began circulating, the departments could see that they shared common
problems that needed a more systemic solution. Lori started floating

ideas about how her firm's expertise in systems and forms management in complex organizations could be brought to bear on the hospital's communication problems.

Before Lori started walking the halls, price was the only way the hospital could define the problem. What she learned about the deeper issues broadened the focus. Opposing, adversarial positions yielded to mutual inquiry. The initial question on the table—the terms of a contract renewal—gave way to a discussion of how the hospital's forms and systems management could be revamped. The collective sense of the issues at stake allowed the systemic problems to surface. These required a solution that had little to do with price or even clever packaging. Instead of being forced to accept or reject additional price concessions, Lori negotiated an expanded contract.

Pushing, Packaging, Mutual Inquiry, and the Shadow Negotiation

Pushing, packaging, and mutual inquiry are models for making agreements. Which process you choose depends on the situation and personal preference. It is also conditioned by what takes place in the shadow negotiation, where bargainers work out how they feel about each other. Their interactions here determine how open they are when they discuss the issues dividing them, how candidly they talk about what matters to them and what they really want. It is in the shadow negotiation, as bargainers relate to each other, that they judge just how willing they are to participate in the problem solving of packaging, much less in the dialogue of mutual inquiry.

Karen was involved in a negotiation that could have played out under any of our three scenarios: pushing, packaging, or mutual inquiry. Each approach calls on advocacy and connection differently and produces very different outcomes. Karen actually tried all three approaches sequentially, shifting the balance between advocacy and connection as she went along.

Karen is something of a contradiction in terms—a bubbly and enthusiastic workaholic. Only in her mid-thirties, she had landed a dream job at a think tank in Washington. Two weeks into her tenure, she stumbled badly in a negotiation with the institute's major contractor. She took Sam, a big, smiling man, at face value, and he proceeded to exploit her lack of familiarity with the institute's past practices to make a great deal for himself.

That first exposure left a bad taste in Karen's mouth. Convinced that Sam's good-natured joviality was all show, she distrusted his numbers and disliked him personally. She was not about to have a repeat performance the next time around. Whatever it took, she would make up for her dismal results the previous fall.

Karen was the first woman to be appointed co-director of the Strategic Information Institute (SII). The institute's programs, marketed through Sam's company, offered programs on strategic modeling to individuals and corporations in the information-technology sector. The success of the institute's basic program had encouraged Karen and her co-director, Rick, to develop advanced seminars for anyone who had completed the introductory course. Sam, who paid SII a fixed fee for each SII program he handled, saw the expanded offerings as another potential source of revenue. The issue on the table was the fee arrangements for the new program. Although the advanced program made sense for both parties, the negotiations did not begin on an auspicious note.

> We met at our usual place for breakfast. Sam handed Rick and me his proposal. After we had a chance to look it over, it was clear to both of us that Sam intended to pay us considerably less for this program than we got for the basic course. Rick asked Sam what was going on. He thought Sam was taking advantage of us. From Rick's vantage point, the institute was the goose that laid golden eggs for Sam and his company.

At this moment, Karen could have pursued the negotiation in three ways. She could have followed Rick's lead and *pushed* for a greater share for the institute. Alternatively, she could have tried to discover what Sam wanted and come up with a *package deal* that suited everyone. She could also have engaged Sam in *mutual inquiry*, although with the hostilities so high that was an improbable approach to take right then.

Karen's negotiation: the pushing option. As soon as Rick and Karen read through Sam's proposal, the stage was set for a win-lose negotiation. Sam had staked out an adversarial position by putting such a ridiculously low number on the table. Predictably, Rick and Karen reacted.

Rick negotiates right from the gut. If he thinks he's being treated unfairly, off he goes. That's what happened. He started to pull his things together, getting ready to leave.

Karen sat quietly while Rick attacked Sam. She was even more cynical. She considered Sam's proposal "just more of his double-speak: talking about partnership and making a lowball offer."

On the defensive, Sam immediately countered. His costs were high. He was taking all the risks. He deserved a bigger slice of the revenues. Rick got up to leave. "Fine," Rick said. "If this proposal is the deal, then it's off. Forget the new product offering—we'll stick with what we have or get another contractor."

At this point Karen took another look at where they were headed in this contest of wills. To her mind, Rick's options left them worse off. SII could end up without a contractor or the new course offering. The prospects had to be equally unappealing to Sam. The best he could hope for was to maintain the present arrangements, with no possibility of increasing his revenues from another program. At worst, he would lose the SII account altogether. Karen set aside Sam's numbers and made a case for greater flexibility. In the early years, no one guessed SII's course would be so successful. The costs and the risks were high. Those days were over, she argued, but Sam was still taking a big cut. The new course would probably have the same life cycle. Sam countered that there were no guarantees that history would repeat itself.

They agreed to table any new offerings for the moment. To increase revenues, they decided to offer more sessions of the introductory course. Everyone felt okay, but not great, about this outcome. Each got something—more revenue from the additional sessions. If no one was dissatisfied, no one was really satisfied, either. In a sense, this is an example of what Mary Parker Follett called a lose-lose outcome. The real issue—how to put on and market the new course—was not settled.

Karen's negotiation: the packaging option. Rick had picked up his papers and was getting ready to leave. Karen's efforts to convince Sam of the need for greater flexibility had been unsuccessful. Instead of pushing further in this direction, Karen changed course and tried to come up with some creative packaging.

I'm not sure what clicked for me, but I started to ask myself: "Why are
we doing this? We both want to make a deal on the new offering. Why
isn't it working?" Something was going on that I just didn't understand.
Why was Sam resisting so hard? Rick was really ticked off. He wasn't
joking when he threatened to get a new contractor.

Karen came right out and asked Sam why the revenue-sharing scheme
for the new program was so skewed in his favor. His explanation was simple. He could only recruit participants from the pool that had already at-
tended the basic course. He was worried that the yield would be low and
he wouldn't make his numbers.

What caught Karen's attention was the risk profile that Sam's remarks revealed. She had not realized the new advanced program was more risky for
Sam than the basic offering. With the entire pool of possible attendees for
the advanced course limited to the 10,000 people who had already completed the introductory course, he had no flexibility in his marketing. Karen
suggested they meet again after she had a chance to talk with Rick. The next
day she gave Sam a proposal. Because he was concerned about the new program's risk, she suggested that the institute's share start low but ratchet up as
the number of seminar participants increased. When enrollments reached a
certain level, SII would begin taking in more. This skewing compensated
SII for its willingness to accept less during the earlier stages. Sam acknowledged the concession, but objected to the rapid ratcheting. Karen then responded by adjusting the proposal—postponing the point at which SII's
share increased but raising its percentage when that threshold was crossed.

The solution produced gains for both sides. The new course would
move forward. Although it would not return as much revenue in the early
stages as Karen and Rick had hoped, it was likely to generate considerable
cash flow in the future—for both Sam and SII. The scheme addressed
Sam's risks and the institute's interest in diversifying its programs and
bringing in more revenue. But Karen and Sam were still preoccupied with
who would get what and when. Sam pushed Karen for a slower ratcheting,
while Karen argued for a higher payout in the later stages.

Karen's negotiation as mutual inquiry. Karen started the negotiation
with Sam with a negative attitude about him as a person and as a negotiator. But as Sam began his litany of objections to the ratcheting in the package deal she proposed, she kept thinking:

I'm still missing something here. We haven't talked enough. This scheme works for both of us, but Sam is really upset. He's not just stonewalling about the money. Maybe I don't understand his business.

This train of thought prompted Karen to ask Sam to talk about his business in more detail.

Well, he did. He told us a lot more. In order to cover his costs, including the institute's fixed fee, he needed to bring in 105 attendees each time a course was run. At the start of a mailing cycle, he could never predict the yield. If the numbers looked low, he'd send out more direct mail. Based on a formula of one per thousand, he knew he could fill the sessions if he sent out enough mail.

Interesting, Karen thought. Sam's problem wasn't just the fee structure. He couldn't fill the new course with a direct mail campaign. He could only approach previous participants. If not enough signed up, he was out of pocket. Karen mentioned that she was only beginning to see how risky the advanced program was for him.

That comment really set him off. He felt he had always borne all the risks. When we started, he said, nobody knew the programs would be so successful. He underwrote them. Now that they had succeeded, not only was the institute unappreciative, we wanted more.

Sam's unguarded remarks brought to the surface a critical element driving the shadow negotiation. Both parties considered the other greedy and interpreted their actions through that screen. Sam's story pulled Rick into the conversation.

The whole mood changed. Sam stopped being so defensive. Rick and I stopped being so negative. We both now realized that Sam had a lot riding on our work together.

Karen inquired more deeply into Sam's business—not just the nuts and bolts but why he made the decisions he did. Her appreciative inquiries broke the impasse. They surfaced the resentments that prevented them from dealing with each other or the problem. Through mutual inquiry all three discovered the real incentives they had to work out an agreement together. They also transformed the problem. No longer focused on the fee arrangements for the new course, they concentrated on the methods they could use to fill the classes. That meant moving outside the limited pool of people who had completed the basic course. But how?

Karen came up with the idea of a two-day course that created "instant alumni." Instead of promoting the new course as a stand-alone offering, they could couple it with the introductory course. That way Sam could approach the 10,000 existing alumni and, at the same time, prospect for new attendees for the basic course. After the first day, new recruits would become "instant alumni" and have the option of remaining for the advanced program.

> Rick loved the idea. Sam was more hesitant. He needed to work it through. I understood that. But it was different this time. Sam was excited about the new course and wanted to make it a go.

The solution was a real winner for everyone. The two-day program played to sellout crowds. Mutual inquiry enabled Sam, Karen, and Rick to look at their differences differently. They actually confronted the conflict setting them at odds. Rather than the lose-lose outcome that came from the pushing approach (there is no new program) or the trade-offs of the packaging scenario (the new program gets off the ground, but the method of sharing revenues remains a bone of contention), mutual inquiry opened new possibilities. As Sam, Rick, and Karen learned about each other and from each other, they gained respect for each other's talents and revalued their initial perspectives together.

Mutual inquiry departs significantly from the exploration into interests that takes place in packaging. That probing focuses almost exclusively on interests as they are currently defined. Had Karen persisted in pursuing only Sam's interests in the fee arrangements, she would in all likelihood have elicited an elaboration of his well-worn themes. Instead, she moved on to more controversial ground by expressing a concern for the risks Sam was taking. Her appreciation of his difficulties was key to opening up the conversation. She learned something critical from Sam that she could build on. Most important, the existing relationship between Sam and Rick and Karen changed through mutual inquiry. Once they looked at each other more charitably, they saw the mutual stake they had in working together.

The solution Karen and Sam came up with cannot be separated from the process of getting there. They created an agreement not by pushing or packaging but by experiencing their mutual interests. As Sam elaborated on his situation and Karen and Rick had an opportunity to talk about their resentment over the existing sharing arrangements, they began to take tentative steps toward a trust missing in their previous relationship. Once they set aside their earlier suspicions, they could listen to and learn from each other. In their previous negotiations, they had given lip service to the notion of partnership. For the first time, they actually began to experience themselves as partners.

Whether a negotiation becomes a learning experience depends equally on effective inquiry and effective advocacy. Strategic moves and turns protect your interests and provide the incentives to keep the negotiation on track. But connection opens the negotiation up by making room for everyone's stories. Resistance, instead of being regarded as a stumbling block, becomes an impetus for more inquiry. Without having to worry about the risks of disclosing too much, negotiators can come at issues in new ways and experiment with new ideas. Very often the issue under dispute acquires a new definition, one that is constructed together. What seem like conflicts of interests often turn out to be shared causes of concern if one probes deeper or shares more.

Advocacy and connection are ways in which bargainers relate to each other in the shadow negotiation. The effects of each and the balance struck between them ripple through the discussion of issues and the kinds of agreements that are reached. In pushing situations, you concentrate on getting the best deal for yourself, and it is here that advocacy plays its most obvious role. The better prepared you are, psychologically and tactically, the better you will do. But even here connection has a part. You have to be able to gauge the effects of your moves and turns. By anticipating obstacles, pushing in a connected way, you make it easier for the other party to say yes.

Packaging is a form of problem solving. It works best when both sides have a healthy respect for the value each brings to the negotiation. That's what gives everyone the incentive to tailor solutions so that they meet the various interests around the table. For your suggestions to be considered, the other party has to think them worth the time and effort. She or he must believe that it is in her or his best interest to deal with you. The tools of advocacy position you to claim what you deserve and need. But you still require a clear picture of the other person's priorities. That information is the key to the kinds of package deals you can put together. You tap into priorities and interests by getting connected.

In mutual inquiry, advocacy and connection are integrated differently. Neither is yoked so exclusively to self-interest. The moves and turns that get you to the table yield to another kind of process. You work together to learn more about each other's experience, and agreements emerge not from floating attractive options but from this exploration. In other words, new ideas don't come from brainstorming, as in problem solving, but from listening, learning, and creating together.

8

NEGOTIATING CHANGE

Every day we negotiate the fabric of our work and our relationships. Sometimes we deliberately direct the process; other times, it takes place without our much noticing. These discrete negotiations taken together create the patterns of our life. Chance, circumstances—all have a hand in their design. But the more conscious we are of our actions the less likely it is that the results will take shape by default.

The tools of advocacy—its strategic moves and turns—help us guard against the temptation to let decisions slide, to avoid conflicts, while it is by using the skills of connection that we open up new possibilities. If advocacy stretches our notions of what is negotiable, connection expands our understanding of what can be achieved by working together.

Linked over time, negotiated outcomes take on a cumulative force. What we actively bargain for or permit others to decide for us determines what opportunities we will be able to negotiate in the future. If every negotiation has a history and a context, every participant in a negotiation also has a history and a context. Their constraints and resources, values and goals both shape and are shaped by the results they have negotiated in the past. As we go about our daily bargainings, the agreements we make cast ripples into the future. If we agree to take that new assignment with no increase in pay, we add to the expectation that we will make the same choice tomorrow.

In previous chapters we selected vignettes from specific negotiation stories or focused on a single negotiation. Stopping the action, so to speak, allowed us to capture bargainers at precise points in a negotiation or within their careers. First, we wanted to show how some of the women we talked with grappled with the demands of advocating for their interests. Then we moved to stories others told about the challenges of getting connected. What, we asked, do these women have to tell us about gaining a voice at the table? How do they use their relational skills to open a dialogue with the other party and not have their efforts written off as an accommodating "feminine" sensitivity?

To make specific points, we isolated aspects of their stories. But generally negotiations are neither so tidy nor so compartmentalized, particularly when it comes to the shadow negotiation. You don't systematically work through all the strategic moves and turns of effective advocacy and then summon your relational skills to foster a collaborative relationship with your counterpart. Then, too, focusing on one aspect of a negotiation can make the outcome seem inevitable. One of the characteristics of any negotiation is that you can never be sure how it is going to turn out. You can only anticipate the ending. The confrontational strategy Brenda Jacklin initially employed in chapter 5 to resist signing a noncompete agreement seems foolhardy at first. But at the time she considered standing firm her *only* option. She was afraid her boss, Alec, would take advantage of the situation if she didn't. Carrie, in chapter 7, was also dead set against giving someone else—in her case, a major client—so much control over her life. Yet each eventually managed to articulate her "no" in a way that kept the job or the client. Their paths to agreement, however, were by no means straight.

As we talked with women around the country, they not only described complex situations and undiluted triumphs, they touched on their feelings about negotiation. They assessed what they had learned about advocating for themselves and connecting with others, what they believed they still needed to learn. They often attributed their success to luck. "Oh, I was in the right place at the right time," they'd say, or "I was lucky." It is not luck. In their stories, success emerges as the product of constant improvisation, negotiating opportunity, evading roadblocks, creating value. It comes from managing both the tools of forceful advocacy and the relational skills of connection. That experience is cumulative, and in this chapter we want to look at negotiation over time—through the eyes of Shannon Galvin.

Shannon, the highest placed woman in a major hotel chain, has the map of Ireland written across her face. Her fair skin blushes easily. Blunt-cut blond hair swings forward when she bends toward someone to listen. Her smile tips up one side of her mouth and goes right to her eyes. Now in her late thirties, Shannon has a directness that can be mistaken for naïveté. Shannon has spent her entire professional life with the same hotel chain. This tenure has plusses and minuses. One big plus is that Shannon knows the organization from bottom to top: "There are lots of people around who met me when I was a kid. There are telephone operators here who were telephone operators when I first worked the reservations desk. They all call me dear."

The executive offices on the third floor of the chain's flagship hotel are an oasis of calm. No one rushes. The telephone rings constantly, but responses are measured, efficient, and warm. There is little hint that in the not too distant past the chain was reeling under the strain of three reorganizations in five years and outside consultants roamed through the corporate ranks, evaluating head counts and efficiency.

A woman wearing a bright red blazer and a charcoal skirt with knife pleats comes out of a corner office. Before she reaches the reception area, she stops to say hello to a deliveryman unloading a case of bottled water. "Thank you, John." It is Shannon. She runs her hotel on a first-name basis: "I get a little help, you know. When I first came, I insisted on name tags—for everyone."

Shannon has been around the organization for twenty years, wearing many hats. For two and a half years, she sat at headquarters shepherding a massive organizational change. Before the shake-up, decisions got stuck someplace in the chain of command. Accountability fell through the cracks at the lower levels, and at the top the hotel managers assiduously tended their turf, spending a good portion of their time on what Shannon describes as political gamesmanship. "To be a service organization, those attitudes had to be turned around. That's quite an assignment in a place that hates change." Over the years Shannon has acquired the reputation of a consensus builder, and she put her energies to work building agreement on the need for change.

Once the reorganization was well under way, Shannon was promoted to head up operations and take charge of the chain's flagship hotel. Aside from her early experiences on the reservations desk and as an assistant manager, Shannon had never been "in the trenches," she says, "actually assigned to an operating hotel." Some members of the hotel staff, aware of her aversion to confrontation, consistently made moves that pushed her toward accommodation. They tried, in effect, to position her as they saw her.

There were no veterans in management's upper ranks when Shannon came to the hotel. Her senior team was all new. "We had to be extremely sensitive to how comments came out of our mouths. If we saw things that were wrong, the people who had been here thought that we blamed them." If the "old hands" at the reservations desk and manning the telephones remembered a shy young kid, the rest of the staff was more distant. They tried to hide information, not maliciously but to protect themselves: "The impulse behind their moves was transparent. They were obviously thinking that what I didn't know couldn't hurt them." No one considered Shannon a strict disciplinarian, but they knew she was a crusader for customer satisfaction. By hoarding their problems, they avoided bringing any attention to them. She'd hear comments like, "Oh, you don't want to be bothered about that." But Shannon is nonconfrontational with people, not issues. "Why wouldn't I want to hear? If there was an issue, it could be a problem for all of us. If we couldn't make something work, then we had to talk about why, not paper over it."

Shannon arrived at the hotel at the beginning of a blustery January storm. The next day, the chief engineer paid her a visit. One of his men objected to shoveling snow. "Excuse me?" she said. "When it snows, everybody shovels, everyone on the team pitches in. This is winter. It snows." The chief engineer shifted from one foot to the other and then proceeded to fill Shannon in on the facts. "I couldn't ask anyone over fifty to shovel. That was my vivid and rude introduction to unions."

A week later the contract with the hotel engineers, members of the International Brotherhood of Firemen and Oilers, came up for renewal. Although there were twelve union hotels in the city, Shannon's two primary competitors were nonunion and likely to remain so. Any contract she negotiated needed to meet two criteria. The agreement had to be fiscally sound for the hotel and at the same time allow its customers to be served well. Shannon identified the two objectives early on. How they could be realized remained a puzzle initially. Behind them lurked a bigger question. Can customers expect and get good service, top-notch service, in a union hotel without bankrupting the treasury?

Typically in the past, bargaining with the union had been conducted by a closed group. The chief engineer made his needs known going in, but the union president and the general manager of the hotel struck the final deal. Shannon was not prepared to negotiate the contract one-on-one, nor did she think the practice served her larger interests. Determined to get a different kind of contract, she realized she had to change the process.

Shannon, new on the job and completely inexperienced in union negotiations, could have relied on the hotel's labor attorney. Instead, she expanded participation on management's side, opening it to members of her advisory team. "My gut instinct told me that I needed to make a symbolic statement and that I needed to make it early." By including the advisory team in the union negotiation, she signaled that management of the hotel, not just those talks, would be a collaborative effort.

> I wanted to run the hotel as a team, and these negotiations had to be conducted that way. This change disturbed our labor lawyer. He is extremely capable, but quite traditional. Suddenly not only were we breaking the mold, but he was dealing with a team with two women in key roles.
>
> I had no desire to negotiate this contract with our attorney telling me what to do. That advice would have come from what happened in the past. But, face it, I also didn't have the experience or the inclination to do it on my own.

If Shannon's own attorney was disturbed by the change, the union president was at a total loss. He had been comfortable with her predecessor, whose confrontational posturing fitted his notion of how negotiations moved forward.

> The previous manager liked the fight. Well, I don't like the fight. Foul language, pounding the table, threatening to walk out—that is not my style.

Concerned, Shannon called the union president and asked him to come by so she could introduce herself.

> We had tea and cookies. The union president had no idea what to expect. He had never negotiated with a woman before. He'd gone out for beers with my predecessor, but a tea party? I had no stated agenda,

but between sips of Earl Grey I let him know what I expected from a
working relationship and that I expected to have one with him. This was
not what he had been used to hearing from my predecessor.

Shannon was essentially telling the union president that they were in
this together. Off-line, before the formal proceedings began, she created
an opportunity for him to get to know her. Equally significant, Shannon
gave herself an opportunity to clarify her own expectations for the upcoming talks. She emphasized her willingness to be reasonable within certain
boundaries. Both the willingness and the boundaries were important to
establish before the negotiations began.

Shannon was taking on a larger task than even she realized. She had a
broader objective than keeping the annual increase in the union's hourly
wage to a minimum. She wanted to focus on performance and tie compensation to that performance.

Every organization has some slugs. Everyone involved in these
negotiations had to be thinking about serving our customers. From my
perspective, the contract needed to sharpen that focus. You cannot
serve customers well if you don't have flexibility, if a plumber cannot
change a lightbulb.

The hotel had just had a terrific year, and prospects looked equally
promising for the current year. The union representatives arrived at the
first session with their confidence swelled by that success. They immediately put their demands—all forty-five of them—on the table. The management team countered by raising the issue of performance-based pay.
Conversations about performance measurement were not new. What was
new was the idea of linking compensation to performance.

I wanted the union members to share my objective for the hotel—to be
number one in service in the city. Starting with a dime, countering with
a nickel, and settling for seven cents was not going to get us even
close to where we needed to be.

Shannon knew from the beginning that she did not want to pursue a
pushing strategy. The most she could hope to achieve by pushing was a

seven-cent compromise. The attitudes about work and the working relationships would remain unchanged. To insure that customer satisfaction
was in the front of everyone's minds, she needed to shake things up a bit.
It could not be business as usual.

Performance-based pay has two components: an hourly wage and a
bonus that is contingent on doing a good job. The union representatives
rejected the concept in the first session. Their reaction came as no surprise to Shannon: "That was how the negotiations had always been conducted. You push, I push back, and we see where everyone is in the end."
In the past, union officials had bargained for hikes in hourly wages across
the board, and the union membership measured success by the rate
achieved. Shannon appreciated the extent to which she was asking the
union members to venture into uncharted territory. Not only would they
have to relinquish a visible and comfortable scorecard, they would have to
give up some of their traditional rights.

Rather than respond as an adversary, Shannon treated that first no as a
starting point. Her tea-and-cookies meeting with the union president had
convinced her that the interests of the union and the hotel converged. The
challenge was to find a way of enabling everyone to see how.

Luisa DiLorenzo, the head of human resources, began working behind the scenes, talking to people in the cafeteria. The message she heard
was loud and clear: The union members wanted to hear from Shannon,
who, thus far, had remained in the background.

> I was the new kid on the block. I wanted to get to know the players
> better, watch, and not take over. Besides, it was important for me that
> this negotiation be perceived as a team effort. If I started inserting
> myself into the sessions right from the beginning, everyone would just
> wait for me to talk.

However low a profile Shannon had kept, the union leadership still
considered her the final authority, and she was an unknown quantity. Until they heard directly from her, they remained unsure of their ground. In
order for her to get them to own the problem with her, she had to be candid about her objectives. To get where she wanted to go, everyone involved in the negotiations needed to recognize the goals they had in
common and not concentrate only on the past practices and contract de-

tails pulling them apart: "The union knew the *what* of performance-based pay. It was now time to talk about the *why*, and they wanted to get it from the horse's mouth. In their mind that horse was me."

Shannon began the "horse's mouth" session by sharing her goals for the hotel and how they were linked to performance: "Right off, I put my three objectives up on a flip chart: serving our customers; looking out for our employees; and insuring our financial health." Shannon considered these goals interconnected. Without satisfied employees they wouldn't get satisfied customers. She also mentioned the changes in company ownership. As a public company, the hotel chain was accountable to its stockholders. Performance was monitored daily in the stock price.

With that introduction, Shannon made what she thought was an impassioned plea for performance-based pay. Until some agreement was reached on performance, she argued, they could not even begin to discuss the union's other forty-five issues. Shannon told the assembled crowd that they had three options in the talks. First, performance-based pay. Second, the traditional hourly pay. And third, contracting out the work based on what made economic sense. She believed the only viable choice was the first option. If they went the traditional route, all they could talk about was dollars, and she would fight as hard as possible for the best deal for the hotel. If they could not come to an agreement that was reasonable economically, she would be forced to contract out the services.

Shannon directly linked the kind of agreement they could forge with the negotiation process itself. Going the traditional route would replay the adversarial win-lose bargaining of the past. In her view, more structured participation, a process driven by dialogue, would lead to joint ownership of the issues on the table.

When Luisa again tapped into the hotel grapevine, she discovered that the union members had interpreted Shannon's remarks very differently than she had intended them. They believed she had drawn a line in the sand. Union leadership and the rank and file heard Shannon's list of options as a thinly veiled threat. If they did not back down on performance, they faced the real possibility of a strike. "I didn't want to position myself that way," Shannon says. "I hadn't intended to send that particular message." A subtle self-deception is at work here. Shannon did fully intend to deliver a tough message; she did not, however, want to be perceived as being intractable or hard. Rather than misunderstanding the message, the union members got their first real glimpse of Shannon's primary objective.

Shannon, a connected negotiator by preference, discovered in the aftermath of that session the importance of strategic moves. Before both sides could work seriously together on a joint solution, the union needed to feel some pressure to cooperate. At first, Shannon was horrified at the way in which union members had interpreted her remarks. Then she watched their effect. Rather than resisting her firm stand, the union members said they appreciated the "straight talk."

That "horse's mouth" session laid out the potential costs to everyone of *not* coming to terms. Shannon's candor, instead of adding to the divisiveness, became the catalyst for more intense and open discussion. No one wanted a strike. This consensus provided a starting point from which both sides could test for other common interests. Behind the scenes, Luisa stepped up her invisible work of connection. In casual meetings with individual union members or small groups, she stressed management's intention to be flexible. Although management was not willing to give in on the performance concept, it was open to any suggestions about the weighting between the hourly figure and the bonus. Luisa more or less gave the union members an open invitation to participate in figuring out what that should be.

At the same time, Shannon decided they could not let themselves get bogged down in specific details: "The most important thing we needed was a buy-in on the concept of performance-based pay itself." In order for joint ownership to evolve, Shannon and her team had to keep the conversation (as opposed to the formal talks) going. Once the union understood why performance-based pay was so important, the details could be bundled or unbundled in lots of ways. "Just getting a performance component into the contract," Shannon believed, "would represent real progress."

This clarity on the goal prevented Shannon from getting mired in the details of implementation. Walking around, talking to people, the management team learned more about what the union wanted. The views of the membership were not monolithic. Differences within the union camp encouraged Shannon to broaden the discussions so that they now included more players on the union side.

At the next session Shannon held out a proposal for the union's consideration. She stressed that the idea was not meant to define a position.

Rather, she suggested, it should be taken as just an idea, something to which they could react. She put muscle behind that statement by establishing work groups to develop other alternatives. Eventually all the engineers participated in these voluntary sessions.

> They came up with truly innovative suggestions. They didn't want anyone to start with a history, and they were dead-on there. They realized right away that poor performers would fare better than high performers under our opening proposal because they had more room for improvement. When they asked if we would be willing to change that, we said, "Sure, come back with a workable formula."

These work groups affected the tenor of the negotiations in three ways. First, they reinforced Shannon's commitment to reaching a joint agreement. Second, because she could act on the recommendations coming out of the work groups, they provided concrete opportunities to back up that commitment. And, most important, everyone involved could build on the ideas the sessions produced.

All the time the hotel's labor attorney was whispering to the management team: "Listen harder. Don't be so concerned about your responses. It's okay to keep your mouth shut and your ears open." Shannon maintains they were listening; they just didn't know what they were listening for. From then on, they made sure that someone on the team just listened. "We got into the habit of rephrasing to make sure that we were hearing what someone actually meant. We would say, 'We hear you. It might work if we did this. Is that okay?'" These kinds of inclusive questions insured that everyone stayed involved. They also encouraged people to participate more actively. Their responses, in turn, contributed greater color and detail, expanding the understanding on both sides. As the various groups worked on specific problems, multiple perspectives emerged, and the discussions shifted imperceptibly in the direction of the subjunctive—from emphatic declarative statements and counterproposals to the inclusive inquiry "What if?"

Listening harder revealed flaws in Shannon's original logic. The discussions had become a learning process. Over the course of these negotiations she came to realize that you must approach dramatic changes gradually. People need time to work through the implications of new ideas. Performance-based pay goes against the union grain, against established patterns of thinking. It is a compensation system that individualizes people and, as a result, runs counter to the group identification that membership in a union encourages.

To be responsive to these concerns, at first Shannon included a team component in the performance measurements, but in the end the engineers themselves decided to eliminate it. "They recognized, as we talked," Shannon says, "that their ability to influence their own performance was greater than their ability to influence a team's." As the union members evaluated various schemes, they were forced to consider how they would be affected on a daily basis. They began to rethink how they worked individually and as members of a team.

After agreement was reached on the performance component, the discussions took on a different rhythm. "The formula wasn't everything I had hoped for," Shannon says, "but it was a start." At this point, she began to share with the union representatives as much financial information as she could. This openness was a major change for her labor attorney and for the union.

> I looked at their original forty-five items and basically said: "It is impossible for us to deliver all of these. We have a budget. This is the pot of money we have. How do you want to spend it? Tell us what demands are most important."

The timing of this sharing is significant. Had Shannon furnished the financial information earlier, the union leadership would probably not have believed they were getting the whole story, and they would have been suspicious about the numbers they were given. Shannon, on the other hand, would have risked having that information used against her to extract concessions. Trust on both sides of the table was a precondition for her candor.

The way in which Shannon shared the information is also significant. With common financial data at hand, the union and management could agree on what was actually in the pot. Shannon left the spending to the union members. It was money available for their benefits. They knew best how to spend it.

If there was a danger in sharing that information, there was an equally potent benefit. It was an act of trust, a signal that they had the makings of a real dialogue.

I was going for trust, telling them as much as I could. Previously getting more was the goal—more concessions, squeezing. We were learning as we went along. This really comes down to how you define success, what it means to win.

Before these negotiations, Shannon had no hands-on experience dealing with unions. Her inexperience with the traditional adversarial model of collective bargaining, where pushing is the rule, worked to her advantage. She chose to define success in terms of shared decision making. Through mutual inquiry, she moved them all to a joint problem and a jointly constructed solution. For that definition of success to take hold, however, Shannon had to stand firm at critical junctures. Had she not, her inexperience would have been used against her. Once she established her authority at the table beyond the dimensions conferred by her position, she could make connected overtures that were interpreted as such, rather than as signs of weakness. "I knew where I wanted to go in these talks," Shannon says, "but I didn't have a clue how to get there." Against a history of adversarial pushing, she fashioned a participatory and collaborative process. Both sides learned together as they went along. They discovered the linkages between their concerns and reframed the issues separating them.

Shannon is an inclusive kind of person. She goes out of her way to draw people in, bends toward them when she listens, instinctively steps back when people are talking to make room so that no one is left standing on the outside of a closed circle. But there are limits to how far participation can be taken within any organization. Shannon has discovered that effective advocacy is not just a prelude for making connection but is important on its own. Before Shannon took over the reins at the hotel, she did not consider consensus building a form of negotiation whose terms and limits needed to be negotiated.

"People want a lot of you. I take consensus to a fault. I'm inclusionary, say, ninety percent of the time and that ten percent when I'm not becomes an issue." The more Shannon puzzled over the criticism she heard about the missing ten percent, the more she realized that people needed boundaries. Without them, they resented the lack of participation or tested her, looking for the limits. Advocacy establishes your place at the table, but it also defines the limits you set.

It has always been my preference to have everyone move forward happily. I will drag people if I need to, but I don't like doing it. I now have a better understanding of what is actually going on. For example, when the union thought I was drawing a line in the sand with my impassioned plea for performance pay, I did not realize how necessary it was to draw that line. I now recognize that it's not only okay to be tough, but actually necessary. They would not have let go of their original positions and moved forward without that strong statement from me.

Shannon does not equate consensus with compliance. Although she still has an aversion to outright conflict, she is not interested in rubbing the rough edges off differences of opinion. She does not want to reach a place where everyone agrees, but rather one where differences can be spoken and heard.

The hotel and its parent have been going through a lot of change, of which performance-based pay for union members is only a part. The last reorganization, which Shannon spearheaded, has been a painful growing process for a lot of people. Shannon is the first to admit that it has not been easy. Negotiating a change in attitude or behavior takes a personal and professional toll. There has been some difficult learning on everyone's part as old habits and sometimes actual turf have had to be surrendered. Change is also ongoing.

I want everyone in the hotel to be thinking about the customer—to know that they are accountable for our customers' satisfaction and do everything they can to make our guests' stays pleasant. But that means we all have to pull in the same direction.

At times Shannon's position gets in the way of the communication she wants. No matter how hard she tries to create an impression of openness, she is still perceived as the boss. And for a very good reason. She is.

It is tough. Last week I had bonus checks in my desk drawer. I'd written letters to each of the managers, but I wanted to give them their checks personally. When I saw one of the managers in the lobby, I asked him to stop by my office whenever he got a minute.

Well, he panicked—all day long. I happened to catch him in the human resources office downstairs with Luisa. She said, "I don't break confidences, but, Shannon, you have got to hear this. Nick has been wound up like a top because you want to see him. I had to tell him you have his bonus check."

That should have been a great day for Nick. Instead he stewed unnecessarily for five hours. I thought, "This is mind-boggling. Sure I'm his boss, but he also needs to understand that I wouldn't approach a problem by saying, 'Hey, when you get a minute, stop by my office.'"

Some managers would have been in my office in a split second, ready to talk. What struck me was his immediate response: He must have done something wrong. He didn't think, "Gee, maybe she wants my opinion on something." It's the same perception that makes it hard for him, and for others, to ask for help. In their minds, it is an admission of incompetence, an acknowledgment that they cannot handle something on their own.

That incident gave Shannon pause. It reinforced her conviction that open communication and a fear of sanctions do not mix. The reaction of the manager was both her problem and his. To help him and others feel more comfortable raising difficult issues, Shannon began to build frameworks for what she calls "programmed communication." These are not occasions for her to channel discussion to her way of thinking. They provide recurrent opportunities for feedback.

If you don't actively seek input from people, provide for it, look for other opinions, where do they come from? How do you get people to the point of knowing they can bring bad news and their heads won't roll?

There is a hidden danger in introducing programmed communication. People instinctively recognize that these techniques can be used for diametrically opposed purposes. They can encourage diverse opinions, but they can also mute dissent. When compliance is the order of the day, people are reluctant to put their opinions out for inspection. They won't take the chance. Their concerns might depart from what is being enforced. Structured opportunities for communication can raise suspicions. They also take time away from "real work." "I rarely dig my heels in," Shannon says, "but I dug my heels in on this issue. These sessions were worth the time and the effort. You have to give people a chance to sit around a table and lay their needs out. They have to know they will have everyone's undivided attention."

Only recently has Shannon admitted to herself that relationships as much as issues must be negotiated.

> Remember at breakfast I told you that I never negotiated, that I was going into my first big negotiation—the labor talks. Well, the other day, two senior staff members came to me with an ongoing issue that they needed to resolve. They wanted me to broker the resolution for them. I told them it was not about either one of them positioning themselves individually with me. They needed to negotiate their relationship. That is part of what they get paid for. To work together. I would never have said that a couple of years ago.

Behind the success of Shannon's negotiations is a conscious struggle. She is a firm believer that "no news is not good news." She subjects her own goals and the process to a hard-edged scrutiny. She explicitly contracts with those around her for the sharing of information and reliable feedback. She reflects on what she hears and constantly revises the way she approaches the practice of negotiation. The union members' reaction to her strong advocacy and its positive effect on the subsequent talks made her think about why she shied away from any appearance of toughness. For Shannon, negotiation has become a learning experience.

Shannon negotiates changes as an insider with a powerful position. She has also benefited from the backing of a powerful mentor. Both her title and her support create perceptions when she negotiates. On the one hand, she has less need to establish her voice in the shadow negotiation. She takes her credentials to the table with her. On the other, she also carries along her reputation for having an aversion to confrontation.

Despite her power (or perhaps because of it), Shannon has been slow to realize the need for continuous advocacy: "I don't like to throw my weight around, tell people what to do. Subconsciously, I did not recognize the difference between being tough and being an empowered advocate. Now I realize they are not the same." That recognition separates her earlier efforts at consensus building from the negotiations of mutual inquiry in which she now engages. Shannon has resolved the Catch-22 most women face when they negotiate—how to be a forceful advocate so you get what you want, but not so tough that you alienate the other person. She has come to grips with the paradox by no longer considering advocacy and connection, strategic moves and responsive inquiry, as mutually exclusive approaches. She has come to see that all are equally necessary to the effective practice of negotiation. Forceful moves and turns, Shannon has discovered, can define the boundaries and set the conditions for a participatory, expansive process that goes beyond consensus.

Every decision carries a potential point to be negotiated, whether she decides to take it up or not. Not every encounter leads to connection. Nor is she as inclusionary in one situation as she might be in another. There are many lessons in Shannon's story, but perhaps the most important is this exercise of choice. "No" begins a process of engagement—with herself, trying to figure out the reasons blocking progress, and with those on the other side of the table.

Shannon Galvin is one particular woman. She builds into the negotiation process the possibility for mutual inquiry. As the tenor of negotiation moves from pushing and defensive posturing or clever packaging, the focus shifts from specific agendas or interests to solutions people hadn't considered before. Together they invent new options. Although not all negotiations contain the seeds of transformative change, they all produce change at some level. The question is whose voices will participate in fashioning those changes.

The story of Shannon Galvin and the experiences of the other women in this book reveal what an inevitable part of our lives negotiation is. It is the way people work their way through conflict and put their stamp on change. Negotiated outcomes all resolve conflict in one way or another. They can reinforce existing relations, including the calculus of power at the table, or they can modulate those relations. There is a choice involved here, but it is one that depends ultimately on the recognition that choice is possible. Outcomes can be purposefully shaped. The decision to play an active role in that shaping is perhaps the most important one you as a negotiator make in coming to the table. That primary decision opens up multiple avenues for effective advocacy and participative inquiry.

Three threads weave through all our stories. The awareness imbedded in each expands not only the choices available to you in a negotiation but the possibilities.

Negotiation is a complex process. The interactions take place on many levels. Bargainers work out relations of power and define their roles in a shadow negotiation that parallels their debate on the issues.

How issues are defined, interpreted, and recast depends fundamentally on the relationships established in this shadow negotiation. The impressions that govern those relationships are not static. They can be confronted, resisted, and modified by active intervention—through strategic moves and turns that empower us as negotiators.

But the outcome of any negotiation is a function of the process used to get there. You can draw the other person into the negotiation conversation in ways that promote collaboration. Through mutual inquiry, bargainers can rethink their biases and expectations together. In what Mary Parker Follett called a constant process of relating and revaluing, they can come to see each other differently and gain new perspectives on the issues dividing them.

These threads, woven together, subtly transform our notions of what it means to be an effective negotiator. When equal weight is granted to the shadow negotiation, it becomes clear how important relational matters are to the outcome of any negotiation. The relationship isn't just "something that women worry about." The ideal negotiator, defined as an individual-istic and analytic problem solver, no longer appears so ideal. That concep-tion ignores half the negotiation equation.

The way out of the double binds negotiation can create for women is not a choice between fitting a model measured against a male standard. Nor is it acceptance of the accommodating relational approach commonly associated with the "feminine." Negotiations involve both self-interest and a concern for others. The balance between them constantly shifts. But, as Shannon Galvin and our other storytellers show us, there are many ways to manage the shadow negotiation, many ways of advocating for our own interests at the same time that we connect with others to give greater depth to our understanding of the issues at stake.

Notes

Preface

1. *Working Woman* (July/August 1999), 42–56.
2. The U.S. Department of Labor, Bureau of Labor Statistics, *Working Women: A Chartbook* and *Employment and Earnings*, table 22.
3. Korn/Ferry International and the UCLA Anderson Graduate School of Management, *Decade of the Executive Woman*, and U.S. Department of Labor, *Report on the Glass Ceiling Initiative*.
4. By no means is gender the only trigger in the shadow negotiation. Race, economic status, class, and ethnicity—all come into play, and the understanding of how those interactions work is muddy at best. White women, for example, suffer 40 percent higher markups when they go to buy a used car than do white men, but women of color face markups three times greater. See Ian Ayers, "Fair Driving: Gender and Race Discrimination in Retail Car Negotiations."
5. Mary Catherine Bateson, *Composing a Life*.

Introduction: Recognizing the Shadow Negotiation

1. Donald Trump, *The Art of the Deal*.
2. Books that have influenced thinking about negotiation include Roger Fisher, William Ury, and Bruce Patton, *Getting to Yes;* William Ury, *Getting Past No;* Howard Raiffa, *The Art and Science of Negotiation;* David Lax and James Sebenius, *The Manager as Negotiator;* and Max Bazerman and Margaret Neale, *Negotiating Rationally*.
3. Anthropologists and linguists emphasize the extent to which meaning in any exchange comes not just from what is said but from how it gets said. See Gregory Bateson, *Steps to an Ecology of Mind*.
4. We are using the concept of "position" in a way that differs from its use in most writing on negotiation. In *Getting to Yes*, for example, a position is a demand a negotiator makes and is to be distinguished from the interests that stand behind that position or demand. We use *position* as a verb. This verbal form suggests how a negotiator comes to be placed in the process, whether she positions herself to advocate for what she wants—the subject-position—or is at the whim

of how others define her—the object position. This object/subject relation has been a primary focus in women's studies. See, for example, Chris Weedon, *Feminist Practice and Poststructuralist Theory,* and Sylvia Gherardi, *Gender, Symbolism, and Organizational Culture.* Sara Cobb takes up its impact on conflict resolution in "A Narrative Perspective on Mediation."

5. When asked what aspects of self are important to them, women are more likely than are men to mention gender as the defining element. See Kay Deaux and Brenda Major, "A Social Psychological Model of Gender"; Alice Eagly, *Sex Differences in Social Behavior: A Social Role Interpretation;* and Roberta A. Sigel, *Ambition & Accommodation: How Women View Gender Relations.*

6. Early examples of this approach are Margaret Hennig and Anne Jardim, *The Managerial Woman,* and Betty Lehan Harragan, *Games Mother Never Taught You.* More recent "rulebooks" include Pat Heim, *Hardball for Women;* Adrienne Mendell, *How Men Think: The Seven Essential Rules for Making It in a Man's World;* and Phyllis Mindell, *A Woman's Guide to the Language of Success: Communication with Confidence and Power.* As is evident simply from the titles, the key is fitting into a "man's world." Harriet Rubin offers a slightly different prescription in *The Princessa: Machiavelli for Women:* "Learn the rules of the man's world and then manipulate them."

7. Linda Carli describes the two-edged sword that assertiveness can be for women in "Gender, Language, and Influence," and Mary Crawford offers a pointed critique of the assertiveness training solution in *Talking Difference: On Gender and Language.*

8. Arguments along these lines are found in Sally Helgesen, *The Female Advantage: Women's Ways of Leadership,* and Judith Rosener, "Ways Women Lead."

9. Catharine MacKinnon, "Feminist Discourse."

10. Jean Baker Miller turns this argument upside-down in *Toward a New Psychology of Women:* "Subordinates . . . know much more about the dominants than vice versa. They have to. They become highly attuned to the dominants, able to predict their reactions of pleasure and displeasure. Here . . . is where the long story of 'feminine intuition' and 'feminine wiles' begins. It seems clear that these 'mysterious' gifts are in fact skills, developed through long practice, in reading many small signals, both verbal and nonverbal. . . . That women are truly much more able to tolerate . . . feelings [of weakness or vulnerability] is a positive strength" (at 10–11, 31–32, 135).

11. For the effects on organizations when masculine values and the experience of men come to be taken as the yardstick, see Joyce Fletcher, *Disappearing Acts: Relational Practice, Power, and Gender in the New Organization.* On the extent to which gender can be suppressed in organizations and the impact on its members, see Joanne Martin, "Deconstructing Organizational Taboos: The Suppression of Gender Conflict in Organizations"; Joan Acker, "Gendering Organizational Theory"; and Marta Calas and Linda Smircich, "From a Woman's Point of View: Feminist Approaches to Organization Studies."

12. The notion of the ideal employee and its negative impact on women (and organizations) are developed in "Relinking Life and Work: Toward a Better Future,"

a report to the Ford Foundation based on collaborative research with three corporations.

13. Experiences in gendered situations can be internalized as an individual problem and whittle away at self-confidence. On this point, see Virginia Valian, *Why So Slow?* and Mary Catherine Bateson, *Composing a Life.* Bateson likens the situation to playing against the "house odds"—no particular hand breaks the bank, but eventually the results stack up.

14. The fish metaphor is borrowed from Sandra Bem, *Lenses of Gender.*

15. *Barron's,* August 16, 1999.

16. J. T. Spence and R. L. Helmreich, *Masculinity and Femininity: Their Psychological Correlates.* Tests like these, by their design, force polarization between the sexes. Individual traits, behaviors, and values get lumped together in a package deal.

17. All comparisons have a defining element. Weak, for example, lacks strength. When the masculine or the male is the defining pole, women become the problem. They are not something or are associated with something negative. Psychologist Rhoda Unger characterizes these dichotomies as metaphors for the ways in which we structure reality: "The terms male and female carry with them beliefs about good and evil, rational and irrational, and so forth. Beliefs about male hardness and female softness probably exert as much social control over the sexes as do societal prescriptions about appropriate gender role behavior. Indeed, these negative beliefs can exert even more social control because they are subject to neither conscious scrutiny nor public debate." "Imperfect Reflections on Reality: Psychology Constructs Gender," 131.

18. The Equal Employment Opportunity Commission has targeted Morgan Stanley in a sex bias inquiry. A female employee who earns more than $1 million a year was denied partnership. The complaint cites a boss who found her "snippy during tense trading sessions" and points to performance reviews in which she is criticized, despite her salary level, for not being "a team player." *New York Times,* July 29, 1999.

A 1991 Supreme Court ruling in the Hopkins case specifically addresses the Catch-22 in which the "unfeminine" woman finds herself: "It takes no special training to discern sex-stereotyping in a description of an aggressive female employee as requiring 'a course at charm school.' . . . An employer who objects to aggressiveness in women but whose positions require this trait places women in an intolerable and impermissible Catch-22: out of a job if they behave aggressively and out of a job if they don't." See Ann Hopkins, *So Ordered: Making Partner the Hard Way,* and Kathleen Hall Jamieson, *Beyond the Double Bind: Women and Leadership.*

19. Barbara Gray takes up the case of the missing women in "The Gender Based Foundations of Negotiation Theory." See also Joyce Fletcher, "Castrating the Feminine Advantage." In *Working with Emotional Intelligence* and the earlier *Emotional Intelligence,* Daniel Goleman stresses the pragmatic importance of relational skills; they are essential to corporate success.

20. It is especially important in negotiation to see gender relations as fluid, not cast

in stone or fixed by characteristics peculiar to one sex or the other. Bargainers work out their gender relations along with their other relations in the shadow negotiation. The fluid characteristics of gender relations are stressed by Jane Flax, "Postmodernism and Gender Relations in Feminist Theory"; Kay Deaux and Brenda Major, "Putting Gender into Context: An Interactive Model of Gender Behavior"; and Judith M. Gerson and Kathy Peiss, "Boundaries, Negotiation, Consciousness: Reconceptualizing Gender Relations."

21. Erving Goffman has refined the idea that people follow social scripts that keep society in balance. Goffman suggests that although people read these scripts, they also act them out. And it is through these performances, he argues, that people construct their identities. One such script is the gender script. Gender thus is, in part, a performance. People "do gender." They do it walking down the street, getting dressed, taking out the garbage, asking for directions. See "The Arrangement Between the Sexes," *The Presentation of Self in Everyday Life,* and *Interaction Ritual.* When bargainers "do gender" in negotiations, they simultaneously perform the gender script and the negotiation script, and the two sometimes come into conflict, as they do for Elizabeth and Will.

Chapter 1: Staying Out of Your Own Way

1. In a summary of early research in *The Social Psychology of Bargaining and Negotiation,* for example, Jeffrey Rubin and B. R. Brown point to studies that conclude that women cannot be or are not sufficiently aggressive or self-interested to negotiate effectively. At the same time, other studies that they consider find women less flexible in negotiations than men and more inclined to dig in their heels. For a different reading of these diverse findings, see Deborah Kolb and Gloria Coolidge, "Her Place at the Table." Analysis of recent work turns up equally inconsistent findings. There is some evidence that, over all, women are slightly more cooperative than men unless they are caught in a tit-for-tat situation. When Alice Stuhlmacher and Amy Walters restricted their analysis to negotiation, however, the studies found that men negotiated better outcomes than women did, but the differences in results were small ("Gender Differences in Negotiation Outcomes: A Meta-Analysis"). Even when gender does not affect a bargainer's results, Carol Watson's research indicates that it does affect the bargainer's feelings. Women tend to feel less confident and less satisfied regardless of the outcomes they achieve.

2. Naomi Wolf, *Fire with Fire,* 237.

3. Lawrence Fouraker and Stanley Siegal first pointed to the determining impact that aspirations—the goals you set and the expectations you have about their success—can have on the outcome of a negotiation in *Bargaining and Group Decisionmaking.*

4. Women are much less likely to use self-promoting tactics like the ones Pat employs in this story than are men, and they make fewer offers and counteroffers. These differences in approach and tactics account, in part, for the lower salaries women negotiate when they compete with men for the same jobs. See Lisa

Barron, "Talk That Pays: Differences in Salary, Negotiator's Beliefs, and Behaviors."

5. Myriad explanations have been put forth for the disparity in the salaries negotiated by men and women. Women have difficulty setting specific salary targets and putting a number on the table (Cynthia Stevens, "Gender Differences in the Acquisition of Salary Negotiation Skills"). Men get more because they ask for more, are more confident of success, and employ a more active strategy than do women (V. S. Kamen and C. E. J. Hartel, "Gender Differences in Anticipated Negotiation Strategies and Outcomes"). Women do badly, in part, because they don't ask for much (Brenda Major and colleagues, "Social Comparisons and Pay Evaluations: Preferences for Same-Sex and Same-Job Wage Comparisons"; "An Investigation of Sex Differences in Pay Expectations and Their Possible Causes"; and "Overworked and Underpaid"). Women determine what they deserve on the basis of what other women are earning rather than what the work itself commands (Faye Crosby, *Relative Deprivation and Working Women*, and Bernice Lott, "The Devaluation of Women's Competence"). Or the work they do simply does not pay well (W. T. Bielby and J. N. Baron, "A Woman's Place Is with Other Women: Sex Segregation Within Organizations").

6. Rhona Mahony, *Kidding Ourselves: Breadwinning, Babies, and Bargaining Power*, and Arlie Hochschild, *The Second Shift*.

7. For more on the concept of BATNA, see *Getting to Yes*.

Chapter 2: Making Strategic Moves

1. Robin Lakoff, *Language and Women's Place;* Deborah Tannen, *You Just Don't Understand: Women and Men in Conversation* and other works; Kathleen Kelley Reardon, *They Don't Get It, Do They?;* and Mary Crawford, *Talking Difference: On Gender and Language*.

2. Growing up, many women learn to display their accomplishments indirectly. They let others sing their praises rather than advertise their talents themselves. A taboo on bragging among women is one of the conversational prohibitions Deborah Tannen isolates in *You Just Don't Understand: Women and Men in Conversation*. See chapter 8, "Damned If You Do."

3. Abba Eban, *Diplomacy for the Next Century*.

4. "Unfreezing" is a concept developed by, among others, Kurt Lewin, *Resolving Social Conflicts: Field Theory in Social Science*.

5. Negotiations to secure the backing of a bargainer's own "side" are so critical to success in the main negotiation that they have been called the "second table." See Thomas Colosi, "Negotiations in the Public and Private Sectors"; Ray Friedman, *Front Stage, Backstage: The Dramatic Structure of Labor Negotiations;* Richard Walton and Robert McKersie, *A Behavioral Theory of Labor Negotiations;* and Robert Mnookin, Lawrence Susskind, and Pacey Foster, eds., *Negotiating on Behalf of Others*.

6. David Lax and James Sebenius, "Thinking Coalitionally."

7. "Clean encounters," conducted one-on-one privately, have another benefit. A negotiator might be willing to explore controversial issues or concessions in private, but feel constrained in a more public forum.

8. On making change without explicit authority, see Allan R. Cohen and David L. Bradford, "Influence Without Authority: The Use of Alliances, Reciprocity, and Exchange to Accomplish Work." Peter Bachrach and Morton S. Baratz differentiate between direct and indirect uses of power in "The Two Faces of Power."

9. Influence in negotiation is relational. It is not fixed, as the notion of bargaining power implies, but fluid, malleable. It can, within limits, be increased through strategic moves. For this reason, we prefer the concept of positioning—the active bettering of your odds at the table—to the static notion of bargaining power. On the intersection of power relations and gender relations, see Joan Scott, *Gender and the Politics of History;* Jane Flax, "Postmodernism and Gender Relations in Feminist Theory" and *Thinking Fragments: Psychoanalysis, Feminism, and Postmodernism in the West.*

Chapter 3: Resisting Challenges

1. Erving Goffman shows in *The Presentation of Self in Everyday Life* the great lengths to which people go to present themselves in a positive light. Bargainers use moves and turns to insure that a positive or flattering view of them prevails in the negotiation.

2. Judith Lorber suggests in *Paradoxes of Gender* that "doing gender" means, in part, that men do dominance while women do deference. The expectation that women will be accommodating causes problems in the shadow negotiation. Women sometimes hesitate to ask for much or to push their own advocacy, and other parties, expecting acquiescence, retaliate when they don't get it.

3. Linda Alcoff, "Cultural Feminism Versus Post-Structuralism: The Identity Crisis in Feminist Theory."

4. Maryanne's story is based on work done in collaboration with the Center for Women and Enterprise, a nonprofit organization in Boston.

5. "Focus on the problem, not the people" is a much-quoted dictum in *Getting to Yes,* and negotiators are urged to ignore personal challenges, rise above them, or deal with them outside the negotiation. Challenging moves in the shadow negotiation frequently carry a gendered and quite personal message to women bargainers that *must* be answered directly.

6. Kathleen Reardon underscores, in *They Don't Get It, Do They? Communication in the Workplace—Closing the Gap Between Women and Men,* the confirming aspect of not confronting these challenges. The label sticks when no objection is raised.

7. Disruptive turns bring gender and sexism to the surface and expose the problems they can cause. Conflicts of this nature are generally avoided in organizations. See Joanne Martin, "Deconstructing Organizational Taboos: The Suppression of Gender Conflict in Organizations."

8. Because gender is transmitted and reenacted through communication, the

tools of language—sarcasm, irony, exaggeration—come in handy in turning the insults of gender. See Kathy Ferguson, "Interpretation and Genealogy in Feminism"; Teresa DeLauretis, *Technologies of Gender: Essays on Theory, Film, and Fiction;* and Sylvia Gherardi, *Gender, Symbolism, and Organizational Culture.*

9. Attractiveness is considered an attribute of success in male executives but is most often taken as a sign of sexuality among females. Madeline Heilman and Melanie Stropek, "Attractiveness and Corporate Success: Different Causal Attributions for Males and Females."

Chapter 4: Laying the Groundwork

1. In "Bargaining and Gender," Carol Rose contends that it does not matter whether women are or are not more inclined to cooperation and connection. The assumption that they are makes it difficult for women to get people to the table without making concessions and even more difficult for them not to be forced to make concessions once they are there. For arguments that specifically link women and connection, see Carol Gilligan, *In Another Voice;* Mary Belenky, Blythe Clinchy, Nancy Goldberger, and Jill Tarule, *Women's Ways of Knowing;* and Judith Jordan, Alexandra Kaplan, Jean Baker Miller, Irene Stiver, and Janet Surrey, *Women's Growth in Connection.*

2. Robert Mnookin, "Why Negotiations Fail: An Exploration of Barriers to the Resolution of Conflict," and Max Bazerman and Margaret Neale, *Negotiating Rationally.*

3. Victor Turner, *Fields and Metaphors;* Jerome Bruner, *Active Minds, Possible Worlds;* Molly Hite, *The Other Side of the Story: Structures and Strategies of Contemporary Feminist Narratives;* Laura Tracy, "Catching the Drift": Authority, Gender, and Narrative; Jill Freedman and Gene Combs, *Narrative Therapy;* and Michael White and David Epson, *Narrative Means to Therapeutic Ends.*

4. Roderick Kramer and David Messick, *Negotiation as a Social Process.*

5. We have adapted this exercise in circular questioning from Sara Cobb, who first introduced the technique to the negotiation field in "Narrative Perspective on Mediation." Alison's story is adapted from "Amelia Rogers at Tassani Communications," a case used at the Harvard Business School.

Chapter 5: Engaging Your Counterpart

1. David Cooperider and Suresh Srivastrva, "Appreciative Inquiry in Organizational Life."

2. Victor Turner, *Drama, Fields, and Metaphor: Symbolic Action in Human Society* and *The Ritual Process;* Clifford Geertz, *Local Knowledge.*

3. Dennis K. Mumby and Linda L. Putnam, "The Politics of Emotion: A Feminist Reading of Bounded Rationality."

4. Deborah Tannen, "Rethinking Power and Solidarity in Gender and Dominance."

5. Amy Sheldon calls this kind of exchange "double-voice discourse" to suggest that self-assertion is expressed without giving offense ("Saying It with a Smile: Girls' Conflict Talk as Double-Voice Discourse").

6. Steven R. Wilson, "Face and Facework in Negotiation," and Erving Goffman, *The Presentation of Self in Everyday Life.*

7. Sandra Gilbert coined the phrase "female female-impersonator" to characterize a literary technique—the practice of aping the culturally constructed feminine.

Chapter 6: Getting Collaboration to Work

1. Mary Parker Follett, *The Prophet of Management,* 42, 75, 189.

2. Jeffrey Z. Rubin, Dean G. Pruitt, and Song Hee Kim, *Social Conflict: Escalation, Stalemate and Settlement.*

3. Joyce Fletcher, *Disappearing Acts: Gender, Power, and Relational Practice at Work,* and Deborah M. Kolb, "Women's Work: Peacemaking Behind the Scenes."

4. Sara Cobb, "A Narrative Perspective on Mediation: Toward the Materialization of the 'Storytelling' Metaphor"; W. B. Pearce and V. E. Cronen, *Communication, Action, and Meaning: The Creation of Social Reality;* and Carlos Sluski, "Transformations: A Blueprint for Narrative Changes in Therapy."

5. Victor Turner, *The Ritual Process: Structure and Anti-Structure,* and *Drama, Fields and Metaphor: Symbolic Action in Human Society.* Reference to "doffing" is in *Drama,* 243.

6. Ann Douglas, *Industrial Peacemaking.*

7. Jeffrey Rubin discusses this and other common traps in negotiation in "Some Wise and Mistaken Assumptions About Conflict and Negotiation." See also Rubin, Pruitt, and Kim, *Social Conflict: Escalation, Stalemate and Settlement.*

Chapter 7: Crafting Agreements

1. More extensive commentary on win-lose or "distributive" negotiations can be found in the works by Howard Raiffa, Thomas Schelling, and David Lax and James Sebenius cited in the bibliography. The most accessible accounts of win-win or "joint-gains" bargaining remain Roger Fisher, William Ury, and Bruce Patton's *Getting to Yes* and William Ury's *Getting Past No.*

2. Peter Senge talks about the learning that comes from "reciprocal inquiry making" in *The Learning Organization,* but this inquiry is about understanding another person's reasoning, about getting the facts.

3. The work of Howard Raiffa and his students David Lax and James Sebenius has clarified how important differences, rather than commonalities, are in providing the ingredients for joint-gain negotiations. See also Dean Pruitt, "Strategic Choice in Negotiation."

4. Mary Parker Follett, *The Prophet of Management,* 69.

5. In *The Manager as Negotiator,* David Lax and James Sebenius characterize all negotiation as a parallel process of claiming value for yourself and creating

value together with your counterpart. There is an inevitable tension between the two impulses in pushing and packaging situations. It abates in mutual inquiry.

6. The authors of *Women's Growth in Connection* consider the asking for and giving of help an essential factor contributing to the way women develop. We do not want to gender mutual inquiry in the sense that it is viewed as a process only women can practice. We do want to point out how valuable women's experience can be in creating mutual inquiry negotiations.

Bibliography

Acker, Joan. "Gendering Organizational Theory," *Gendering Organizational Theory,*" eds. Albert J. Mills and Peta Tancred (Newbury Park, Calif.: Sage, 1992).

Ayers, Ian. "Fair Driving: Gender and Race Discrimination in Retail Car Negotiations," *Harvard Law Review,* 104:4 (1991), 817–72.

Alcoff, Linda. "Cultural Feminism Versus Post-Structuralism: The Identity Crisis in Feminist Theory," *Signs,* 13:3 (1988), 405–36.

Bacharach, Samuel, and Edward Lawler. *Bargaining* (San Francisco: Jossey-Bass, 1981).

Bachrach, Peter, and Morton Baratz. "The Two Faces of Power," *American Political Science Review,* 56 (1962), 947–52.

Bailyn, Lotte. *Breaking the Mold: Women, Men and Time in the Corporate World* (New York: Free Press, 1993).

Barron, Lisa. "Talk That Pays: Differences in Salary, Negotiator's Beliefs, and Behaviors" (unpublished dissertation, Anderson School, UCLA, 1998).

Bateson, Gregory. *Steps to an Ecology of Mind* (New York: Ballantine, 1972).

Bateson, Mary Catherine. *Composing a Life* (New York: Plume, 1990).

Bazerman, Max, and Margaret Neale. *Negotiating Rationally* (New York: Free Press, 1992).

Belenky, Mary Field, Blythe McVicker Clinchy, Nancy Rule Goldberger, Jill Mattuck Tarule. *Women's Ways of Knowing: The Development of Self, Voice, and Mind* (New York: Basic Books, 1986).

Bem, Sandra. *The Lenses of Gender: Transforming the Debate on Sexual Inequality* (New Haven: Yale University Press, 1993).

Bielby, William T., and James N. Baron. "A Woman's Place Is with Other Women: Sex Segregation Within Organizations," *Sex Segregation in the Workplace: Trends, Explanations, Remedies,* ed. B. F. Reskin (Washington, D.C.: National Academy Press, 1984).

Boulding, Kenneth. *Three Faces of Power* (Newbury Park, Calif.: Sage, 1989).

Bruner, Jerome. *Active Minds, Possible Worlds* (Cambridge: Harvard University Press, 1986).

Butler, Judith. *Gender Trouble: Feminism and the Subversion of Identity* (New York: Routledge, 1990).

Bylsma, Wayne H., and Brenda Major. "Social Comparisons and Performance Evaluations," *Psychology of Women Quarterly*, 16 (1991), 193–200.

Calas, Marta, and Linda Smircich. "From a Woman's Point of View: Feminist Approaches to Organization Studies," *Handbook of Organization Studies*, eds. S. Clegg, C. Hardy, and W. Nord (Newbury Park, Calif.: Sage, 1996).

Carli, Linda. "Gender, Language, and Influence," *Journal of Personality and Social Psychology*, 59 (1990), 941–51.

Chodorow, Nancy. *Feminism and Psychoanalytic Theory* (New Haven: Yale University Press, 1989).

Chusmir, L. H., and J. Mills. "Gender Differences in Conflict Resolution Styles of Managers: At Work and at Home," *Sex Roles*, 20 (1989), 149–63.

Cobb, Sara. "A Narrative Perspective on Mediation: Toward the Materialization of the 'Storytelling' Metaphor," *New Directions in Mediation*, eds. Joseph P. Folger and Tricia S. Jones (Thousand Oaks, Calif.: Sage, 1994).

———. "Empowerment and Mediation: A Narrative Perspective," *Negotiation Journal*, 9 (1993), 245–59.

Cohen, Allen R., and David L. Bradford. "Influence Without Authority: The Use of Alliances, Reciprocity, and Exchange to Accomplish Work," *Negotiation*, eds. Roy Lewicki et al. (Minneapolis: Richard Irwin, 1994).

Colosi, Thomas. "Negotiation in the Public and Private Sectors," *American Behavioral Scientist*, 27 (1983), 229–55.

Connell, R. W. *Gender and Power* (Stanford: Stanford University Press, 1987).

———. "Theorising Gender," *Sociology*, 19:2 (1985).

Cooperrider, David, and Suresh Srivastva. "Appreciative Inquiry in Organizational Life," *Research in Organizational Change and Development*, vol. 1 (Greenwich, Conn.: JAI Press, 1987), 129–69.

Crawford, Mary. *Talking Difference: On Gender and Language* (London: Sage, 1990).

Crosby, Faye J. *Juggling: The Unexpected Advantages of Balancing Career and Home for Women and Their Families* (New York: Oxford University Press, 1991).

———. *Relative Deprivation and Working Women* (New York: Oxford University Press, 1982).

Deaux, Kay. "Putting Gender into Context: An Interactive Model of Gender-Related Behavior," *Psychological Review*, 94:3 (1987), 369–89.

———. "From Individual Differences to Social Categories: Analysis of a Decade's Research on Gender," *American Psychologist*, 39 (1984), 105–16.

———, and Brenda Major. "A Social Psychological Model of Gender," *Theoretical Perspectives on Sexual Difference*, ed. Deborah Rhode (New Haven: Yale University Press, 1990).

Degler, Carl N. *At Odds: Women and the American Family from the Revolution to the Present* (New York: Oxford University Press, 1980).

DeLauretis, Teresa. *Technologies of Gender: Essays on Theory, Film, and Fiction* (Bloomington: Indiana University Press, 1987).

Derrida, Jacques. *Writing and Difference* (Chicago: University of Chicago Press, 1978).

Douglas, Ann. *Industrial Peacemaking* (New York: Columbia University Press, 1962).

DuPlessis, Rachel Blau. *Writing Beyond the Ending: Narrative Strategies of Twentieth-Century Women Writers* (Bloomington: Indiana University Press, 1985).

Eagly, Alice. *Sex Differences in Social Behavior: A Social Role Interpretation* (Hillsdale, N.J.: Erlbaum, 1987).

———. "The Science and Politics of Comparing Women and Men," *American Psychologist*, 50 (1995), 145–58.

Eban, Abba. *Diplomacy for the Next Century* (New Haven: Yale University Press, 1998).

Eco, Umberto. *The Role of the Reader: Explorations in the Semiotics of Texts* (Bloomington: University of Indiana Press, 1979).

Ely, Robin. "The Power of Demography: Women's Social Constructions of Gender Identity at Work," *Academy of Management Journal*, 38 (1995), 589–634.

Epstein, Cynthia Fuchs. *Deceptive Distinctions: Sex, Gender, and the Social Order* (New Haven: Yale University Press, 1988).

Ferguson, Kathy. "Interpretation and Genealogy in Feminism," *Signs*, 16 (1991), 322–39.

———. *The Feminist Case Against Bureaucracy* (Philadelphia: Temple University Press, 1984).

Fisher, Helen E. *The First Sex* (New York: Random House, 1999).

Fisher, Roger, William Ury, and Bruce Patton. *Getting to Yes: Negotiating Agreement Without Giving In* (Boston: Houghton Mifflin, 2nd ed. 1992, 1st edition, 1981).

Fisher, Roger, and Scott Brown. *Getting Together* (New York: Penguin, 1987).

Flax, Jane. *Thinking Fragments: Psychoanalysis, Feminism, and Postmodernism in the Contemporary West* (Berkeley: University of California Press, 1990).

———. "Postmodernism and Gender Relations in Feminist Theory," *Signs*, 12 (1987), 621–43.

Fletcher, Joyce. *Disappearing Acts: Gender, Power, and Relational Practice at Work* (Cambridge: MIT Press, 1999).

———. "Castrating the Feminine Advantage: Feminist Standpoint Research and Management Science," *Journal of Management Inquiry*, 3 (1994), 74–82.

Follett, Mary Parker. *The Prophet of Management*, ed. Pauline Graham (Cambridge: Harvard Business School Press, 1995).

Fouraker, Lawrence, and Stanley Siegal. *Bargaining and Group Decisionmaking* (New York: McGraw-Hill, 1960).

Freedman, Jill, and Gene Combs. *Narrative Therapy* (New York: W. W. Norton, 1996).

Friedman, Ray. *Front Stage, Backstage: The Dramatic Structure of Labor Negotiations* (Cambridge: MIT Press, 1994).

———. "Interaction Norms as Carriers of Organizational Culture: A Study of Labor Negotiations at International Harvester," *Journal of Contemporary Ethnography*, 18 (1989), 3–29.

Fuchs, Victor R. *Women's Quest for Economic Equality* (Cambridge: Harvard University Press, 1988).

Geertz, Clifford. *Local Knowledge: Further Essays in Interpretive Anthropology* (New York: Basic Books, 1983).

Gerhart, B. "Gender Differences in Current and Starting Salaries: The Role of Performance, College Major, and Job Title," *Industrial and Labor Relations Review,* 43 (1990), 418–33.

———, and S. Rynes. "Determinants and Consequences of Salary Negotiations by Male and Female MBA Graduates," *Journal of Applied Psychology,* 76 (1991), 256–62.

Gerson, Judith M., and Kathy Peiss. "Boundaries, Negotiation, Consciousness: Reconceptualizing Gender Relations," *Social Problems,* 32:4 (1985), 317–31.

Gherardi, Sylvia. *Gender, Symbolism, and Organizational Culture* (Newbury Park, Calif.: Sage, 1996).

Gilbert, Sandra. "Female Female Impersonators: The Sardonic Heroinism of Edna St.-Vincent Millay and Marianne Moore." Lecture given at Cornell University, March 23, 1986.

Gilligan, Carol. *In a Different Voice* (Cambridge: Harvard University Press, 1982).

———, and Lyn Mikel Brown. *Meeting at the Crossroads: Women's Psychology and Girls' Development* (Cambridge: Harvard University Press, 1992).

Goffman, Erving. "The Arrangement Between the Sexes," *Theory and Society,* 4 (1977), 301–31.

———. *Frame Analysis* (New York: Harper and Row, 1974).

———. *The Presentation of Self in Everyday Life* (Woodstock, N.Y.: Overlook Press, 1973).

———. *Interaction Ritual: Essays in Face-to-face Behavior* (New York: Doubleday/Anchor, 1967).

Goleman, Daniel. *Working with Emotional Intelligence* (New York: Bantam, 1998).

———. *Emotional Intelligence* (New York: Bantam, 1997).

Goodwin, Marjorie Harness. *He-Said-She-Said: Talk as Social Organization Among Black Children* (Bloomington: Indiana University Press, 1991).

Gray, Barbara. "The Gender-Based Foundations of Negotiation Theory," *Research on Negotiation in Organizations,* 4 (Greenwich, Conn.: JAI, 1994).

Griscomb, Joan. "Women and Power: Definition, Dualism, and Difference," *Psychology of Women Quarterly,* 16 (1992), 389–414.

Harrigan, Betty Lehan. *Games Mother Never Taught You* (New York: Warner, 1977).

Hartsock, Nancy. *Money, Sex, and Power: Toward a Feminist Historical Materialism* (New York: Longman, 1983).

Heilman, Madeline E., and Melanie H. Stopeck. "Attractiveness and Corporate Success: Different Causal Attributions for Males and Females," *Journal of Applied Psychology,* 70:2 (1985), 379–88.

Heim, Pat. *Hardball for Women* (New York: Plume, 1993).

Helgesen, Sally. *The Female Advantage: Women's Ways of Leadership* (New York: Doubleday, 1990).

Henley, Nancy. *Body Politics, Sex, and Nonverbal Communication* (Englewood Cliffs, N.J.: Prentice-Hall, 1984).

Hennig, Margaret, and Anne Jardim. *The Managerial Woman* (New York: Anchor, 1977).

Hite, Molly. *The Other Side of the Story: Structures and Strategies of Contemporary Feminist Narratives* (Ithaca, N.Y.: Cornell University Press, 1989).

Hochschild, Arlie. *The Second Shift: Working Parents and the Revolution at Home* (New York: Viking Press, 1989).

Hopkins, Ann. *So Ordered: Making Partner the Hard Way* (Amherst: University of Massachusetts Press, 1996).

Hyde, Janet. "Meta-analysis and the Psychology of Differences," *Signs,* 16:1 (1990), 55–73.

Ibarra, H. "Homophily and Differential Returns: Sex Differences in Network Structure and Access in an Advertising Firm," *Administrative Science Quarterly,* 37 (1992), 422–47.

Jamieson, Kathleen Hall. *Beyond the Double Bind: Women and Leadership* (New York: Oxford University Press, 1995).

Jordan, J. V., A. G. Kaplan, J. B. Miller, I. P. Stiver, and J. L. Surrey. *Women's Growth in Connection: Writings from the Stone Center* (New York: Guilford Press, 1991).

Kamen, V. S., and C. E. J. Hartel. "Gender Differences in Anticipated Pay Negotiation Strategies and Outcomes," *Journal of Business and Psychology,* 9 (1994), 183–97.

Keashley, L. "Gender and Conflict: What Does Psychological Research Tell Us?" *Gender and Conflict,* eds. Anita Taylor and Judi Beinstein Miller (Cresskill, N.J.: Hampton Press, 1994), 167–90.

Kessler-Harris, Alice. *A Woman's Wage: Historical Meanings & Social Consequences* (Lexington: Kentucky University Press, 1990).

Kolb, Deborah M. "Women's Work: Peacemaking Behind the Scenes," *Hidden Conflict in Organizations: Uncovering Behind-the-Scenes Disputes,* eds. Deborah M. Kolb and Jean Bartunek (Newbury Park, Calif.: Sage, 1992).

———, and Linda L. Putnam. "Through the Looking Glass: Negotiation Theory Refracted Through the Lens of Gender," *Frontiers in Dispute Resolution in Industrial Relations and Human Resources,* ed. S. Gleason (Ann Arbor: Michigan State University Press, 1997).

———, Lisa Jensen, and Vonda Shannon. "She Said It All Before, or What Did We Miss About Ms. Follett in the Library?" *Organizations* (January 1996).

———, and Judith Williams. "Professional Women in Conversation: Where Have We Been and Where Are We Going?" *Journal of Management Inquiry,* 2 (1993), 14–26.

———, and Gloria Coolidge. "Her Place at the Table: A Consideration of Gender Issues in Negotiation," *Negotiation Theory and Practice,* eds. J. W. Breslin and Jeffrey Rubin (Cambridge: Program on Negotiation, Harvard Law School, 1991).

Korn-Ferry International. *Decade of the Executive Woman: A Joint Study by Korn/Ferry International and UCLA Anderson Graduate School of Management* (Boston: Korn/Ferry International, 1993).

Kramer, Roderick, and David Messick, eds. *Negotiation as a Social Process* (Newbury Park, Calif.: Sage, 1995).

Kriesberg, Louis, and Stuart Thorson. *Timing and the De-escalation of International Conflicts* (Syracuse, N.Y.: Syracuse University Press, 1991).

Kunda, Gideon. *Engineering Culture: Control and Commitment in a High-Tech Corporation* (Philadelphia: Temple University Press, 1992).

Lakoff, Robin. *Language and Woman's Place* (New York: Octagon Books, 1976).

Lax, David, and James Sebenius. *The Manager as Negotiator* (New York: Free Press, 1986).

————. "Thinking Coalitionally," *Negotiation Analysis*, ed. P. Young (Ann Arbor: University of Michigan Press, 1992).

Lewicki, Roy, Joseph Litterer, John Minton, and David Saunders, eds. *Negotiation* (Minneapolis: Richard Irwin, 1994).

Lewin, Kurt. *Resolving Social Conflicts: Field Theory in Social Science* (Washington, D.C.: American Psychological Association, 1997).

Loden, Marilyn. *Feminine Leadership or How to Succeed in Business Without Being One of the Boys* (New York: Times Books, 1985).

Lopresti, Pamela J. "Gender Differences in Wage and Job Mobility," *American Economic Review*, 82:2 (May 1992), 821–31.

Lorber, Judith. *The Paradoxes of Gender* (New Haven: Yale University Press, 1994).

Lott, Bernice. *Women's Lives: Themes and Variations in Gender Learning* (Monterey, Calif.: Brooks Cole, 1987).

Maccoby, Eleanor E., and Carol Jacklin. *The Psychology of Sex Differences* (Stanford: Stanford University Press, 1974).

MacKinnon, Catharine A. *Only Words* (Cambridge: Harvard University Press, 1993).

————. *Toward a Feminist Theory of the State* (Cambridge: Harvard University Press, 1989).

————. "Feminist Discourse," *Buffalo Law Review* (1985).

Mahony, Rhona. *Kidding Ourselves: Breadwinning, Babies, and Bargaining Power* (New York: Basic Books, 1995).

Major, Brenda, and B. Forcey. "Social Comparisons and Pay Evaluations: Preferences for Same-Sex and Same-Job Wage Comparisons," *Journal of Experimental Social Psychology*, 21 (1985), 393–405.

————, and E. Konar. "An Investigation of Sex Differences in Pay Expectations and Their Possible Causes," *Academy of Management Journal*, 27 (1984), 777–92.

————, D. McFarlin, and D. Gagnon. "Overworked and Underpaid," *Journal of Personality and Social Psychology*, 47 (1984), 1399–1412.

Maniero, L. "Coping with Powerlessness: The Relationship of Gender and Job Dependency to Empowerment Strategy Usage," *Administrative Science Quarterly*, 31:4 (1986), 633–53.

Martin, Joanne. "Deconstructing Organizational Taboos: The Suppression of Gender Conflict in Organizations," *Organization Science*, 1 (1990), 339–59.

Menkel-Meadow, Carrie. "Portia Redux: Another Look at Gender, Feminism, and Legal Ethics," *Virginia Journal of Social Policy & the Law*, 2:1 (Fall 1994), 75–113.

————. "Portia in a Different Voice: Speculating on a Woman's Lawyering Process," *Berkeley Women's Law Journal,* 1:1 (1985), 39–63.

Meyerson, Debra. "From Discovery to Resistance: A Feminist Read and Revision of the Stress Discourse," *Organization Science,* 9 (1998), 103–18.

Miller, Barbara. *Sex and Gender Hierarchies* (New York: Cambridge University Press, 1993).

Miller, Jean Baker. *Toward a New Psychology of Women* (Boston: Beacon Press, 1976).

Mills, Albert J., and Peta Tancred, eds. *Gendering Organizational Theory* (London: Sage, 1992).

Mindell, Phyllis. *A Woman's Guide to the Language of Success: Communication with Confidence and Power* (Englewood Cliffs, N.J.: Prentice-Hall, 1995).

Mnookin, Robert H. "Why Negotiations Fail: An Exploration of Barriers to the Resolution of Conflict," *Ohio State Journal of Dispute Resolutions,* 8:2 (1993), 235–49.

————, Scott Peppet, and Andrew Tulumello. "The Tension Between Empathy and Assertiveness," *Negotiation Journal,* 12:3 (1996).

————, Lawrence Susskind, and Pacey Foster, eds. *Negotiating on Behalf of Others* (Newbury Park, Calif.: Sage, 1999).

Monk, Gerald, John Winslade, Kathie Crocket, and David Epston, eds. *Narrative Therapy in Practice: The Archaeology of Hope* (San Francisco: Jossey-Bass, 1997).

Mumby, Dennis K., and Linda L. Putnam. "The Politics of Emotion: A Feminist Reading of Bounded Rationality," *Academy of Management Review,* 17 (1992), 465–86.

Neale, Margaret, and Max Bazerman. *Cognition and Rationality in Negotiation* (New York: Free Press, 1994).

Offerman, Lynn R., and Cheryl Beil. "Achievement Style of Women Leaders and Their Peers," *Psychology of Women Quarterly,* 16 (1992), 37–56.

Parry, Alan, and Robert Doan. *Story Revisions: Narrative Therapy in the Postmodern World* (New York: Guilford Press, 1994).

Pearce, W. B., and V. E. Cronen. *Communication, Action, and Meaning: The Creation of Social Reality* (New York: Praeger, 1980).

Pierce, Jennifer. *Gender Trials: Emotional Lives in Contemporary Law Firms* (Berkeley: University of California Press, 1995).

Pruitt, Dean. "Strategic Choice in Negotiation," *American Behavioral Scientist,* 27:2 (1983), 167–94.

————. *Negotiation Behavior* (New York: Academic Press, 1981).

Raiffa, Howard. *The Art and Science of Negotiation* (Cambridge: Harvard University Press, 1982).

Rapaport, Rhona, Lotte Bailyn, Deborah Kolb, and Joyce Fletcher. *Relinking Life and Work: Toward a Better Future: A Report to the Ford Foundation on a Research Project in Collaboration with Xerox Corporation, Tandem Computers, Inc., and Corning, Inc.* (New York: Ford Foundation, 1996).

Reardon, Kathleen Kelley. *They Don't Get It, Do They? Closing the Gap Between Women and Men* (Boston: Little, Brown and Company, 1996).

Rhode, Deborah, ed. *Theoretical Perspectives on Sexual Difference* (New Haven: Yale University Press, 1990).

Rose, Carol. "Bargaining and Gender: Feminism, Sexual Distinctions, and the Law," *Harvard Journal of Law and Public Policy*, 18:2 (1995), 547–63.

Rosener, Judith. *America's Competitive Secret: Using Women as a Competitive Strategy* (New York: Oxford University Press, 1997).

———. "Ways Women Lead," *Harvard Business Review* (November/December 1990).

Rubin, Harriet. *The Princessa: Machiavelli for Women* (New York: Doubleday, 1997).

Rubin, Jeffrey, Dean G. Pruitt, and Song Hee Kim. *Social Conflict: Escalation, Stalemate and Settlement* (New York: McGraw-Hill, 1993).

———, and B. R. Brown. *The Social Psychology of Bargaining and Negotiation* (New York: Academic Press, 1975).

Schon, Donald. *The Reflective Practitioner: How Professionals Think in Action* (New York: Basic Books, 1984).

Schwartz, Felice N. "Management Women and the New Facts of Life," *Harvard Business Review* (January/February 1989), 65–76.

Scott, Joan Wallach. *Gender and the Politics of History* (New York: Columbia University Press, 1988).

Senge, Peter. *The Fifth Discipline: The Art and Science of a Learning Institution* (New York: Doubleday, 1990).

Sheldon, Amy. "Saying It with a Smile: Girls' Conflict Talk as Double-Voice Discourse," *Current Issues in Linguistic Theory*, eds. M. Eid and G. Iverson (Amsterdam: John Benjamins, 1993).

Sigel, Roberta A. *Ambition & Accommodation: How Women View Gender Relations* (Chicago: Chicago University Press, 1996).

Sluski, Carlos. "Transformations: A Blueprint for Narrative Changes in Therapy," *Family Process* (1992), 217–30.

Smeltzer, Larry, and Kittie W. Watson. "Gender Differences in Verbal Communication During Negotiations," *Communication Research Reports*, 3 (1986), 74–79.

Spence, Janet T., and R. L. Helmreich. *Masculinity and Femininity: Their Psychological Correlates* (Austin: University of Texas Press, 1978).

Stamato, L. "Voice, Place and Process: Research on Gender, Negotiation, and Conflict Resolution," *Mediation Quarterly*, 9:4 (1992), 375–86.

Stevens, Cynthia, K. Bavetta, and M. Gist. "Gender Differences in the Acquisition of Salary Negotiation Skills: The Role of Goals, Self-Efficacy, and Perceived Control," *Journal of Applied Psychology*, 78:5 (1993), 722–35.

Stuhlmacher, Alice F., and Amy E. Walters. "Gender Differences in Negotiation Outcomes: A Meta-Analysis," *Personnel Psychology*, 52:3 (1999), 653–67.

Tannen, Deborah. *Talking from 9 to 5: Women and Men in the Workplace: Language, Sex and Power* (New York: Avon, 1994).

———. *You Just Don't Understand: Women and Men in Conversation* (New York: Ballantine, 1990).

———, ed. "Rethinking Power and Solidarity in Gender and Dominance," *Gender and Conversation Interaction* (New York: Oxford University Press, 1993).

Tracy, Laura. *"Catching the Drift": Authority, Gender, and Narrative* (New Brunswick, N.J.: Rutgers University Press, 1988).

Turner, Victor. *Drama, Fields, and Metaphor: Symbolic Action in Human Society* (Ithaca, N.Y.: Cornell University Press, 1974).

———. *The Ritual Process* (Ithaca, N.Y.: Cornell University Press, 1969).

———, and Jerome Bruner, eds. *The Anthropology of Experience* (Chicago: University of Chicago Press, 1986).

Trump, Donald, and Tony Schwartz. *The Art of the Deal* (New York: Random House, 1987).

Unger, Rhoda K. "Imperfect Reflections on Reality: Psychology Constructs Gender," *Psychology and the Construction of Gender,* eds. Rachel T. Hare-Mustin and Jeanne Maracek (New Haven: Yale University Press, 1990).

U.S. Department of Labor. *Employment and Earnings* (Washington, D.C.: U.S. Government Printing Office, 1993).

———. *Working Women: A Chartbook* (Washington, D.C.: U.S. Government Printing Office, 1991).

———. *Report on the Glass Ceiling Initiative* (Washington, D.C.: U.S. Government Printing Office, 1991).

Ury, William. *Getting Past No* (New York: Bantam, 1990).

Valian, Virginia. *Why So Slow? The Advancement of Women* (Cambridge: MIT Press, 1998).

Walton, Richard, and Robert McKersie. *A Behavioral Theory of Labor Negotiations* (New York: McGraw-Hill, 1965).

Watson, Carol. "Gender versus Power," *Women, Men and Gender,* ed. Mary Roth Walsh (New Haven: Yale University Press, 1997).

———. "Gender Differences in Negotiating Behavior and Outcomes: Fact or Artifact?" *Conflict and Gender,* eds. Anita Taylor and Judi Beinstein Miller (Cresskill, N.J.: Hampton Press, 1994).

———, and L. R. Hoffman, "Managers as Negotiators: A Test of Power vs. Gender as Predictors of Feelings, Behaviors and Outcomes," *Leadership Quarterly,* 7:1 (1996), 63–86.

Weedon, Chris. *Feminist Practice and Poststructuralist Theory* (Oxford: Blackwell, 1987).

West, Candace, and Diane Fenstermaker. "Doing Difference," *Gender & Society,* 9:4 (1995), 8–37.

———, and D. H. Zimmerman. "Doing Gender," *Gender & Society,* 1 (1987), 125–51.

White, Michael, and David Epston. *Narrative Means to Therapeutic Ends* (New York: W. W. Norton, 1990).

Wilson, Steven R. "Face and Facework in Negotiation," *Communication and Negotiation,* eds. Linda Putnam and Michael E. Roloff (Newbury Park, Calif.: Sage, 1992).

Wolf, Naomi. *Fire with Fire: The New Female Power and How to Use It* (New York: Fawcett Columbine, 1993).

Zimmerman, Don, and Candace West. "Sex Roles, Interruptions and Silence in Conversations," *Language and Sex,* eds. Barrie Thorne and Nancy Henley (Rowley, Mass.: Newbury House, 1979).

Index

Action
    translating thoughts into, 154, 156
Active listening, 159
Adversarial relationships, 30–31, 118,
        204, 214, 215, 218, 219–20, 229–31,
        250
Advice
    seeking objective, 65–66, 68
Advocacy, 21–23, 35–38, 41–136, 240, 254
    appreciative overtures tools of, 179
    and connection, 36–37, 211–12, 219,
        220, 222–23, 224, 231, 237, 238,
        255
    continuous process of, 253–54
    in mutual inquiry, 224
    in packaging, 220–22
    pushing and tools of, 215–16, 223
    and relationship building, 141
Agenda, 94, 99
    single-minded concentration on,
        139–40
Agreement(s), 103, 136, 140, 238
    building blocks of, 144
    collaborative, 208
    cooperation needed for, 176
    crafting, 211–38
    models for, 231, 237
    paths to, 240
    timing and, 199
Albright, Madeleine, 16
Allies, strategic, 74, 75
    roles of, 89–93
Alternatives, 74
    developing, 48, 61–64
    considering, of other person(s), 63–64

as pressure lever, 82, 84
    see also BATNA
Anticipation, 55
    of problems, 60
    of reactions, 94–96
    of resistance, 74
Appreciation, 159–77, 180, 213
    making explicit, 161
    of other person's face, 160, 173–77
    of other person's feelings, 160,
        166–69
    of other person's ideas, 160, 169–73
    of other person's situation, 160,
        161–65
    used tactically, 179
Art of the Deal, The (Trump), 16
Aspirations, 260n3
Attribution errors, 142
Attractiveness, 263n9
Authority, 73–74, 84, 99, 103, 174
    challenge to, 125–26
    establishing, 74–75
    establishing, when negotiating for
        others, 85–89
    lack of, 98
Authorization
    explicit, 85–86, 88, 89
    as ongoing activity, 87–89

Back channels
    using lulls to work, 202–04
Backed into a corner, 106, 160, 174–75,
        176
Backing (support), 88
    maintaining, 86–87